A WESTERN HORSEMAN B(

CW00968174

LEGENDS
VOLUME 5

Outstanding Quarter Horse Stallions and Mares

Contributors
Frank Holmes
Ty Wyant
Alan Gold
Sally Harrison

Edited by Pat Close

LEGENDS

VOLUME 5

Published by
Western Horseman Inc.

3850 North Nevada Ave.
Box 7980
Colorado Springs, CO 80933-7980

www.westernhorseman.com

Design, Typography, and Production
Western Horseman
Colorado Springs, Colorado

Cover painting by
Orren Mixer

Printing
Publisher's Press
Salt Lake City, Utah

First Printing: July 2001

ISBN 0-911647-58-9

INTRODUCTION

WE ARE pleased to publish this fifth volume in our popular *Legends* series about outstanding Quarter Horses. This book is the largest so far, with 248 pages, and features 18 stallions and mares who have had a significant impact on the breed.

Four free-lance writers — Frank Holmes, Ty Wyant, Alan Gold, and Sally Harrison — handled the writing, with Frank authoring the majority. Many photographers gave us permission to use their work, as did *The Quarter Horse Journal* and *The Quarter Racing Journal*, and we are very grateful to them. We know that the many photographs we use in our *Legends* books contribute greatly to their popularity.

The Web-site of the American Quarter Horse Association was a tremendous help in preparing this book. The association, as many of you know, has all pedigrees, performance summaries, and sire and dam production records of registered Quarter Horses readily available to those with Internet access. This was a huge time-saver.

One problem in preparing this volume, as with previous volumes, was the confusion between names of many horses. For example, in the Jackie Bee chapter, a horse named Gold Fingers is mentioned. Gold Fingers was a 1972 gray stallion. Yet there is also a Gold Finger, a 1972 brown stallion.

In the early years, AQHA allowed punctuation in names, such as apostrophes or a period after a single letter in a name; for example, Skipper's Lad, Hank H, Queen H., etc. Then AQHA eliminated punctuation marks in names. So in the early studbooks, a name might have a period after an initial, or a name might be possessive. But in the records today those same names do not have a period after an initial, and are not possessive. In this volume, we have eliminated the period after an initial in some of the names.

There are also cases in which two horses have the very same name, except one is possessive and the other is not. For example, Triple's Image was a 1969 stallion, and Triples Image was a 1988 gelding.

As another example of confusing names, Panzarita was a 1931 chestnut mare, and Pan Zareta B was a 1944 mare. And long before either of those mares saw the light of day and also before the AQHA was organized, there was a great race mare named Pan Zarita.

Here's another example that gives headaches to proofreaders: Years ago there was a darn good sire named Beetch's Yellow Jacket. AQHA records now list him as Beetch'syellowjacket.

I mention all this in case some of you question names in the book. We've tried our darndest to be accurate, and we have printed names and pedigrees according to AQHA official records. But in a book this size and with so many names, we know we might have slipped up in a few places. As we have done with the previous volumes, we can correct mistakes in subsequent printings, so if you spot a mistake, we'd appreciate hearing from you.

Cover Artist

The renowned Orren Mixer, of Arcadia, Okla., graciously painted the beautiful cover for this book—just as he did for the first four *Legends*.

For more than 50 years Orren has been photographing and painting horses who have helped build the Quarter Horse industry. Orren was born in Oklahoma City in 1920, and he believes it was 1949 when he did his first portrait of a horse, on commission. He's been at it ever since. Orren and his wife, Evelyn, have a small ranch near Arcadia.

Titles

Contemporary Quarter Horse owners and enthusiasts may not be familiar with some of the titles AQHA used in years gone by. One example is Honor Roll, which was given to year-end high-point horses in the various events.

Speed classifications of A, AA, AAA, and Top AAA (which was abbreviated as TAAA or AAAT) were used before AQHA switched to speed index (SI) ratings.

ROM stands for Register of Merit, a title that horses today can still earn. A horse earns an ROM in halter, performance, and/or racing after he wins a certain number of points in competition.

The AQHA Champion title is awarded to a horse after he earns a certain number of points in both halter and performance.

If you would like more information on the history of the AQHA and its early registration rules and standards for grading Quarter running horses, refer to the "Introduction" in *Legends 1*. It was written by Jim Goodhue, who was the AQHA registrar for many years.

Special Thanks

I want to again thank the many photographers who gave us permission to use their photographs in this book. Their names appear as a credit line with each of their photos. I also want to thank our assistant art director, Jeanne Mazerall, who did the design and layout of the book, and Glenn Mattingly and Richard Smith who handled the photographic work in our production department. It's amazing what Glenn and Richard can do with their computers to restore old, faded pictures to usable ones.

Happy reading!

Patricia A. Close
Consulting Editor
Western Horseman Inc.

CONTENTS

1

LITTLE JOE

By Ty Wyant

His name can still be found in the extended pedigree of many outstanding contemporary horses.

IN 1905 Lacrucia Clegg peered into a crate holding a newly purchased colt later to be named Little Joe. "You gave $250 for that thing that I could put in a chicken coop?" she reportedly asked her husband, George.

George probably didn't say a thing.

Although George had a good eye for promising horseflesh, even he could never have imagined the impact the undersized colt would later have when the Quarter Horse breed was established.

It should be noted that through the

years there were several horses named Little Joe, but far and away the most important one was the little brown colt foaled in 1904. This is the Little Joe whose name can be found in the extended pedigrees of many outstanding contemporary horses. For example: the 2000 World Champion Quarter Running Horse named A Ransom, the 2000 NCHA Futurity winner Royal Fletch, the 1998 and 2000 AQHA Superhorse Acadamosby Award, the 2000 NRHA Futurity winner Von

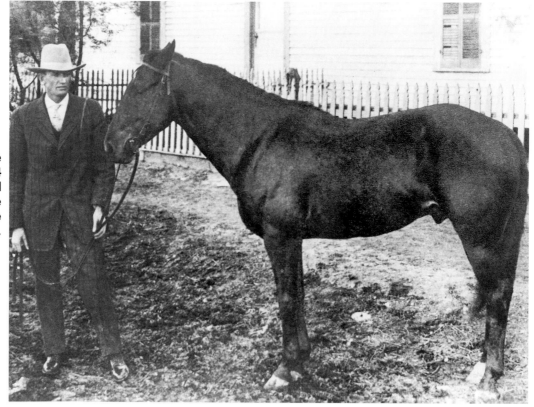

The legendary Little Joe, foaled in 1904 or 1905, has helped shape Quarter Horse breeding ever since the early 1900s.

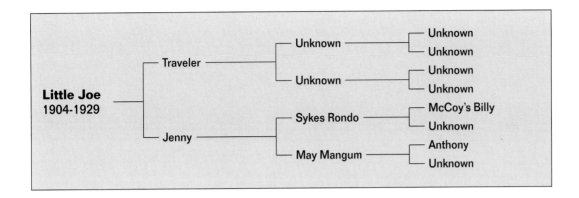

```
                                    ┌── Unknown
                        ┌── Unknown ┤
            ┌── Traveler ┤          └── Unknown
            │            │          ┌── Unknown
            │            └── Unknown ┤
Little Joe ─┤                        └── Unknown
1904-1929   │                        ┌── McCoy's Billy
            │            ┌── Sykes Rondo ┤
            └── Jenny ───┤            └── Unknown
                         │            ┌── Anthony
                         └── May Mangum ┤
                                      └── Unknown
```

Reminic, and the 2000 NRCHA Snaffle Bit Futurity winner Smokums Prize.

Not a bad legacy for a colt who fit in a crate.

George, who died in 1959, is probably still bragging about his $250 purchase to horsemen in the hereafter.

Described by owner Ott Adams as having a "short back and big britches," Little Joe came from the hardscrabble south Texas brush country that produced the Shilohs and Billys. These were terms for Quarter Horses before the name Quarter Horse was coined.

Nobody ever called Little Joe a Quarter Horse while he was alive. Yet, by the 21st century, his blood had helped shape nearly every current racing and performance champion.

The Shely Years

Foaled in 1904 or 1905, Little Joe was bred by the well-known breeders Dow and Will Shely of Alfred, Texas. He was by their great stallion Traveler (*Legends 2*), the horse of unknown breeding who gained racing fame after being discovered pulling a road scraper in east Texas.

Little Joe's dam was the Shelys' top mare Jenny. She, in turn, was by Sykes Rondo and out of the great producer May Mangum. Called "Old May," May Mangum was a bay foaled in 1882. She produced six notable foals when bred to Sykes Rondo. Her top racing offspring was a gelding also named Little Joe, who was nearly unbeatable in match races. Little Joe (the gelding) was defeated by Blue Jacket in a Mexican match race, and Blue Jacket's statue was placed in the

Mexican Jockey Club in Mexico City.

Jenny proved to be a great cross with Traveler. In addition to Little Joe, Jenny produced the Traveler son called King (not to be confused with King P-234), the mare's final foal and an orphan. King was sold to Jim J. Kennedy of Bonita, Ariz., for the fancy sum of 100 head of sound young horses and from then on was called Possum.

Little Joe and King (Possum), the only two colts from the Traveler-Jenny cross, became the potent force in the Traveler line.

In 1940 O.W. Cardwell wrote Bob Denhardt, first secretary of the AQHA, and said, "Openly by many and secretly by more, (Little Joe) is considered the greatest, most ideal sire of this century. Men who have his blood do not wish to change, and outsiders are hunting for it."

The Clegg Years

George Clegg, a cattle rancher from nearby Alice, was in the market for a colt who would be a useful cow horse sire. Clegg needed horses who were tough enough to move cattle in extreme working conditions, and he also liked horses with speed. Little Joe filled Clegg's need for cow horses and his desire for fast horses. Little Joe was fast

Halter and Performance Record: None.

Progeny Record:

Foal Crops: 9   Race Starters: 2
Foals Registered: 74

This is the official AQHA record. Since Little Joe was foaled nearly 50 years before AQHA was formed, he had many performers not in AQHA's records.

Zantanon was one of Little Joe's greatest sons. Zantanon sired, among others, the great King P-234 and Ed Echols.

PHOTO COURTESY *THE QUARTER HORSE JOURNAL*

Traveler, who is featured in *Legends 2*, sired Little Joe.

enough to dominate match races and tough enough to sire offspring who would thrive for south Texas cowboys.

Little Joe, with his short back and powerful hindquarters, was built to sprint. Quickness was his game and he won about every competition.

"I am the only one who raced Little Joe," Clegg once told author Nelson Nye. "He was very fast—could run the quarter in :22.0 (seconds). I ran him as a 3-year-old against all ages, and the only horse to ever beat him was Ace Of Hearts. There were four horses in this race, and Joe was beaten by not more than a foot."

That lone defeat was supported by superstition.

The night before the fabled race, Clegg dreamed that Ace Of Hearts defeated Little Joe by a nose. He told his wife about the dream at breakfast, and the superstitious Lacrucia scolded him for telling a dream at breakfast. Yet, the dream came true.

Ace Of Hearts' people wouldn't allow Clegg to use his regular jockey. With the substitute jockey, Little Joe broke prematurely from the starting line twice and ran the entire quarter mile each time. The third time, Little Joe—who was surely tired—

PHOTO BY FRANKLIN REYNOLDS

Joe Moore, another outstanding son of Little Joe, did not have an attractive head, but became a great sire whose influence is still felt today.

PHOTO COURTESY THE QUARTER RACING JOURNAL

Ace Of Hearts was the only horse ever to defeat Little Joe in a race.

Tobin Joe, an own son of Little Joe, was reported to be an excellent ranch horse, but opinions varied regarding his success as a sire.

Ott Adams may have been of small stature, but he is a giant in Quarter Horse breeding history.

broke at the right moment, but was beaten by a scant head.

Although there are no official records and reports vary, it is believed that Clegg raced Little Joe for four or five years, and Little Joe dominated his rivals every year.

Denhardt said in his classic book, *Quarter Horses: A Story of Two Centuries,* that Little Joe made his racing debut against the famous mare Carrie Nation in San Antonio. (Note: Other reports indicate he had several races before meeting Carrie Nation.)

Little Joe beat the great mare and his fame spread throughout Texas. For the rest of Little Joe's career, Clegg was probably unable to match Little Joe against weak competition. Simply put, Little Joe probably faced the fastest horses in the Lone Star State until an injury ended his racing career.

Clegg owned Little Joe until 1913. He had purchased Hickory Bill (the sire of the King Ranch's foundation sire Old Sorrel) to match race and didn't want two stallions.

The renowned cutting horse sire Peppy San Badger (aka Little Peppy) traces to Little Joe through San Siemon, a son of Zantanon.

Tailor Fit, by Strawfly Special, by Special Effort, and out of Silk Shirt, a granddaughter of Dash For Cash, was the 1999 World Champion Quarter Running Horse. He traces back to Little Joe through his paternal pedigree. The brand on his shoulder is read as Double Bar S, although reading it as a dollar sign would also be appropriate.

A Ransom, the 2000 World Champion Quarter Running Horse, is shown here winning the $400,000 Champion of Champions at Los Alamitos. He traces back to Little Joe through his sire, First Down Dash. A Ransom is owned by Kathie and John Bobenrieth.

The Adams Years

Ott Adams was a small man, standing about 5 feet, with features weathered from the Texas sun and wind. But set in his parched face were the eyes of a horseman.

Adams was looking for a proven race horse to breed to his fast mares. When he found Little Joe, he found his stallion. Later in his life, Adams said that Little Joe was the best horse he ever saw. Adams and Little Joe were made for each other, and they made each other legends in Quarter Horse breeding history.

Adams never raced Little Joe, but used him to build a breeding dynasty.

Adams wanted speed in his horses. "The true value of a Quarter Horse is decided when you break him out of a start and clock his speed at a quarter mile," Adams told author Nelson Nye in 1949. "The value placed on Quarter stock as judged in the ring and practiced today is a fake value, pure and simple—a form of inflation that has no justification in the light of performance."

Strong words. But, their practice has led to a breeding line that still thrives after nearly a century.

Among Little Joe's famous offspring were Zantanon (*Legends 4*), Old Poco Bueno, Cotton Eyed Joe, and Pancho Villa. All still hold prominent places in many Quarter Horse extended pedigrees.

Old Poco Bueno achieved special distinction as the sire of Miss Taylor. When she was bred to King P-234, she produced the outstanding Poco Bueno, plus horses such as Cactus King, Old Taylor, Old Grandad, and Miss Hankins.

Little Joe's great match-racing son Zantanon sired Ed Echols and King P-234, the sire of Poco Bueno, Royal King, and many other great horses. The blood of King P-234 and Poco Bueno is still highly sought today by performance-horse breeders.

Cotton Eyed Joe was a flashy sorrel stallion foaled in 1920. He eventually ended up on the Waggoner Ranch in Texas where he sired several top horses, among them Sue and Billy Van.

The family of San Siemon traces to Little Joe. This family has produced Peppy San, Peponita, Mr San Peppy, and Peppy San Badger.

But no horse illustrates the breeding program Adams built with Little Joe more than Joe Moore, who is featured in the following chapter.

Ott Adams (left) and George Clegg stand beside Little Joe's grave. Several historians believe Little Joe was foaled in 1904 and died in 1929, but this headstone gives the dates as 1905 and 1930.

Adams purchased the mare Della Moore just to breed to Little Joe and, he hoped, to get the replacement stallion for Little Joe. Della Moore was bred to Little Joe four times. After having a filly and then not getting in foal one year, she produced two colts. The first colt, Grano de Oro, became a useful sire. The second colt, Joe Moore, helped define a breed.

Foaled in 1926, Joe Moore was Della Moore's next-to-final foal and from one of Little Joe's last crops. Horsemen acknowledge that Joe Moore's head left a lot to be desired, but otherwise he had classic Quarter Horse conformation for those years.

Used extensively for breeding, Joe Moore sired Monita, Stella Moore, Joe Less, and countless horses who excelled on the track and in the rodeo arena.

The same year that Joe Moore was foaled, Adams went through financial hard times and was forced to sell Little Joe to O.W. Cardwell of Junction, Texas.

Adams always regretted the sale. Three years later Little Joe injured himself in a chute, and Cardwell put him down.

Cardwell buried Little Joe on his ranch. The next year Adams visited Cardwell to ask for the stallion's bones. Cardwell, knowing how much Little Joe meant to Adams, consented.

Adams brought Little Joe's bones back to his ranch and buried them next to a tree that had been planted by his mother nearly 100 years earlier. Years later Joe Moore was buried next to Little Joe.

2

JOE MOORE

By Frank Holmes

He was one of the most influential, albeit little-known, fountainheads of the breed.

IN 1922, with Little Joe getting old, Ott Adams began to entertain thoughts of raising a replacement for him. To Adams, accomplishing that meant but one thing.

Throughout his career as a horse breeder, the little man from Alice had held firm to his belief that the only way to get a sprinter was to breed for one on both sides of the pedigree. In Little Joe, Adams already had the top half of his speed equation in place. All he needed now was to locate and acquire the best race mare he could find for the bottom.

He did just that when he bought Della Moore.

Della Moore was a 1905 sorrel mare, bred by Ludovic Stemmons of Scott, Louisiana. She was sired by Old D.J. (Dedier) and was out of LA Hernandez, by Dewey. This was celebrated Cajun running blood, so it was almost a foregone conclusion that Della would be given the opportunity to race.

Her first chance came pretty quick. The occasion was a "milk race," in which a group of foals was lined up at one end of a straightaway, and then turned loose to race

Although not a good-headed horse, Joe Moore possessed enough good conformation to cause his breeder, Ott Adams, to choose him as Little Joe's replacement.

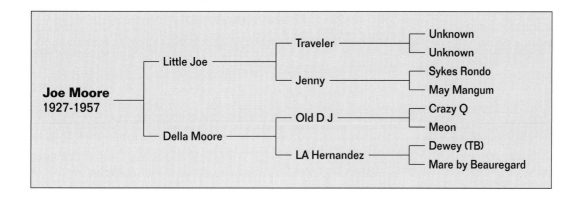

```
                                                 ┌─ Unknown
                              ┌─ Traveler ────────┤
                              │                   └─ Unknown
               ┌─ Little Joe ─┤
               │              │                   ┌─ Sykes Rondo
               │              └─ Jenny ───────────┤
  Joe Moore ───┤                                  └─ May Mangum
  1927-1957    │                                  ┌─ Crazy Q
               │              ┌─ Old D J ─────────┤
               │              │                   └─ Meon
               └─ Della Moore ┤
                              │                   ┌─ Dewey (TB)
                              └─ LA Hernandez ────┤
                                                  └─ Mare by Beauregard
```

to the opposite end where their anxious dams awaited them. Della was entered and won.

The promising youngster's career subsequently progressed to the more sophisticated venues of lap-and-tap match racing, and even starting out of gates. Over the course of the next decade or so, Della became *the* horse to beat in the Cajun State. That proved hard to do, and her fame spread to the point where she could no longer attract any competitors. She was sold to Henry Lindsay of Granger, Texas.

In 1920, while competing at a race meet in San Antonio, Della was stabled next to the celebrated sprinting Thoroughbred Joe Blair. Bred to him on the spot, she foaled Joe Reed P-3 the following year.

With his deep and abiding interest in race horses of every ilk, Ott Adams was well aware of Della Moore, her breeding, and her race record. On June 21, 1922, he managed to purchase the then-17-year-old mare from Henry Lindsay for $600.

Shortly after getting her home, Adams bred Della to Little Joe for the first time. On August 16, 1923, she foaled a sorrel filly named Aloe, who was sold as a yearling to John Dial of Goliad, Texas.

Bred back to Little Joe, Della did not settle. Rebred the following year, she produced the solid bay colt named Grano de Oro in 1925. He was also initially sold to Dial.

Adams bred Della to Billy Sunday, his good son of Horace H (TB) and Carrie Nation, in 1925. Again she failed to settle. Bred to Little Joe for the last time in 1926, she foaled Joe Moore on March 23, 1927.

The great mare had one more foal for Adams before she died in 1930. This was

Halter and Performance Record: None.

Progeny Record:

Foal Crops: 28	Performance Registers of Merit: 1
Foals Registered: 187	Race Starters: 29
Halter Point-Earners: 3	Race Money Earned: $79,077
Halter Points Earned: 4	Race Registers of Merit: 16
Performance Point-Earners: 3	Superior Race Awards: 2
Performance Points Earned: 7	World Champions (Racing): 2
Leading Race Money-Earner: Monita ($44,296)	

the filly named Panzaretta, foaled in 1929 and sired by Paul Ell.

In the end, Della Moore did for Adams exactly what he had hoped she would. In producing Joe Moore, she had given the south Texas short horse aficionado the stallion prospect he had been striving to breed.

Joe Moore never got the chance to personally prove his mettle on the track. Although Ott Adams was a premier racehorse breeder of his day, he never ran his own horses. He sold them instead, and let their new owners prove them out.

As a result, Joe Moore never had the opportunity to show the world how much of his celebrated forebears' speed he had inherited. Fate decreed that he would have to prove that through his get and grandget. But he almost didn't get that chance either.

After breeding Joe as a 2-year-old to some of his best mares, Adams sold him in 1930 to a man named Rogers, who ranched near Menard, Texas.

Joe's first foals hit the ground that same

hip. He was also clean-limbed, with flat cannon bones and low-set knees and hocks.

In Adams' oft-stated opinion, Joe Moore was perfectly built to be a race horse sire.

As was the case with Little Joe before him, Joe Moore had the benefit of an exceptional set of race-bred mares. At the time Joe entered service, Ott Adams' broodmare band contained own daughters of Hickory Bill, Little Joe, Billy Sunday, Paul Ell, and Spokane. In due time, they were joined by a number of top Chicaro Bill mares.

The Adams theory, as it always had been, was still "breed speed to speed to get speed." And, as it had always done, it continued to turn out champions. But those racing champions were a long time coming. In fact, Joe Moore's first two horses to make a name for themselves did it in cutting.

The first was Pay Day, a 1937 bay stallion out of Paulita, by Paul Ell. The earner of $1,148 in NCHA competition, Pay Day also went on to become a top sire.

Ott, a 1943 bay stallion by Joe Moore and out of Lula, by Paul Ell, followed his three-quarter brother into the cutting arena. He fared even better, earning $19,505 and a Bronze Certificate of Achievement. In 1955, he also finished the year as the eighth highest money-earner.

It wasn't until Joe Moore's 1945 foal crop that the speed began emerging in his foals. The pattern held for the rest of his breeding career.

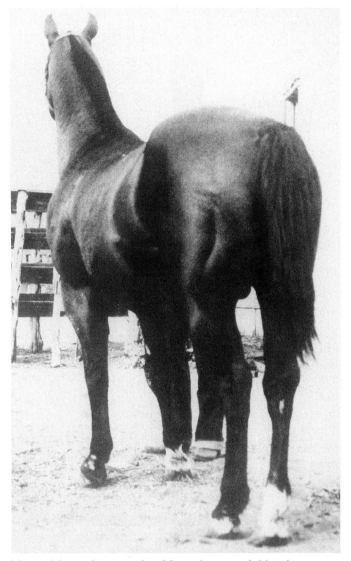

Viewed from the rear, Joe Moore's powerful hindquarters and long, tapering forearms lent further credence to the stallion's potential as a sire of early speed.

year. As they developed into a promising set of young horses, Adams realized that he had made a huge mistake in letting their sire go. In 1932 he successfully negotiated to get him back. The price of the trade was a 5-year-old sorrel stallion named Pal-O-Mine, a full brother to Rialto P-2.

By this time, Joe Moore was in his prime. A dark bay standing between 14.2 and 14.3 hands, he was often described as being as "stout as a bull." From a negative standpoint, there was no denying that he was decidedly rough in the head and neck. On the positive side, he was deep-hearted and strong-backed, with an exceptionally long

Stella Moore

Stella Moore was a 1945 bay mare by Joe Moore and out of Canova, by Chicaro Bill, and she was her sire's first AAA runner and his first world champion. Bred by Adams, Stella was owned by Q.I. Roberts of Palatka, Florida. She broke her 2-year-old maiden race in about as tough a fashion as could be conceived.

The setting was the Del Rio, Tex., racetrack, and the distance was a full quarter-mile. Stella's competition was the awesome Woven Web, a Thoroughbred also known as Miss Princess (*Legends 4*), who was in her prime.

Here is Della Moore, the famed Louisiana race mare who produced both Joe Moore and Joe Reed P-3.

COURTESY *THE QUARTER HORSE JOURNAL*

Ott (on the right), a 1943 bay stallion by Joe Moore and out of Lula, by Paul Ell, earned more than $19,000 in the cutting arena. At the 1959 State Fair of Texas, the leggy stallion tied for first with Poco Stampede (left) in the open cutting. That's Jack Newton on Poco Stampede and Bubba Cascio on Ott.

Yucca King, a 1953 black stallion, was sired by R. Joking and was out of R. Hobo's Mona, by Hobo, by Joe Moore. This photo was used in an ad for Purina Omolene in the July 1960 issue of *Western Horseman*. The flashy stallion was a top show horse and had just recently sold for $50,000.

PURINA SALUTES...
A champion of the horse world
YUCCA KING
Jim Huwaldt—
former owner
Oshkosh, Nebraska

Ben Jay was the first of the four Joe Moore-Yokohama full brothers to achieve stardom. Rated AAA on the tracks, he was also a AAA sire. This photo was taken circa 1959.

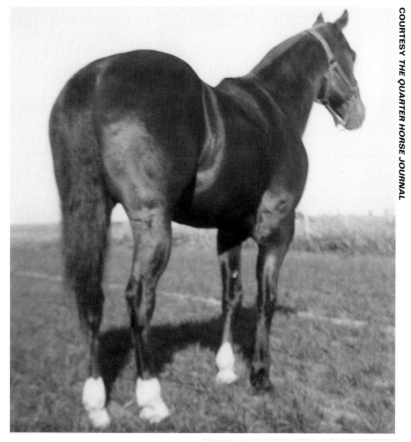

It was a race that should never have been run—a green, untested 2-year-old against the greatest quarter-miler of her time. But, in the end, Stella Moore acquitted herself admirably. She actually led the race until a few yards from the finish, and pushed Woven Web to setting a world's record for the distance.

From 1948 through 1951, Stella raced mostly in Louisiana and south Texas—at the Del Rio and Eagle Pass tracks. The bald-faced, stocking-legged mare set 3-year-old records for 330 and 440 yards and narrowly edged out Leota W. and Miss Pinkie for 1948 Champion Quarter Running 3-Year-Old Filly honors in the American Quarter Racing Association.

In 1949 she placed second in the Del Rio Sweepstakes. The following year she ran third in the Eagle Pass Feature and in 1951 won the Del Rio Championship.

Stella's 1952 campaign proved to be her most memorable. In August at Raton, N.M., she defeated Maddon's Bright Eyes in the 400-yard Raton Handicap. A second-place

Stella Moore, a 1945 bay mare by Joe Moore and out of Canova, by Chicaro Bill, was the 1952 Champion Quarter Running Mare. The durable runner went to the post 50 times, placing first 21 times, second 9 times, and third 3 times. She had a SI rating of 100.

Here's another shot of Stella Moore, reprinted from the American Quarter Racing Association's 1948 Yearbook. The bald-faced mare had just won the 440-yard New Mexico Championship Handicap at Albuquerque, defeating Scooter W. and Leota W. and setting a 3-year-old world record. At the time Stella was owned by Q.I. Roberts of Palatka, Florida.

finish in the 440-yard Gage Boot and Saddle Purse at Ruidoso, N.M., and four track records at Raton, Ruidoso, and Pawhuska, Okla., earned her the title of 1952 AQHA Champion Quarter Running Mare.

Stella continued to be a straightaway threat for two more racing seasons. In 1953, she won the 440-yard New Mexico State Fair Championship and finished second in the 400-yard Parker Handicap

Smuggler was featured in this ad reprinted from the April 1953 issue of *The Quarter Horse Journal*. Smuggler, another son of Joe Moore and Yokohama, looked to be a well-made, athletic horse. Among his noteworthy get were Burks' Red Frost, SI-95, and Baca Reed, a Superior barrel horse.

and 440-yard Rillito Championship—both run at Rillito Park outside Tucson. She received her Superior in racing in 1953 and was retired in 1954.

From 50 official lifetime starts, Stella Moore tallied 21 wins, 9 seconds, and 3 thirds, and earned $12,041. She had an official speed index of 100, and was graded AAA at five distances ranging from 220 to 440 yards.

She was what Ott Adams had bred her to be—a race horse.

More Speedsters

Ben Jay, a 1945 brown stallion by Joe Moore and out of Yokohama, by Spokane, by Paul Ell, was also a speedster. The first of four full brothers who would be influential in some fashion, Ben Jay achieved a speed index of 95, won the 1950 Eagle Pass Feature, and set or equaled track records at 220 and 330 yards. From 29 official starts, he won 6 races, placed second in 5, and third in 5.

Lee Moore, a bay full brother to Ben Jay, was foaled in 1946. Also a AAA race horse and a track record-holder, he accounted for 12 wins, 2 seconds, and 4 thirds in 26 lifetime starts. (The other two full brothers were Poquito Mas and Smuggler; more on them later.)

Monita was Joe Moore's next sprinting superstar. One of Quarter racing's most memorable world champions and a top producer, she is featured in the following chapter.

Sadie Parker was Joe Moore's fifth and final AAA runner. A 1947 bay mare out of Fay Parker, by Chicaro Bill, Sadie had a speed index of 95 and, from 45 lifetime starts, tallied 6 firsts, 10 seconds, and 7 thirds.

In addition to his five AAA-rated get, Joe Moore had eleven others who qualified for their Register of Merit in racing. They were Stevy, Johnny Moore, Ottie Adams, V Day, Lena, Miss Della Moore, Senorita Bonita, Yours Truly, Big Booger, Liz Parker, and Joe Jet.

Three of Joe's get—Hobo, Poquito Mas, and Annie B.—were halter point earners, and

Hobo was arguably the best-looking son of Joe Moore. The flashy bay stallion is shown with owners Mr. and Mrs. B.L. Smith of Junction, Tex., after being named grand champion stallion at the 1951 San Angelo show.

The elegant Monita was without a doubt Joe Moore's greatest racing offspring. A world champion runner and top producer, her story is chronicled in the following chapter.

Under the ownership of one-time AQHA President Bob Kieckhefer of Prescott, Ariz., Poquito Mas was both an outstanding rope horse and a top sire.

No Butt, a paternal granddaughter of Joe Moore, was the 1962 Champion Quarter Running Horse. One of the hardest-knocking competitors of her time, she started 103 times and won 29, including 13 stakes and feature events.

three—Ottie's Brother, Poquito Mas, and High Lonesome—earned performance points.

High Lonesome, a 1955 bay stallion out of Dark Damsel, by King P-234, was Joe's sole performance ROM qualifier. The bay was also an NCHA money-earner, as was the race ROM-earner Lena.

His Greatest Contributions

Like his sire before him, Joe Moore did not inundate the Quarter Horse world with race or show point-earners. And also like his sire, Joe's greatest contributions to the breed came through the siring and producing abilities of his sons and daughters.

Heading the list of Joe Moore's top-siring sons are the four full brothers—Lee Moore, Ben Jay, Poquito Mas, and Smuggler.

Lee Moore, proving his speed was no fluke, sired 17 race ROM-earners. Among his top sprinters were Miss Pitapat, the 1953 AQHA Quarter Running Champion 2-Year-Old Filly and a Superior race horse; Tidy Too, SI-95 and a Superior race horse; and Vegas Moore, SI-95.

Lee also excelled as a broodmare sire, with his daughters producing 55 race ROMs, 8 Superior race horses, 6 performance ROMs, 1 AQHA Champion, 2 Superior halter horses, and 1 Superior performance horse.

Ben Jay, although not as successful a sire as Lee Moore, did put 10 race ROMs into the record books, including the AAA runners Moore Cider, Iron Be, and Bay Ben Jay. He was also the maternal grandsire of 29 race ROMs, 2 Superior race horses, 3 performance ROMs, and 1 AQHA Champion.

Poquito Mas proved to be an excellent sire of both speed and good looks. Among his 10 race ROM get were the AAA runners Betty Dooley, Vindication, and Katy Kan. On the show and performance side of the ledger, Poquito Mas sired such standouts as K4 Gigi, an AQHA Champion and Superior halter horse, and Blazing River, an AQHA Champion and 1966 AQHA High-Point Trail Horse Stallion.

As a maternal grandsire, Poquito is

credited with 37 race ROMs, 11 performance ROMs, 2 AQHA Champions, 1 Superior halter horse, and 4 Superior performance horses.

Smuggler—who was the fourth of the full brothers—accounted for four race ROMs and two performance ROMs, including Burks' Red Frost, SI-95, and Baca Reed, a Superior in barrel racing.

As a maternal grandsire, Smuggler tallied 26 race ROMs, 12 performance ROMs, and 2 AQHA Champions.

Joe Moore had other top-siring sons as well.

Pay Day, the cutting horse, sired three race ROMs, including Vinegar Bend, SI-95 and a Superior race horse, and one performance ROM. More important, he sired such top broodmares as Double Life and Miss Pay Day.

Double Life produced Two D Two, an AQHA Champion who, in turn, sired Two Eyed Jack (*Legends 3*). Miss Pay Day produced Miss Pay Bracket, SI-95, and Magnolia Pay, an AQHA Supreme Champion.

Joe Less and No Butt

Joe Less, a 1943 chestnut stallion by Joe Moore and out of June, by Universe (TB), also made his mark as a sire. Bred by George Clegg, Joe Less was one of the better-looking members of his family. He also sired 13 race ROMs and 11 performance ROMs.

His most renowned offspring was the mare with the unflattering name of No Butt. She was a 1955 bay out of Red Bottom, by Barney Owens. Guy Purinton of Tipton, Calif., owned her in her early years and for most of her racing career.

Purinton had acquired Red Bottom as partial payment on a training bill and was so unimpressed with her that he unsuccessfully tried to sell her, while she was carrying No Butt, for $200. When No Butt was a youngster, Purinton described her as being "not a large filly but beautifully balanced ... (who) did not set any woods afire as a 2-year-old."

The second part of that description changed in a hurry.

The next year, No Butt was named the 1958 AQHA Champion Running 3-Year-Old

Parr Passum, a maternal grandson of Joe Moore, was a AAA-rated race horse who went on to become both a leading sire and a leading maternal grandsire of ROM race horses.

Filly, and in 1959 and 1960, she won five stakes. In 1961 No Butt made all of her 15 starts in stake and feature events. She emerged victorious in four races, defeating such world champions as Go Man Go, Vanetta Dee, Pap, Breeze Bar, First Call, Triple Lady, Vandy's Flash, Clabber's Win, and Table Tennis. There were many who thought she should have been named champion Quarter running mare that year, but the honor went to another. The Joe Moore granddaughter rectified that situation the following year.

From 18 starts in 1962, No Butt won 4 stakes, finished second in 4 more, and third in another. Sixteen of her races were run in AAA time, and she again met and bested such top world champions as Pap, Fly Straw, Caprideck, Straw Flight, Rebel Cause, Pokey Bar, Arizonan, Tonto Bars Hank, and Golden Note.

She wound up the year as the 1962 Champion Quarter Running Horse, Champion

Quarter Running Mare, and Champion Quarter Running Aged Mare.

Raced for six full seasons, No Butt went to the post 103 times. She emerged victorious 29 times, finished second 15 times, and third 14 times.

Retired to the broodmare band, she capped off her storied racing career by producing four top runners: More Cause, SI-100; Go Man No, SI-100; Mr. Wes, SI-95; and No Butts About It, SI-91.

Getting back to Joe Less, in addition to No Butt he also sired Sly Joe, SI-100 and a Superior race horse; Moore Or Less, SI-95 and a Superior race horse; Moless Badger, SI-95; and Babe's Gray, an AQHA Champion.

As a maternal grandsire, Joe Less is credited with 44 race ROMs, 9 performance ROMs, and 2 Superior performance horses. Included among his top performing grandget were Bruce's Shadow, SI-95 and a Superior cutter and chariot

Bar Adams, a 1965 bay stallion by Three Bars (TB) and out of Little Marina Adams, by Joe Moore, achieved a speed index of 100. A Superior race horse, he won the 1967 Juvenile Handicap at the state fairgrounds track in Albuquerque.

race horse; and Bruce's Shadow, Superior western pleasure.

Joe Moore's final son to make a big name for himself as a sire was Hobo. A 1940 bay full brother to Pay Day, Hobo was colored a great deal like Stella Moore. Bald-faced with high stocking legs, he gained early fame as a sire of conformation, quality, and—from time to time—a little extra chrome.

Among Hobo's top racing get were the ROM qualifiers Bo El, Bo Gay, Bo Jet, Bolo, Happy Hobo, Hobo Joe, Jamie Boy, Miss Sequin, and Vagabond.

Among his top arena performers were Bo Bo Cee, AQHA Champion, and the ROM qualifiers Chief Moore, Jo Bo, Operation, and Stembo.

Like most of the males in his family, Hobo was also a superior broodmare sire. All told, his daughters produced seven AAA race horses, six AQHA Champions, three Superior halter horses, and five Superior performance horses.

Hobo Sue produced four AQHA Champions—Dollie Pine, Pine's Penny, Poco Texas Sue, and Pine Bo. Hobo Sue was also the maternal granddam of Zippo Pine Bar (*Legends* 4) through her daughter Dollie Pine.

Miss Bo produced Tom B Man, AQHA Champion and Superior halter horse, and Hobo Chick, SI-90.

Del Rio Belle produced Pepper Del Rio, who earned Superiors in western pleasure, western riding, and trail.

R. Hobo's Mona produced Yucca King, an AQHA Champion who sold for $50,000.

Everita was the dam of Ever Rapids, a Superior halter horse and earner of 296 halter points.

Bo Essie, Botation, Jenny Bo Bruce, and Sissy Bo were AAA producers as well.

All in all, from Lee Moore to Hobo, the sons of Joe Moore were above average sires and did their part to solidify the family's claim to fame.

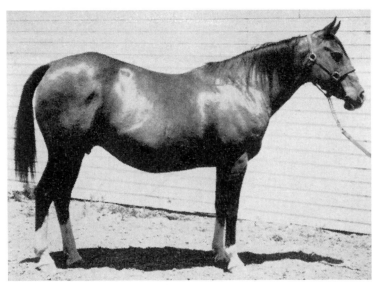

Flicka, a maternal granddaughter of Joe Moore, produced three AAA race horses: Black Easter Bunny, Flicka Hyloah, and Kid Viersen. Foaled in June 1941, Flicka was by Chicaro Bill and out of Kitty Wells, by Joe Moore.

Joe Moore Daughters

In racing, the daughters of Joe Moore produced 117 starters who amassed 453 wins, 99 ROMs, 8 Superior race awards, and $698,726 in winnings.

Stella Moore and Monita, Joe's two greatest racing daughters, were also two of his greatest race producers. Bred exclusively to Thoroughbreds, Stella produced Segura Miguel, SI-95; Thymus Moore, SI-95; and Ima Moore, SI-95.

Monita, on the other hand, was bred to several top Quarter race sires, and she produced 10 ROM race horses, all of whom will be chronicled in the following chapter.

Among Joe Moore's remaining race-producing daughters, Jody Mo and La Price deserve special attention.

Jody Mo, a 1958 sorrel mare out of Lahoma Bruce, by Starway, produced Jody Oh, SI-105 and a Superior race horse; Adams Gain, SI-100 and a Superior race horse; Miss Alberghetti, SI-100; Jody Quest, SI-94 and a Superior race horse; Call Me John, SI-95; Jodys Deck, SI-94; and Jody Ohla, SI-94.

La Price, an AQHA appendix-registered mare out of a daughter of Hickory Bill, was the dam of Parr Passum. A 1949 sorrel stallion sired by Danger Boy, Parr Passum

achieved a speed index of 95 and had five wins, two seconds, and three thirds from fifteen lifetime starts.

As a sire Parr Passum did much better, accounting for 108 ROMs, 2 world champion running horses, 13 Superior race horses, and the earners of $973,588. As a maternal grandsire he put the frosting on the cake with 247 ROMs, 18 Superior race horses, and the earners of $2,249,841.

Kitty Wells, a 1937 bay mare out of Lady Lou, by Little Joe, produced Flicka. A 1941 bay mare sired by Chicaro Bill, and thus a triple-bred Little Joe, Flicka was an A-rated runner and the dam of Black Easter Bunny AAA and the 1952 Champion Quarter Running 3-Year-Old Filly. Kitty Wells also produced Flicka Hyloah and Kid Vierson, both AAA.

Black Easter Bunny, in turn, produced Bunny's Bar Maid AAAT, the 1961 Co-Champion Quarter Running 2-Year-Old Filly; Bunny's Bar Boy AAA; Harlequin AAA; and Pink Mink AAA.

Flicka Hyloah went on to produce Flicka Bars AAA and Flicka's Request AAA.

The descendants of these and other Joe Moore race-bred horses continue to make their presence felt on the Quarter tracks of today.

Show Producers

To a somewhat lesser degree, the Joe Moore daughters also excelled as show producers. All told, they were the dams of three AQHA Champions, one Superior halter horse, and three Superior performance horses. And they also produced earners of 39 performance ROMs, 245 halter points, and 486 performance points.

Little Marina Adams and Little Lulubelle Adams produced both runners and arena horses.

- Little Marina Adams, a 1950 brown mare out of Marina, by Chicaro Bill, produced Bar Adams, SI-100 and a Superior race horse; Three Bargains, SI-95; and Brown Marina, AQHA Champion.
- Lulubelle, a 1949 dun mare out of Lula Belle Adams, produced Bambit, SI-95;

Little Deedy, AQHA Champion; and Bell Bob Jr., a Superior reining horse.

- Sally Moore, a 1954 bay mare out of Betty Seger, by Billy Joe, was the dam of Mr. Gillmoore, the 1976 High-Point Junior Calf Roping Horse and a Superior calf roping horse.
- Flaxie Moore, a 1931 sorrel mare out of an Old Joe Bailey mare, produced Mitzi M., a Superior halter horse.
- Annie B., a 1940 sorrel mare out of Ramona, by Paul Ell, produced Miss Nan Play, a Superior cutting horse.
- Finally, there was Fairy Adams, a 1949 bay mare out of Fairy, by Chicaro Bill. Remembered by many horsemen as Three Bars' blind, inseparable companion during his twilight years (*Legends 1*), Fairy Adams had several more claims to fame.

To begin with, she produced six performers, including Cona Bars, SI-96; Three Jingles, SI-85; The Last Son, who earned a performance ROM; and Wacker, an NCHA money-earner.

Fairy Adams was also the dam of Vila, a 1960 bay mare by Leon Bars. Vila earned five halter points and went on to produce the great Te N' Te. He earned 22 halter points and, from only five foal crops, sired one open world champion and the earners of 4,254.5 halter points, 1,308.5 performance points, 38 Superior halter awards, 8 Superior performance awards, and 30 performance ROMs.

The world champion was Sierra Te, a 1980 bay stallion out of Miss Snoflurry, by Missle Step. The 1984 World Champion Aged Stallion, Sierra Te has sired six open world champions. His get have earned 4,312 halter points, 619 performance points, 31 Superior halter awards, 2 Superior performance awards, and 6 performance ROMs.

And so the Joe Moore story goes. In some ways, it is a tale of untapped potential. Joe Moore was not an especially good-looking horse. As a result, he never attracted the top show and performance mares of the day. He was bred but sparingly to a very narrow range of mares.

Still, when you begin to stack up his

PHOTO BY GRESSETT, COURTESY *THE QUARTER HORSE JOURNAL*

Mitzi M. was proof that when the Joe Moore daughters were bred to the right type of stallions, they could produce both show and performance horses. A 1946 bay mare by Scooter S. and out of Flaxie Moore, Mitzi M. was a Superior halter horse with 63 points, and was one of the Southwest's premier halter mares during the early to mid-1950s.

accomplishments as a sire, and add on those of his sons and daughters, and their sons and daughters, the final tally is impressive.

Joe Moore was born to be a race sire. That he fulfilled that part of his destiny is unquestioned. But he wound up being much more than the one-dimensional sire Ott Adams intended him to be.

Given the accomplishments of just three of his thousands of descendants— Two Eyed Jack, Zippo Pine Bar, and Te N' Te—Joe Moore emerges as one of the most influential, albeit little-known, fountainheads of the breed.

If he were still around, and although he probably wouldn't admit it, Ott Adams would probably be proud.

3

MONITA

By Ty Wyant

She was one tough competitor who became a good producer.

IN THE barn area of a racetrack, when a race horse is called a *race* horse, it is the highest compliment. A *race* horse is fast, durable, and, most importantly, a game competitor.

Foaled in 1947 in the south Texas brush country, Monita was a *race* horse. She had speed to burn. A daughter of Little Joe's top son Joe Moore, Monita wasted no time in showing off her talents.

In her very first start at the wind-blown Val Verde Downs in Del Rio, Tex.—just a long toss from the Rio Grande—Monita set a world record at 250 yards (13.4 seconds). By the time she retired, she had equaled or set seven track records from south Texas to northern California.

Monita was also durable. Her career spanned 1949 to 1955, and she had 89 official starts and an unknown number of match races. She undoubtedly felt the aches and pains that any horse would have with so many races. But she was a strong, hardy mare in an era when horses did not have the advantages of high-tech veterinary care.

With all the racing and travel from track to track, Monita was tough enough to win 30 races and an impressive 10 stakes races at a half-dozen tracks.

Monita was one of the toughest Quarter racing mares of all time. She's shown here in the winner's circle at Centennial in Denver in 1951. The identification on the photo lists L.M. Blackwell as the owner, E. Harris as the trainer, and Ike Garza as the jockey.

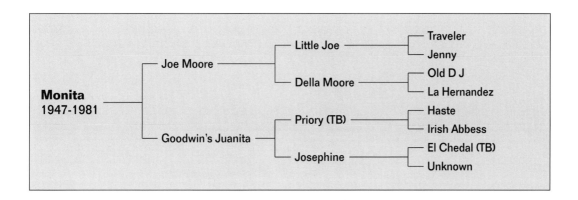

Monita 1947-1981

Joe Moore
- Little Joe
  - Traveler
  - Jenny
- Della Moore
  - Old D J
  - La Hernandez

Goodwin's Juanita
- Priory (TB)
  - Haste
  - Irish Abbess
- Josephine
  - El Chedal (TB)
  - Unknown

Monita was truly a competitor. After setting a world record in her career debut, Monita faced the best horses to be found on western straightaways over the next six years. From her 3-year-old year through her 8-year-old season, she won at least one stakes race each year.

Distances didn't matter to Monita. She won stakes at distances of 250 yards to 440 yards. The racing surface could be super quick or boggy mud. Nothing mattered. She just gave her all every time she broke from a starting gate.

Yes, Monita was a *race* horse.

Monita, Spanish for little cutie, was a filly with a willing disposition who quickly responded to training. Some old-timers believe that Monita was bred by Ott Adams, but her official AQHA record names J.F. Goodwin as her breeder. Monita was raised and started by Goodwin on his ranch near George West, Texas.

According to an article in the May 1966 issue of *Western Horseman*, Goodwin sent Monita to trainer Claude Bourland in San Antonio in 1949. Bourland, who also trained Thoroughbreds, believed that Monita needed plenty of work and lots of feed.

She thrived during her early training and grew into a 15-hand, 1,000-pound sorrel with plenty of sprinting muscle. But she was a smooth mare with long muscles that probably came from her dam, who was registered as a Quarter Horse called Goodwin's Juanita. Although she was officially a Quarter Horse, Juanita's sire was Priory, a Thoroughbred.

In her second start for Bourland, at

Halter and Performance Record: Had 89 official starts on the racetrack. Won 30, placed second 9 times and third 11 times. Earned $44,296. 1951 Co-World Champion Quarter Running Mare; 1951 Co-Champion Quarter Running Horse.

Produce of Dam Record:

Della's Queen	1957 mare by Leo Tag Racing Register of Merit
Fly Man Fly	1959 stallion by Vandy Racing Register of Merit
Flyita	1960 mare by Jet Flight (TB)
Mon Go	1962 stallion by Go Man Go Racing Register of Merit
Triple Money	1963 stallion by Triple Chick
Chickamona	1964 mare by Triple Chick Superior Race Horse Racing Register of Merit
Gotebo	1965 stallion by Go Man Go Racing Register of Merit
Scoot Deck	1966 stallion by Top Deck (TB) Racing Register of Merit
Mongo Bird	1967 stallion by Good Bird (TB) Racing Register of Merit
Go Again	1969 stallion by Triple Chick Racing Register of Merit
Here Again	1970 stallion by Go Man Go Racing Register of Merit
Gallant Heritage	1971 stallion by Go Man Go Racing Register of Merit

Frederickburg in August 1949, Monita easily defeated a seven-horse field at 220 yards in 12.4 seconds. Then at Del Rio in October, Monita set a world record of 13.4 seconds for 250 yards.

Monita edged past Barbara L. and Diamond Bob to win this 1951 race at Centennial.

Lewis Blackwell used his horse-trading skills to acquire Monita for $5,000 instead of the asking price of $10,000.

According to the *WH* article, "After Monita had set a new world record, some skeptics did not believe what they heard and other race-horse men, certain of their own speedsters, still wanted a chance at her. One of the best sprinters in that area was Jo Hanna, owned by George Pharr, Alice, Texas.

"On March 12, 1950, at the track in Premont, Tex., Pharr matched Jo Hanna against Monita for 300 yards, betting $12,000 to $7,000. Monita beat Jo Hanna by nearly two open lengths of daylight by racing down the laned track (lanes separated by a rope). She covered the 300 yards in 15.9, a new record for the Premont track."

Despite his mare's loss, Pharr still couldn't believe that Monita was the faster mare. So there was a rematch a couple of months later at Del Rio, and again Monita easily won.

Later in 1950, Monita won the Bay Meadows (Calif.) Handicap by racing the 440 yards in 22.6.

A New Owner

Lewis Blackwell of Amarillo, Tex., owner of a liquor dealership and a taxicab company, loved to acquire fast horses. He had owned and raced Hard Twist and Miss Panama when Monita came to his attention.

Blackwell loved a deal and the action that came with buying and selling fast horses. Perhaps the only thing that he en-

The great
Maddon's
Bright Eyes
battled Monita
five times
in 1951,
winning three.

Monita's
daughter
Chickamona,
by Triple Chick,
placed second
to Go Dick Go
in the 1966
All American
Futurity.

The great Maddon's Bright Eyes and Monita staged several heroic battles in 1951.

joyed more than racing horses was acquiring horses for as little money as possible.

Monita was building her reputation in south Texas, and Blackwell was in northwest Texas. Yet Monita's reputation had spread northward after just a few starts.

Blackwell got the word about the gritty little mare when she was a 3-year-old. Several months before Blackwell died in 1991, he told *The Quarter Racing Journal*'s editor, Rich Chamberlain, "I had some cattle on pasture in Kansas, and I was up there getting ready to ship. I ran into this ol' fella from south Texas who said, 'We got a little mare down in our part of the country named Monita that sure can run.'

"My ears went up. I remembered when she ran as a 2-year-old and set that world record, and a friend of mine who was down there came back telling me how fast she was—she'd run off and left all those other colts."

Blackwell sensed he could add another star to his already well-stocked stable. But he also wanted a deal.

Initially, Blackwell planned to buy Monita and send her to California to race. When he called the Goodwin home, Mrs. Goodwin told Blackwell that Goodwin and Monita had already gone to Bay Meadows in northern California.

Blackwell knew that if Monita started winning regularly at Bay Meadows her price would rise. However, if she lost, Goodwin might soften on the price.

Blackwell called his trainer at Bay Meadows, Walt Harris, and told him to keep an eye out for Monita. Harris reported back and told Blackwell that just a week after Monita was hauled from San Antonio to the track near San Francisco, she was entered in a race. Goodwin and his buddies had bet a bunch of their bankroll and the mare lost.

Monita was obviously getting tired. Harris told Blackwell that he felt Monita's connections had made a major training error. Then they compounded the mistake by repeatedly giving Monita hard workouts. Now she was tired and grouchy. Blackwell said that they even had to "ear" the filly in the paddock to saddle her.

Blackwell knew Monita was becoming more affordable. He went to Bay Meadows to see another of his horses run, but didn't even talk to Goodwin about Monita. He didn't want to appear overly interested in the mare.

Goodwin knew that Blackwell had talked to his wife about Monita and, upon returning to Texas, called Blackwell and priced Monita at $10,000.

Blackwell was not about to pay the asking price; he didn't like to do that for any horse. So they dickered back and forth. Blackwell finally said he'd pay $5,000 for Monita if she was sound. Goodwin agreed and Blackwell hitched up his trailer and headed south (the mare was back in Texas).

"They had her tied under a tree... she was a little mare just turning 4," Blackwell recalled. "She'd run at you with her mouth open, just sour. I couldn't see where she was

Monita as a 2-year-old with jockey Larry Jackson and (we think) trainer Claude Bourland.

Monita and her foal by Jet Flight (TB) at the E.L. Gosselin sale in Oklahoma in 1960 where she brought $27,000. She was 13 years old.

crippled, though, couldn't see anything wrong with her, so I bought her."

Blackwell knew the mare needed some rest and good care. He hauled her to Tucson where Harris was wintering with Hard Twist.

Upon seeing the mare come out of the trailer, Harris told Blackwell that she needed about 200 pounds, some rest, and "to be treated like a horse."

Harris started hand-grazing Monita on alfalfa and hand-feeding her grass cut from the roadside. The tired little mare started feeling friskier, and in a matter of weeks she was bucking and playing.

The sorrel was ready to make history.

Building Her Legacy

Many times legends are built with the help of a rival. In Monita's case, her legacy was built — in a large part — on her confrontations with the great Maddon's Bright Eyes, known at every track as Bright Eyes.

Named after a pale blue right eye, Bright Eyes was the 1949 World Champion Quarter Running Horse and the 1949 and 1950 World Champion Quarter Running Mare. Her dominance at any distance was overwhelming. She equaled the world record at 220 yards and was a futurity winner at 440 yards.

Bright Eyes was Quarter racing's queen when Monita started to feel like running again.

In 1951, the year of their showdown, Monita had begun the year racing while Bright Eyes started the year by resting. When they met for the first time, in mid-August, Monita had been loaded into the gates seven times; Bright Eyes just once.

The 1951 confrontations between Monita and Bright Eyes spanned five races in less than two months. After those five races, they only raced against each other once more.

Their first meeting took place on August 19 at La Mesa Park, which is in northeastern New Mexico on the south side to Raton Pass. Bright Eyes lived up to her high-profile reputation and raced to a 1-length victory over Monita in the 400-yard Raton Handicap.

Score: Bright Eyes 1, Monita 0.

The two mares were then shipped to Centennial Park, just south of Denver, and lined up against each other at a quarter-mile on August 31. This time Monita showed she could handle the two-time champion Bright Eyes. Monita raced the 440 yards in 22 seconds flat to win by 1½ lengths.

Score: Bright Eyes 1, Monita 1.

Bright Eyes was given another start at Centennial, which she won, and then was shipped to La Mesa Park.

After her Centennial victory, Monita shipped back to La Mesa.

In the 440-yard Sangre de Cristo Handicap at La Mesa Park on September 9, Monita showed she was in peak form. She blazed the quarter mile in 21.8 seconds for

In the second match race between Monita and Jo Hanna (right), the latter broke on top. But Monita soon swept by her. Note the rope separating the two lanes.

A headshot of Chickamona, Monita's most successful offspring.

the win. Bright Eyes could only manage fifth place after racing just six days earlier at Centennial.

Score: Monita 2, Bright Eyes 1.

Their final two meetings in 1951 took place during the New Mexico State Fair in Albuquerque.

In the 300-yard Shue Fly Stakes on September 30, Bright Eyes prevailed in the battle over Monita to win by three-fourths of a length in 15.7 seconds, a track record.

Score: Monita 2, Bright Eyes 2.

Their final meeting of 1951 took place over the classic distance of 440 yards in the New Mexico State Fair Championship, one of Quarter Horse racing's leading events of the era. It was a hard-fought duel over the classic Quarter Horse distance, and Bright Eyes prevailed by less than a length over Monita.

Score: Bright Eyes 3, Monita 2.

The voters for the 1951 championships could not separate the two mares, so they shared the titles of 1951 World Champion Quarter Running Horse and 1951 World Champion Quarter Running Mare.

Bright Eyes, the sport's reigning queen, had defended her titles won in 1949 and 1950. Monita had proved her equal.

In a period of five races over less than two months, Monita showed she had championship mettle. She had successfully battled the great Bright Eyes and shared the world title.

Monita raced four more years and was a stakes winner each year, but her competitions with Bright Eyes in 1951 defined

Go Man Go, to whom Monita was bred four times.

her class. (For more on Maddon's Bright Eyes, see *Legends 3*.)

Offspring

As a broodmare, Monita proved to be a useful producer. She had 12 foals, 10 reached the track, and they were each winners. However, none of them won a stakes race.

Monita's leading performer was Chickamona, her 1964 filly sired by Triple Chick. Chickamona was among the best of her foal crop despite not winning a stakes race. Chickamona ran second in the Raton Futurity at La Mesa Park and was second to Go Dick Go in the All American Futurity.

The sorrel mare earned her ROM and a Superior in racing.

Monita's 10 starters earned $126,472 with $111,671 of that total earned by Chickamona.

Other Monita foals to earn an ROM in racing included:

- Della's Queen, by Leo Tag.
- Fly Man Fly, by Vandy.
- Mongo, Gotebo, and Gallant Heritage, all by Go Man Go.
- Scoot Deck, by Top Deck (TB).
- Mongo Bird, by Good Bird (TB).
- Go Again, by Triple Chick.
- Triple Money, Monita's 1963 son by Triple Chick, never earned an ROM but did have 12 wins on the track and earned 17 halter points in the show ring.

According to AQHA records, Mel Hatley bought Monita in 1967. Hatley was a prominent breeder of Quarter racing horses at the time, and Monita produced three foals for him.

Although Monita did not set the world on fire as a broodmare, she set a world record in her first start and never ducked a rival over seven years of winning from south Texas to northern California.

Monita was a *race* horse. She died in 1981, according to AQHA records.

BILL CODY

By Frank Holmes

He was the AQHA's first Honor Roll halter horse.

AS THE AQHA's first Honor Roll halter horse and one of its first Superior halter award winners, Bill Cody helped set the standards for generations of show-ring stars to come.

Then, after his show days were over, he went on to found a family of halter and performance horses whose influence is still being felt. As a result of both of these accomplishments, he ranks as one of the breed's premier foundation horses.

Bill Cody was foaled in 1944 on the vast expanses of the King Ranch of Kingsville, Texas. As were all the King Ranch horses of that era, the chestnut stallion was the product of an intricate line-breeding program built almost solely on the blood of Old Sorrel (*Legends 4*).

Wimpy P-1, Bill Cody's sire, was by Solis, by Old Sorrel, and out of Panda, by Old Sorrel. Pesetita, his dam, was by Old Sorrel, and out of Peseta, by Cardenal, by Old Sorrel. Old Sorrel was a son of Hickory Bill, by Peter McCue. With

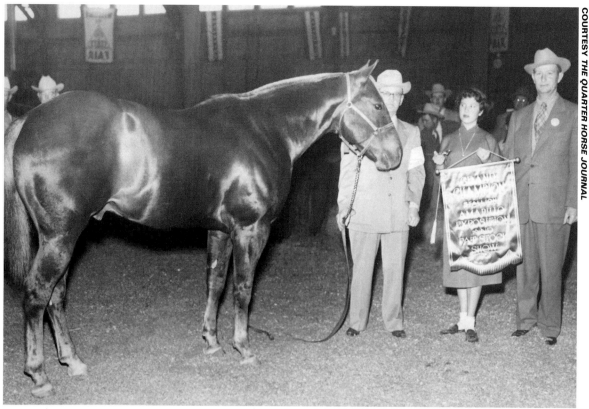

Bill Cody was one of the breed's first halter superstars. He is shown here with owner Glen Casey of Amarillo after earning grand champion stallion honors at either the 1952 or 1953 Amarillo Exposition and Fat Stock Show.

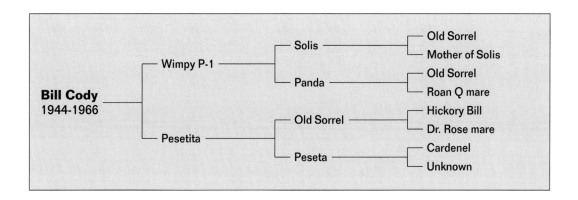

			Old Sorrel
		Solis	Mother of Solis
	Wimpy P-1		Old Sorrel
		Panda	Roan Q mare
Bill Cody 1944-1966			Hickory Bill
		Old Sorrel	Dr. Rose mare
	Pesetita		Cardenel
		Peseta	Unknown

Wimpy's dam, Panda, also being out of a daughter of Hickory Bill, this gave Bill Cody five close-up doses of Peter McCue's potent blood.

In January 1946 Joe "Watt" Hardin of Fort Worth purchased the then-unnamed 2-year-old chestnut colt from the King Ranch and registered him with the AQHA. Named in honor of the famous Indian fighter and Wild West showman, William F. "Wild Bill" Cody, Hardin's young stallion was assigned registration number 3244.

Hardin owned Bill Cody for more than 3½ years and showed him at halter throughout that time. Due to the fact that the AQHA point system was not yet in place, few records exist of those early outings.

But it is a matter of record that Bill Cody won the 2-year-old and 3-year-old stallion classes at the 1946 and 1947 Southwestern Livestock Expositions held in Fort Worth.

Also, in the May 1950 issue of *Back In The Saddle*—a Texas-based horse publication—Bill Cody and Hardin are pictured after winning grand champion stallion honors at the third annual Cisco, Tex., horse show on March 25.

The pair no doubt combined to win numerous other awards, but few official records exist of them.

In addition to showing him at halter, Hardin also had Bill Cody broke to ride, and even had him shown in performance by Roy Savage. Savage, who currently lives in Benbrook, Tex., remembers the stallion well.

"I'm not sure who actually broke Bill

Halter and Performance Record: Superior Halter (97 points); 1952 AQHA High-Point Halter Horse.

Progeny Record:

Foal Crops: 21	Performance Point-Earners: 47
Foals Registered: 255	Performance Points Earned: 679
AQHA Champions: 12	Performance Registers of Merit: 28
Halter Point-Earners: 68	Superior Performance Awards: 1
Halter Points Earned: 1,194	Race Starters: 3
Superior Halter Awards: 8	

Cody," he says. "Watt had a Mexican working for him during the mid- to late 1940s, and I'm pretty sure he started the horse under saddle.

"In the fall of 1948 or 1949, Watt got in touch with me and asked if I would take Cody for the winter and rope off him at some rodeo and jackpot roping events. Watt wanted to get Cody out before the public, to drum up interest in him. So I took him, and he made a better-than-average rope horse.

"As I remember him, Bill Cody stood around 15 hands and weighed in the neighborhood of 1,150 pounds. He was a nice horse for that day and age—nice-headed and well balanced with a lot of muscle in both his front and rear ends. And he was an even-dispositioned, willing horse.

"One of the first rodeos I took Cody to," he continues, "was at Ardmore, Oklahoma. Gene Autry used to produce the Madison Square Garden rodeo every winter, and he'd always stop by with his stock on the way to New York and put on the Ardmore

The King Ranch line-breeding horse program was designed to produce top working stock that was consistent in type and coloring. As evidenced by this photo of Wimpy P-1, and the preceding shot of Bill Cody, the ranch succeeded on both fronts.

"For as heavily made as he was, Cody had a lot of speed."

rodeo. Cody and I won the roping at Ardmore that year, and we did well in several others over the course of the winter. One roping I especially remember took place at Texhoma, Oklahoma.

"It was a jackpot roping and featured a pretty long score. For as heavily made as he was, Cody had a lot of speed. We won a go-round and the average there."

From September 1950 through September 1952, Savage did a stint in the U.S. Army. Upon his discharge he got one last chance to team up with Bill Cody.

"On September 6, the very day I got home from the Army," he says, "Watt called me and said that Glen Casey of Amarillo, Tex., who owned Bill Cody then, was coming to an AQHA show the next day in Fort Worth. Watt asked if I'd show Cody in the roping, and I said I would. There is a photo of us competing at that show, which was actually held at the HorseShoe Club's show grounds in Mesquite. That's the only shot I've ever seen of Cody as a rope horse, and that show was the last time I competed on him."

In the fall of 1950, Watt Hardin had sold Bill Cody to Dr. Darrell Sprott, a highly respected veterinarian from Killeen, Texas. Sprott continued with Cody's halter career and showed him to championships at Uvalde, Tex., and at the Texas State Fair in Dallas.

The pair picked up in early 1951 where they had left off the fall before. A win at Phoenix was followed by yet another grand championship at the Southwestern Livestock Exposition.

One of the duo's most impressive wins in 1951 came on May 18 at the Pacific Coast Quarter Horse Association's 7th Annual Spring Show, held in Santa Barbara, California.

There, Cody won the aged stallion class over such top West Coast stallions as Quicksand, Bras d'Or, Kelly, Tiptop, and Brown Bob. He then came back to earn grand champion stallion honors over J.B. King, the great AA AQHA Champion owned by Jay Parsons of Benson, Arizona.

And, as reported in a feature article on

PHOTO BY SKEET RICHARDSON

Dr. Darrell Sprott of Killeen, Tex., purchased Bill Cody from Watt Hardin in the fall of 1950 and showed him to some of his biggest halter victories. This photo was taken after Sprott showed Bill Cody to the grand champion stallion title at the 1951 Southwestern Exposition & Fat Stock Show in Fort Worth.

Sprott also exhibited Bill Cody to grand champion stallion honors at the 1951 Pacific Coast Quarter Horse Association's 7th Annual Spring Show, held in Santa Barbara. Note the tail length that was the style in those days.

the show, which appeared in the June-July 1951 issue of *The Horse Lover*, "Darrell Sprott saddled up Bill Cody on Saturday afternoon. With Bill Combs of San Luis Rey in the saddle, the stallion put on an exhibition of calf stopping that earned him loud applause from the crowd."

Several months prior to Bill Cody's foray to the West Coast, the AQHA executive committee had, during their March

PHOTO BY POTTS, COURTESY THE QUARTER HORSE JOURNAL

After standing champion at the 1951 Santa Barbara show, the 7-year-old stallion was then teamed with Bill Combs of San Luis Rey, Calif., to "put on an exhibition of calf stopping that earned him loud applause from the crowd."

PHOTO BY GRESSETT STUDIO

Miss V O H, a 1950 sorrel mare by Bill Cody and out of Sorrel Farr, is shown after earning grand champion mare honors at Killeen, Tex., as a weanling. She went on to earn 10 halter points and win the grand champion mare title at the 1952 National Western Stock Show in Denver.

annual meeting held at Colorado Springs, forever changed the face of Quarter Horse showing with their final approval of a national point system. Included among its features was the establishment of the Register of Merit, AQHA Champion, and Honor Roll (year-end high-point) awards.

The system was made retroactive to the beginning of the year, and Bill Cody was one of the first horses to achieve national recognition through it.

Unfortunately Sprott would not be around to see his faith in Bill Cody — as both a show horse and sire — justified. In the fall of 1951, he was killed in a car accident, and Cody was then sold to the man who would be his final owner — Glen Casey of Amarillo.

Even before he purchased Bill Cody, Casey was well known in Quarter Horse circles. As the owner and exhibitor of Jole Blon S. and Wilson's Lady — two top mares with more than 50 grand championships to their credit — Casey knew the halter horse game. And he figured Cody to be just the horse to take his show and breeding program to the next level.

With Casey hauling and exhibiting him, 1952 proved to be Bill Cody's most successful show year.

The pair began their 1952 campaign by

Lee Cody, a 1950 sorrel stallion by Bill Cody and out of Rodgers' Rockey, was an outstanding double-threat show horse. An AQHA Champion with Superiors in halter and cutting, he went on to sire six AQHA Champions and horses earning 15 Registers of Merit, 5 halter and performance Superiors, and 928 AQHA points.

earning grand champion honors at Vernon and Stamford, Tex., and reserve champion honors at Amarillo.

Then it was on to the New Mexico Spring Horse Fair, held June 13-15 in Albuquerque. There Cody took the blue in an aged stallion class that included Settle Up, owned by Rose Fulton of Dragoon, Ariz., and Nugget McCue S., owned by Warren Shoemaker of Watrous, New Mexico.

Bill Cody was then named grand champion stallion over a field that included Shoemaker's Pay Day, owned by Jack Kyle, Vaughn, N.M., and G-Fern Dashing Cat, owned by Ed Honnen of Denver.

Next came championships at Post, Vernon, and Olney, Tex.; Enid, Okla.; and a reserve at Odessa, Texas. Finally, the show season was ended with a championship at the fall Fort Worth show.

Cody's official AQHA show record for 1952 reveals that he was exhibited at 11 shows, winning 9 grands, 2 reserves, and 38 halter points. By today's standards, this was not an overly extensive campaign, but it was enough back then to secure him a spot in the AQHA record book as the 1952 Honor Roll Halter Horse—the first in the association's history.

With 60 official halter points to his credit by the end of the year, he was also

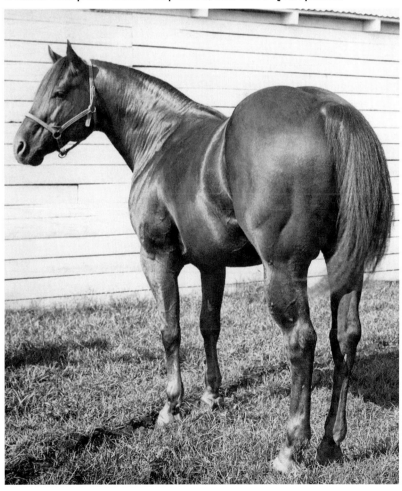

Glen Casey of Amarillo was an accomplished exhibitor. He's shown here with Jole Blon S., a Chubby daughter and one of Casey's top halter mares, after she earned grand champion honors at an early 1950s AQHA show.

Glen Casey was the last owner of Bill Cody and showed him to the grand champion stallion title at the 1955 New Mexico State Fair in Albuquerque.

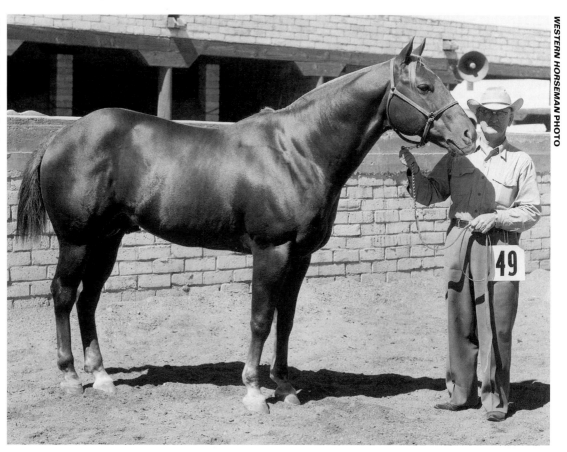

WESTERN HORSEMAN PHOTO

Town Crier, a 1951 sorrel stallion by Bill Cody and out of Watt's Niki, was owned by Paul Curtner of Jacksboro, Texas. They are shown here after Town Crier earned grand champion honors at the 1956 Santa Rosa Roundup. Curtner, of course, went on to even greater heights as the owner of both Poco Pine and Zippo Pat Bar.

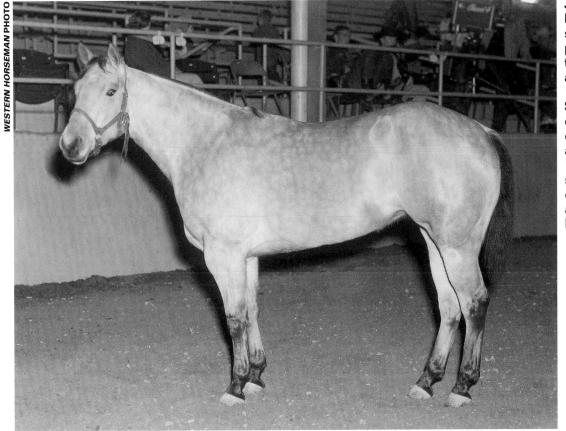

WESTERN HORSEMAN PHOTO

Jole Blon S. was bred to Bill Cody seven times and produced such top individuals as Blon Cody, a 1953 dun mare. Shown here after earning grand champion honors at the January 1957 Amarillo show, Blon Cody earned 59 points and a Superior halter award.

PHOTO BY STEWART'S

Unk Cody, a 1953 sorrel stallion, by Bill Cody and out of Sally Goodinlawrence, was an AQHA Champion. He is shown here after winning his halter class at the Colorado State Fair in Pueblo, circa 1955.

COURTESY THE QUARTER HORSE JOURNAL

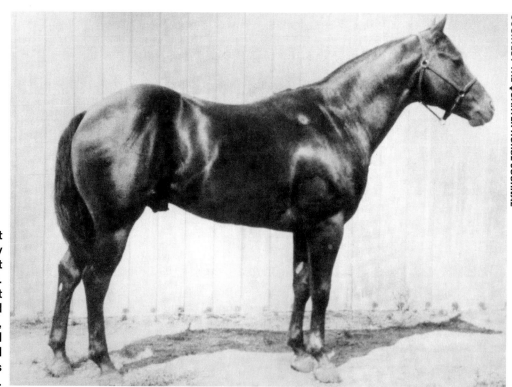

Babe Cody was yet another of the Bill Cody sons to greatly impact the Quarter Horse breed. A 1953 sorrel stallion out of Ormega, Babe sired 11 AQHA Champions, 9 Superior halter and performance horses, and the earners of 20 ROMs and 1,440 AQHA points.

Strole's Cat, a 1953 sorrel mare, by Bill Cody and out of Trammell's Little Bit, was an AQHA Champion and AQHA Champion producer. That's E.J. Freeman at the halter, according to the information on the back of the photo.

presented with one of the registry's first Superior awards in halter.

After the 1952 campaign, Cody was campaigned even more sparingly. In 1953, for instance, AQHA records list him as attending only two shows — Amarillo and Houston. He went grand at both.

In 1954 he was again hauled to two shows. At the National Western Livestock Show in Denver, he stood reserve champion to Monsieur Joe. At San Angelo, Tex., he was named grand champion over such good horses as Toots Mansfield, Poco Dell, and Easter King.

Finally, in 1955, AQHA records credit Cody with appearing at three shows. At the New Mexico State Fair in Albuquerque, he was named the grand champion stallion.

Bill Cody's complete show record, from AQHA records that are sketchy at best, reveal him to have earned 18 grand championships and 97 halter points in a show

career that spanned, officially, from 1951 through 1955.

It was enough, as it turns out, to give him a firm stake to the claim of being one of the breed's first official halter stars.

Sire Record

As good as he was in the show ring, however, Bill Cody's most lasting impact on the breed would come as a sire.

While owned by Watt Hardin, he sired a number of top show and breeding horses.

Lee Cody, a 1950 sorrel stallion out of Rodgers' Rockey, by Revenue, was an AQHA Champion and also earned Superiors in halter and cutting.

Miss V O H, a 1950 sorrel mare out of Sorrel Farr, by Jazz, by Harmon Baker, stood grand champion as a 2-year-old at the National Western Stock Show in Denver.

O'Meara's Scotty, a 1950 sorrel gelding

Blair Cody, a 1960 brown stallion, by Bill Cody and out of Sarah Robinson, was an AQHA Champion and Superior halter horse with 162 points, and had 73 performance points to his credit. He is shown here after being named grand champion stallion at the March 1965 Riverside, Calif., AQHA show.

From Cody's 1954 foal crop, Babe Cody was the star.

out of Miss John Scott, by Silver King; Cody's Pet, a 1951 bay mare out of Pet Squaw, by Revenue; and Town Crier, a 1951 sorrel stallion out of Watt's Niki, by Nicky, by Sheik P-11, were all AQHA Champions and Superior halter horses.

Sue Cody, a 1951 sorrel mare out of Sterling City Sue, by Dodger, by Harmon Baker, was also an AQHA Champion.

Getting back to Bill Cody himself, he sired only one crop of foals while owned by Darrell Sprott. Foaled in 1952, that crop included such hallmark producers as Joe Cody and Codalena.

Joe Cody, a 1952 sorrel stallion out of Taboo, by King P-234, was an AQHA Champion who went on to rewrite Quarter Horse history under the ownership of C.T. Fuller of Catasauqua, Pa., (see following chapter).

Codalena, a 1952 sorrel mare, was a full sister to Town Crier. Unshown herself, she became one of the breed's premier producers with six AQHA Champions to her credit.

After Dr. Sprott's death, Bill Cody was purchased by Glen Casey in February of 1952 and remained under his control for the remainder of his life.

From Casey's first crop of Bill Cody foals—born in 1953—came the likes of Blon Cody, Strole's Cat, and Unk Cody.

Blon Cody, a dun mare out of Jole Blon S., by Chubby, was a Superior halter horse. Both Strole's Cat, a sorrel mare out of Trammell's Little Bit, by Joe Green, and Unk Cody, a sorrel stallion out of Sally Goodinlawrence, by Cowboy Mike, were AQHA Champions.

From Cody's 1954 foal crop, Babe Cody was the star. Under the ownership of the Sutton Brothers of Agar, S.D., he became one of the Northern Plains' most influential early sires.

Over the course of the next five years— from 1955 through 1959—the Bill Cody foal crops were exceptionally small. Averaging in the single digits, they managed to put only two performers in the AQHA record books.

Casey Cody, a 1955 sorrel stallion out of Wilson's Lady, by Dan Waggoner, earned 17 halter points. Winfred Cody, a 1959 palomino stallion out of Jole Blon S., was an AQHA Champion and a Superior halter horse.

The 1960 and 1961 foal crops were slightly larger—averaging 11—but they, too, only

This Bill Cody get-of-sire entry featured three champions. From the left, they are Winfred Cody, a 1959 palomino stallion out of Jole Blon S.; Casey Cody, a 1955 sorrel stallion out of Wilson's Lady; and Blon Cody, a 1953 dun mare out of Jole Blon S.

PHOTO BY ESTER

The product of powerful genetics, Bill Royal was by Bill Cody and out of White Sox Lady, by Royal King. The 1963 sorrel stallion lived up to his heritage by becoming an AQHA Champion and Superior halter horse.

Clif Cody Jr., a 1959 gray stallion by Clif Cody and out of Blue Eye Cox, was a double-bred Bill Cody and an AQHA Champion.

PHOTO BY JACK STRAYHORN, COURTESY *THE QUARTER HORSE JOURNAL*

contributed two foals to Bill Cody's list of AQHA point-earning performers.

Blair Cody, a 1960 brown stallion out of Sarah Robinson, by Jubilee Joe, was an AQHA Champion and a Superior halter horse. Chub Cody, a 1961 bay stallion out of Cutie, by Chub, earned 31 halter and 9 performance points.

For the 1961 and 1962 breeding seasons, Bill Cody was leased by Victor Orsinger's North Wales Quarter Horse Farm in Warrenton, Virginia. This move resulted in renewed interest in the 17-year-old stallion and made the 1962 and 1963 foal crops, numbering 16 and 7 respectively, two of the largest of Cody's breeding career.

From them came the AQHA Champions Cash Cody, a 1962 buckskin stallion out of Poco A Poco, by Poco Bob, and Bill Royal, a 1963 sorrel stallion out of White Sox Lady, by Royal King.

In addition, Gigi Bon Cody, 1963 chestnut mare out of Replica, by Rey Del Rancho, earned 12 halter and 6.5 performance points, and Ninita Cody, a 1963 dun mare out of Nina Kleberg, by Lowder, earned 4 halter and 29.5 performance points.

For the 1963, 1964, and 1965 breeding seasons, Bill Cody returned to West Texas. Again, he was lightly bred. With his final three foal crops averaging fewer than four,

PHOTO BY WALLOT, COURTESY THE QUARTER HORSE JOURNAL

Here's Bill Cody (right) and his daughter Blon Cody, photographed at the North Wales Quarter Horse Farm, Warrenton, Va., in either 1961 or 1962.

he put his last point-earning performer in the record books in 1970.

Kip Cody has the dual distinction of being both Bill Cody's last registered get and his last AQHA performer. A 1966 sorrel stallion out of Ma Koy, by V. Day Koy, he earned 36 halter points.

Bill Cody died in July of 1966 as a result of colic. He was 22 years old.

From 21 foal crops, he sired 255 foals, of which 101 were performers. They earned 12 AQHA Championships, 8 Superior halter awards, 1 Superior performance award, 28 ROMs, and 1,194 halter and 679 performance points.

As a show horse and a sire, Bill Cody made his mark. In terms of his lasting influence on the breed through successive generations, he accomplished even more.

Through his sons Lee Cody, Joe Cody, and Babe Cody, Bill Cody helped reshape the Quarter Horse halter and reining industries.

Through such daughters and granddaughters as Codalena, Annie Lee Cody, Mickey's Cody, Crier's Betty, Pines Plaudit, and Georgia Cody, he did the same to the western pleasure and cutting industries.

All in all, Bill Cody was one of the great early trailblazers of the Quarter Horse breed, and a horse whose descendants are still finding new roads to explore in virtually every phase of the industry.

JOE CODY

By Frank Holmes

He was the patriarch of the Quarter Horse breed's first great reining horse dynasty.

SINCE JOE CODY was sired by Bill Cody, the AQHA's first Honor Roll halter horse, it seems logical Joe would have been groomed for a halter career as well.

Instead, he was pointed to the performance arena where he became one of the top cutting horses of his day. Then he went on to become an all-time leading

Joe Cody is shown here as an aged stallion at Willow Brook Farms in Catasauqua, Pennsylvania.

COURTESY NRHA

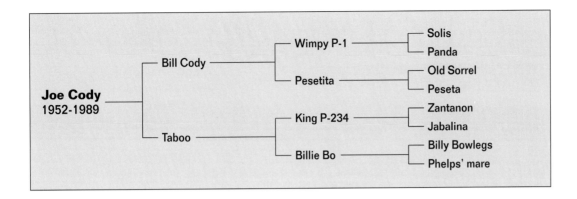

sire of performance horses, especially reining horses..

Joe Cody, a 1952 sorrel stallion out of Taboo, by King P-234, was bred by Tom Cochran of Belton, Texas.

Bill Cody, as discussed in the previous chapter, was the great King Ranch-bred halter champion and sire. And Taboo, as a direct daughter of King P-234, also came from a very accomplished and highly respected line. In any study of Joe Cody's pedigree, it's generally overlooked what Billie Bo — his maternal granddam — contributed to his genetic makeup.

Billie Bo was a 1934 bay mare, sired by Billy Bowlegs and out of a Phelps mare. Bred by AQHA Hall of Fame inductee George Clegg of Alice, Tex., she was purchased in the late 1930s by Doc Spence of Belton, Texas.

Spence was a well-known rodeo contestant at the time and, in short order, Billie became his primary calf roping, bulldogging, and match-racing mount. In addition, the talented mare served as a barrel racing horse for Spence's wife, Bennie Lee.

Doc and Bennie Lee's son, Sam Ed Spence — former staff member of *The Quarter Horse Journal* and executive secretary of the American Paint Horse Association — remembers Joe Cody's granddam very well.

"When dad brought Billie home from Mr. Clegg's," he says, "she was one of the first Quarter Horses in our part of the country. She was an Old DJ-bred mare, and showed a lot of Thoroughbred in her conformation.

"Dad rodeoed off of Billie for years, throughout the Southwest and as far east as Florida. One year at Kissimmee, Fla.—it was either 1944 or 1945 — he entered her

Halter and Performance Record: Performance ROM; AQHA Champion; 1995 AQHA Hall of Fame Horse; 1996 NRHA Hall of Fame Horse.

Progeny Record:

Foal Crops: 23	Performance Point-Earners: 156
Foals Registered: 324	Performance Points Earned: 5,600.5
AQHA Champions: 13	Performance Registers of Merit: 80
World Champions: 5	Superior Performance Awards: 30
Halter Point-Earners: 41	Race Starters: 2
Halter Points Earned: 455	Race Money Earned: $3,383
Superior Halter Awards: 1	Race Registers of Merit: 1
Leading Race Money-Earner: Cajun Cody ($2,853)	

in a series of match races against some Thoroughbreds.

"She won her preliminary races and was set to run in the finals. The day before that race, dad rode her in the bulldogging. A steer set up on them and hooked Billie in the shoulder.

"Dad went ahead and ran her the next day, and later told me she had the race won up until the final few strides. Then he felt Billie's shoulder give way. She faltered and was narrowly defeated.

"Darrell Sprott, of Killeen, Tex., was my dad's closest friend," he continues. "After he came back from World War II, Dr. Sprott registered Billie with the AQHA for Dad. For some reason, he put the mare in his name, but he never owned her. She was always Dad's horse.

"Billie was kind of a legend in our neck of the woods, and it's nice to see that her blood has been carried on to the present."

In 1942, looking to breed his rodeo mount for the first time, Doc Spence hauled her 350 miles southwest, to the Rocksprings, Tex., ranch of Jess Hankins and King.

"When Daddy bred to King," Sam Ed says, "the stud fee was only $50. Mr. Hankins had only owned King for five years or so, and he was just beginning to make a name for himself as a sire. Before too long, the stud fee would go up."

But $50 it was at the time, and well worth it as it would turn out. In the spring of 1943,

COURTESY SAM ED SPENCE

Doc Spence roping on Billie Bo, the granddam of Joe Cody. The picture was taken in the mid-1940s in central Texas, either at Belton or in that vicinity. Doc also used Billie Bo for bulldogging.

Here's a nice three-quarter-rear conformation study of Joe Cody, taken shortly after he was acquired by C.T. Fuller.

Although he founded an all-time great family of reining horses, Joe Cody's own specialty was cutting. This shot of him is reprinted from an article entitled "Comeback Horse: Joe Cody" that appeared in the May 1965 issue of *Western Horseman*.

the mating of King and Billie Bo resulted in a brown filly named Taboo. Tom Cochran, a neighbor of Spence, purchased the King filly when she was a yearling.

Squaw H, another King daughter who would become a south Texas racing legend,

was a year older than Taboo and just beginning to make her presence felt on the straightaways. No doubt influenced by Squaw's early showings, Cochran put his King mare in race training.

Taboo's official AQHA performance

PHOTO BY BERT BOLLINGER, COURTESY *THE QUARTER HORSE JOURNAL*

Janna Cody was the first get of Joe Cody to excel as a show horse. A 1958 dun mare out of Miss Black Jacket, Janna earned an AQHA Championship in 1962 and a Superior at halter in 1963.

Like her mother, Taboo was blessed with a certain amount of speed and athletic ability.

record reveals that, from five starts, she placed first once, second once, third once, and achieved a speed index of 65.

In an account published in the February 1956 issue of *The Quarter Horse Journal*, however, Taboo is portrayed as "an outstanding Quarter Horse race mare, having been raced at Del Rio and in Arizona." The piece further states, "She holds the track record at Del Rio, and was defeated in only one race out of nineteen starts."

No matter which version of her racing career is more accurate, one thing is certain. Like her mother, Taboo was blessed with a certain amount of speed and athletic ability. In 1950, with her racing career behind her, it was time to turn Taboo into a broodmare.

The stallion Cochran chose to breed her to first was King Raffles (TB). From this cross came the 1951 chestnut stallion Tab Raff. Next, and for the only time, Taboo was bred to Bill Cody—with Joe Cody as the result.

Seemingly unable to decide whether to raise race horses or arena performers out of Taboo, Cochran and a subsequent owner,

George Glascock of Cresson, Tex., bred the mare to such race sires as Lightning Bar and Hy Balmy and such performance-bred horses as Fourble Joe and Wimpy Leo. From these efforts would come only one additional performer. Taboo Leo, a 1964 bay mare by Wimpy Leo, achieved a speed index of 75.

Several of Taboo's foals did go on to sire and produce well. Tab Raff sired four ROM arena performers, and Taboo Bar, a 1957 bay mare by Lightning Bar, produced two ROM race horses.

But Joe Cody was the sole superstar that Taboo produced. And, as fate would have it, he would be shown to some of his highest achievements by the man who had bred his dam.

The Youngest Champion

Shortly after Joe Cody was foaled, he was acquired by Watt Hardin of Aledo, Tex., the man who had purchased Bill

Sappho Cody, a 1959 dun mare out of Hapgood's Sal, was Joe's first Honor Roll (high-point) champion. Shown here with Bob Anthony up, Sappho was the 1963 AQHA High-Point Reining Horse.

Easter Cody, a 1960 dun full sister to Sappho Cody, was the 1965 AQHA High-Point Reining Horse, and the 1966 and 1967 AQHA High-Point Working Cow Horse. Also an AQHA Champion, the good-looking mare earned 32 halter and 244.5 performance points. That's Bob Anthony in the saddle.

Cody from the King Ranch. In July 1954, when Joe was 15 months old, Hardin sold him to Robert F. Roberts of Joaquin, Texas. Roberts had earlier purchased Lee Cody, a 1950 sorrel stallion by Bill Cody and out of Rodgers Rockey, from Hardin and Sam Rodgers of Fort Worth.

With the acquisition of Joe, Roberts now owned two of Bill Cody's most promising sons.

"My father went to work as the ranch manager and trainer for Mr. Roberts in the fall of 1954," Sam Ed Spence says. "Lee Cody and Joe Cody had both been started

under saddle and even been shown some by that time. Willis Bennett did most of the early training on Lee, and he, Jack Hat, Eldon McCloud, and L.N. Sykes all put in time on Joe.

"My dad finished the AQHA Championships on both horses, with Lee getting his toward the end of 1954 and Joe being awarded his on January 1, 1955. Those two studs were the first AQHA Champions sired by Bill Cody and, at the time he earned his championship, Joe Cody was the youngest one in the history of the association.

"Those first three full years that he

Sal Cody was yet another top result of the Joe Cody-Hapgood's Sal cross. A 1961 dun mare, she earned her AQHA Championship in 1968.

worked for Mr. Roberts—1955 through 1957—were probably the most successful years my dad ever enjoyed as a trainer and showman.

"When Dad went to work for Mr. Roberts, he brought with him a half-Thoroughbred, appendix-registered gelding named Knocky. He sold half-interest in him to Mr. Roberts and then campaigned him to the 1956 Honor Roll titles in both reining and calf roping. At the time, that had never been done on any horse. He also showed Knocky to his AQHA Championship and a Superior in reining.

"Then, in 1957, he showed Lee Cody to

ninth place in the NCHA Top 10. Dad was a top hand with a horse, and Mr. Roberts saw to it that he had some good ones to ride."

Among those good ones, of course, was Joe Cody.

The Show Horse

As is the case with a number of Quarter Horses shown in the early to mid-1950s, Joe Cody's AQHA show record does not necessarily reflect the true extent of his placings. Shows often did not send their results to AQHA, which added to the association's difficulties in keeping accurate records in that era.

Officially, Joe is credited with 10 halter points, no firsts, and no grands or reserves. But in a full-page ad in the November 1955 issue of *The Quarter Horse Journal*, the Roberts Ranch credits Joe with earning 10 firsts, 7 seconds, 5 thirds, and 3 reserve championships at halter.

Joe's official record in performance shows that in cutting, he earned 46 points and had nine wins. In reining, 4 points and one win. Three of Joe's four reining points were garnered in his one official win at the January 24, 1960, AQHA show in Trenton, New Jersey. The AQHA record also reveals that he won his first reining point at a 1954 Abilene, Tex., show. The Roberts Ranch ad further credits him with being the champion reining horse of that show.

Both accounts reveal that the sorrel stallion's most impressive outing of his AQHA Championship run occurred in January 1955 at the Southwestern Exposition and Livestock Show in Fort Worth. There, he tied for third in a class of 51 junior cutting horses, and earned 4 points.

Joe was shown on a very limited basis after earning his AQHA Championship and in March 1958 was sold to Mrs. Virginia Epes Harper of Long Island, New York. Although Doc Spence helped orchestrate the sale, the loss of Joe Cody was something that he viewed with a certain amount of trepidation.

"Dad was fond of both Lee Cody and Joe Cody," Sam Ed says. "Mr. Roberts tended to

Here's Workman's Joe, a 1961 sorrel stallion by Joe Cody and out of Paprika Nicha. Shown by Bob Anthony, he was the 1966 AQHA High-Point Reining Stallion.

Josie Cody, a 1963 sorrel mare by Joe Cody and out of Twisty Whiz, achieved her fame in the cutting arena. The earner of 80 points and a Superior in cutting, she was also an AQHA Champion.

favor Lee and, as a result, he got the most opportunities as a show and cutting horse. I'm sure Dad was a little prejudiced toward Joe because of the bottom side of his pedigree, but I think Dad always felt that Joe would go on and make the best breeding horse.

"I was a teenager when we moved onto the Roberts Ranch," he continues. "I got to cut cattle with Joe Cody a couple of times. The one time I remember in particular occurred when I was 16. I had cut out a pretty salty cow for Joe to work and, at one point, she made a quick move to dive past him along the fence. Joe dropped to his knees to block the cow. That was the first time I'd ever seen a cutting horse do that, let alone be atop one when it happened.

"It remains as one of the most awesome horseback experiences I've ever experienced.

"Joe Cody was as cowy as they come, and it was always a great source of pride to my dad that, in some small way, he had something to do with the horse's background and show career."

Eastward Bound

Once she got Joe Cody safely settled in at his new home — the Indian Field Ranch located near Montauk Point on the eastern tip of Long Island, Mrs. Harper continued his show career.

Shown exclusively in performance, Joe racked up five firsts, eight seconds, and one third in AQHA-approved cutting events. As

High Proof, a 1970 sorrel gelding by Joe Cody and out of Liz Five, was a two-time world champion. Shown here with Bob Loomis, High Proof was the 1974 AQHA World Champion Junior Reining Horse and the 1976 AQHA World Champion Senior Reining Horse.

Red God, a 1969 sorrel gelding by Joe Cody and out of Tiara Bar, was the 1973 AQHA High-Point Reining Horse. The beautifully balanced gelding was also an AQHA Champion and a Superior reining horse.

noted earlier, he was shown once in reining and placed first.

Mrs. Harper also had Joe campaigned in NCHA-sanctioned events. He twice won the NCHA trophy presented to the top horse of the East Coast Cutting Horse Association, and had $2,251 in NCHA earnings.

In 1961 he even became a Quarter Horse ambassador when Mrs. Harper accepted an invitation by the Bermuda government to bring Joe to their agricultural fair to give a cutting and reining exhibition. He was reported to have performed flawlessly before an enthusiastic and appreciative crowd.

In August 1964, Joe Cody sold for the third and final time. His new owner, C.T. "Tom" Fuller of Catasauqua, Pa., had gotten in the Quarter Horse business several years earlier at the urging of his horse-crazy daughter.

With Joe Cody's arrival at Fuller's Willow Brook Farms, the stage was set for a combination of human and equine talent that would rewrite the Quarter Horse record books and establish one of the most accomplished performance horse dynasties of all time.

Ride 'N' Slide Time

Shortly after acquiring him, Fuller briefly brought Joe out of retirement to show him at the Syracuse, N.Y., fall horse show. The 12-year-old stallion acquitted himself well, making the finals in the cutting and defeating his stablemate, Hardy's Jessie, in the process.

But at Willow Brook the emphasis on Joe Cody was to be as a sire. What's more, he was destined to become a sire of not just halter and cutting horses, but also of reiners: a highly successful sire of reiners.

Even before heading east, Joe Cody had begun to establish himself as a sire. Consistently forced to play second fiddle to Lee Cody in terms of numbers and quality of mares bred, Joe still managed to sire Janna Cody, a 1958 dun mare and a Superior halter horse, and Jose Mellis, a 1958 chestnut gelding and a Superior cutting horse.

COURTESY THE QUARTER HORSE JOURNAL

Sapphire Cody, a 1967 dun mare by Joe Cody and out of Hapgood's Sal, was the 1971 AQHA High-Point Reining Horse. The cross of Joe Cody and Hapgood's Sal was one of the greatest in Quarter Horse history, producing the earners of five Honor Roll titles, three AQHA Championships, three Superior reining awards, and one Superior working cow horse award.

From Joe's first two eastern foal crops, before Fuller bought him, came his first two reining superstars. Sappho Cody, a 1959 dun mare, and Easter Cody, a 1960 dun mare, were full sisters out of Hapgood's Sal, a 1948 dun mare by Sappho's Bertie.

Both mares were bred by Marion Harper Jr. of New York and purchased by C.T. Fuller as yearlings. As to why they were

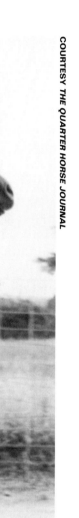

Benito Paprika, a 1975 sorrel mare by Doc's Benito Bar and out of Paprika Cody, was shown by Bob Loomis to the 1977 AQHA World Champion Junior Reining Horse title. The Joe Cody granddaughter was also the 1978 AQHA Reserve World Champion Senior Reining Horse.

developed as reiners, the answer can be boiled down to two words: Bob Anthony.

"I got into the Quarter Horse business in the early 1960s because my daughter Holly wanted some horses around," Tom Fuller says. "After I bought a couple of horses for her, I advertised for someone to help take care of them. Bob Anthony applied and it all just sort of snowballed from there. Bob was a Quarter Horse man whose primary interest was reining, so that's the direction the Willow Brook program took."

Upon arriving at the Fuller farm, Sappho Cody and Easter Cody were turned over to Anthony to be readied for show careers.

Sappho was shown to her AQHA Championship in 1963, with Easter earning

hers the following year. In 1963, Sappho earned a Superior in reining and was the AQHA High-Point Reining Horse. Easter earned the same honors in 1965, and was also the 1966 and 1967 AQHA High-Point Working Cow Horse.

By the fall of 1964, C.T. Fuller and Bob Anthony could see that Joe Cody, the sire of their champion mares, belonged at Willow Brook. The deal was made and the rest is history.

Sal Cody, a 1961 dun mare, was the third member of the Joe Cody-Hapgood's Sal family to make her mark in the show ring. Bred by Mrs. Virginia Harper, she was purchased by Willow Brook Farms and shown to her AQHA Championship by Anthony in 1963.

Here's Croton Cody, a
1972 sorrel stallion by Joe
Cody and out of
Crotonette. An AQHA
Champion, Croton was
also a Superior western
pleasure horse.

**The deal was
made and the
rest is history.**

Workman's Joe was also foaled in 1961. A sorrel stallion out of Paprika Nicha, by Burnett Hancock, Workman's Joe earned a Superior in reining and was the 1966 AQHA High-Point Reining Stallion.

Josie Cody, a 1963 sorrel mare out of Twisty Whiz, and Bo Cody, a 1963 sorrel gelding out of Go Silvertone, earned their AQHA Championships, with Whiz tacking on a Superior in cutting for good measure.

More great horses were quick to follow:

- Paprika Cody, a 1964 sorrel full sister to Workman's Joe, was the 1968 AQHA High-Point Junior Reining Horse and the overall high-point reining horse. She was also an AQHA Champion and a Superior reining horse.

- Big Red Cody, a 1965 gelded full brother to Paprika Cody and Workman's Joe, was the 1975 AQHA High-Point Hunter Under Saddle Gelding and earned Superiors in open and youth hunter under saddle.

- Big Bob Cody, a fourth performer from the Joe Cody-Paprika Nicha cross, was the 1975 AQHA Reserve World Champion Senior Reining Horse.

- Baby K Cody and Mano Cody were AQHA Champions.

- Mando Cody earned a Superior in trail.

- Jetarrow Cody earned Superiors in youth western pleasure and western horsemanship.

- Sapphire Cody, a 1967 buckskin mare

Here's a Joe Cody granddaughter of a different color. Las Vegas Moon, a 1979 gray mare by Cypress Moon and out of Vegas Cody, was the 1984 Youth AQHA World Champion Trail Horse. The elegant performer also earned Superiors in trail and western riding, and amassed 536.5 AQHA points.

PHOTO BY LEROY WEATHERS, COURTESY *THE QUARTER HORSE JOURNAL*

out of Hapgood's Sal, followed her three full sisters into the record books as the 1971 AQHA High-Point Junior Reining Horse and overall high-point reining horse. And, like her sisters, she also earned a Superior in reining.

- Tawny Cody, a 1968 dun mare out of Tiara Bar, by Steel Bars, became Joe Cody's seventh high-point or world champion reining horse when she was named the 1974 AQHA World Champion Senior Reining Horse. She, too, was an AQHA Champion.

- Kafka, a 1969 brown gelding out of Beth Ann King, was the 1973 AQHA High-Point Junior and All-Ages Hunter Under Saddle Horse, the 1974 AQHA Reserve World Champion Senior Hunter Under Saddle Horse, a youth AQHA performance champion, and the earner of 5 youth Superiors and 715 AQHA points.

- Cody Squaw, a 1969 sorrel mare out of Squaw Ballerina, was a Superior youth

western pleasure horse who earned 228 total AQHA points.

- Red God, a 1969 sorrel gelding out of Tiara Bar, was the 1973 AQHA High-Point Junior Reining Horse and overall high-point reining horse, an AQHA Champion, and a Superior reining horse.

- Pat's Pal, a 1969 sorrel gelding out of May Band, was the 1979 Youth AQHA Reserve World Champion Reining Horse.

- Rachel Forrest, a chestnut mare out of Liz Five, earned a Superior in trail.

- High Proof, a 1970 sorrel gelding out of Liz Five, was the 1974 AQHA World Champion Junior Reining Horse, 1975 NRHA Open Horse of the Year, and the 1976 AQHA World Champion Senior Reining Horse.

- Solar Cody, foaled in 1970, earned a Superior in western pleasure.

- Cheyenne Joe Cody, another 1970 foal, earned a Superior in trail.

- Barbie Cody, still another 1970 foal,

earned a Superior in youth western horsemanship.

- Guitar Mama, a 1972 palomino mare out of Wofford's Sable, was the 1976 AQHA World Champion Junior Reining Horse.
- Cody Nine, a 1974 bay stallion out of Paprika Nicha, was the 1978 AQHA World Champion Junior Reining Horse.
- Jody Cody Power, a 1975 sorrel mare out of Honey Power, was the 1979 AQHA Reserve World Champion Junior Reining Horse.
- Croton Cody, a 1972 sorrel stallion out of Crotonette, was an AQHA Champion and a Superior western pleasure horse.
- Guru Cody, a 1972 sorrel gelding, earned a Superior in hunter under saddle.
- Cassandra Cody, a 1976 sorrel mare out of Dudes Baby Doll, by Blondy's Dude, won the 1979 NRHA Futurity.
- Topsail Cody, a 1977 chestnut stallion out of Doc Bar Linda, by Doc Bar, won the 1980 NRHA Futurity. He was also the 1981 AQHA World Champion Junior Reining Horse, a 1996 inductee into the NRHA Hall of Fame, and a legend in his own right.

And he was Joe Cody's last performer.

A Life of Leisure

Joe Cody was retired from breeding after the 1976 season. Pensioned to a two-stall barn and a spacious paddock surrounded by the giant willows that gave his long-time home its name, Joe had as a companion the aged mare Wofford's Sable. Sable had been Holly Fuller's equitation horse at one time, and was the dam of the world champion reining horse Guitar Mama.

When Sable died in 1984, she was replaced by Dream Girl, a 35-year-old Shetland mare.

Joe Cody passed away on July 1, 1989, at the age of 37. He died on the morning of the first day of the Joe Cody Classic, a three-day reining show named in his honor and held at Willow Brook Farms. He was buried that evening on the hill overlooking the farm's outdoor arena.

A Summary

Joe Cody's final record as a sire was nothing short of phenomenal. In halter, 41 of his get earned 1 Superior and 455 points. In performance, 156 of his get earned 30 Superiors, 80 ROMs, and 5,600.5 points.

Nine Joe Cody sons and daughters amassed six AQHA world championships and four reserves, while six of his get accounted for eight AQHA high-point awards.

Two of his get were NRHA Futurity winners, and more than 30 were NRHA money-earners.

And the next generation did as well or better.

Topsail Cody, as noted earlier, went on to become a legendary sire in his own right (see next chapter). As of early 2001, he had sired the earners of more than $1 million in NRHA competition.

Such other sons as Corona Cody, Bonac Cody, Heza Banjoe, Cody Nine, Kid Five Cody, and Three Star Cody also sired NRHA money-earners.

Through December 1999, Joe Cody daughters had produced six AQHA world champions, four reserve world champions, four AQHA Champions, and the earners of 33 Superior halter and performance awards and 7,758 AQHA points.

They have also produced the earners of $411,336 in NRHA competition and $79,038 in NCHA-sanctioned events.

As the son of the Quarter Horse breed's first Honor Roll halter champion, and out of a family of mares who had proven their mettle, Joe Cody did not rest on the laurels of his forebears.

He carved his own niche, first as a performer, and then as a legendary reining horse sire. In recognition of his many contributions, he was inducted into the AQHA Hall of Fame in 1995 and the NRHA Hall of Fame in 1996.

Joe Cody, through his abilities as a sire, changed the landscapes of both the Quarter Horse breed and the reining horse industry for the better.

His grandmother would have been proud.

6 TOPSAIL CODY

By Frank Holmes

His story is one of great success, and the final chapters have yet to be written.

IN HORSE breeding, the paramount goal is to have each generation come out a little better than the preceding one. In the Quarter Horse family that originated with Bill Cody and continued with Joe Cody, that's what happened.

Topsail Cody — a member of the family's third generation — continued the trend. And, even more than with his predecessors, his has been a case of powerful genetics being given every opportunity to excel.

Topsail Cody was bred by C.T. "Tom" Fuller and foaled on his picturesque Willow Brook Farms near Catasauqua, Pa., on March 11, 1977. The horse was sired by Joe Cody and was out of Doc Bar Linda, by Doc Bar.

For the first two-thirds of his life, Topsail was owned by NRHA Hall of Fame member Bob Loomis of Marietta, Oklahoma. Loomis' relationship with the Joe Cody horses goes back a long way.

"I've been breeding, training, and showing reining horses for more than 35 years," Loomis says. "I started riding reining horses for Mr. Fuller in 1976. He and Joe

This 1995 conformation study of Topsail Cody shows the compact, well-balanced look so typical of the Joe Codys.

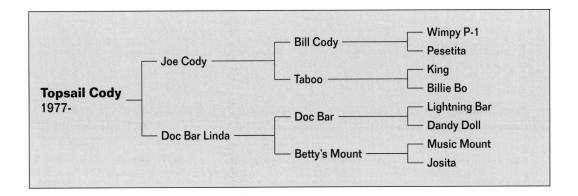

Topsail Cody
1977-
├── Joe Cody
│   ├── Bill Cody
│   │   ├── Wimpy P-1
│   │   └── Pesetita
│   └── Taboo
│   ├── King
│   └── Billie Bo
└── Doc Bar Linda
    ├── Doc Bar
    │   ├── Lightning Bar
    │   └── Dandy Doll
    └── Betty's Mount
        ├── Music Mount
        └── Josita

Cody are probably the two greatest things to happen to my career.

"I was living in Bee, Neb., at the time and High Proof and Benito Paprika were the first two horses Mr. Fuller sent to me. In 1977, at the All American Quarter Horse Congress in Columbus, Ohio, I won the open reining with High Proof, and the NRHA Futurity with Benito Paprika. And my relationship with, and respect for, the Joe Cody horses just took off from there."

As he would for years to come, Loomis made a trip back to Willow Brook Farms in the fall of 1978 to ride and evaluate the coming crop of Joe Cody futurity prospects. It was on that trip that the Nebraska horseman first laid eyes on the yearling chestnut colt who would change his life forever.

"Back then, Dick Herr was starting Mr. Fuller's 2-year-olds," Loomis says. "Then I would go there and pick the ones I wanted to train. It was a perfect situation for me and wound up paying big-time dividends for us all.

"After my success at the 1977 Congress, I became a big believer in the Joe Codys from that point on. They were such pretty stoppers. They'd just lift their shoulders and then bury their rear ends in the dirt. And they had more heart and more try than any line of horses I've ever ridden."

As interested as he was in training and showing top reining horses, Loomis' interests in the discipline extended even further. For as far back as he can remember, he admits to always wanting to breed top reiners as well.

"I started out in the performance horse breeding business with a stallion named Red Bee Moore. After him, I stood a son of

Halter and Performance Record: Performance ROM; 1980 NRHA Reining Futurity Champion; 1996 NRHA Hall of Fame Horse.

Progeny Record: (As of June 2001)

Foal Crops: 22	Performance Points Earned: 5,399
Foals Registered: 756	Performance Registers of Merit: 172
World Champions: 5	Superior Performance Awards: 13
Halter Point-Earners: 8	Total NCHA Earnings: $878
Halter Points Earned: 15.5	Total NRHA Earnings: $1,107,483
Performance Point-Earners: 431	

Okie Leo. And then I owned Boss' Nowata Star. He was the best of the three. He was a 1972 bay, sired by Range Boss and out of Fritzy's Star, by Nowata Star, and he was a good horse. I won more than $3,000 on him in NRHA competition and he was the 1976 AQHA Reserve World Champion Junior Reining Horse.

"But I knew even he wasn't the ultimate horse for me, the horse I wanted to wrap a breeding program around. So I kept looking."

In the fall of 1978, Loomis found what he'd been searching for.

A Different Kind of Cody

"For the most part," he says, "the Joe Codys all looked alike. They were mostly compact little sorrels, with maybe a small star on their foreheads. Every once in a while, there'd be a buckskin because of that great line of buckskin mares that

In addition to having a Hall of Fame sire, Topsail Cody had an equally great dam. Doc Bar Linda, shown here with youth rider Robin Severinsen, was a durable show mare known for both her talent and her independent character.

band, Doc Bar Linda, a 1967 chestnut mare out of Betty's Mount, by Music Mount, was a highly accomplished show horse in her own right.

Shown primarily in youth competition by Robin Severinsen Merrill of Branchville, N.J. — the daughter of Grammy-winning music director Doc Severinsen — Doc Bar Linda proved to be a tough, albeit temperamental, competitor.

"Linda was an intense mare," recalls Merrill, who with husband Frank owns and operates Windward Stud of Purcell, Oklahoma. "In fact, she was a bit of a hot-head. She was like riding a stick of dyna-mite. You never knew when she was going to go off. You had to prepare her correctly. You had to put a few miles on her before she went into the arena.

"But she was above average. She had ability. And she was very sensitive, very 'feely.' If I had to do it over, I probably would have used her in reining, or kept a cow in front of her. She would have been happier.

"But I learned a lot about riding and showing horses through Linda. I learned to be patient, and I learned to be 'eloquent' with my hands. As Mr. Fuller's trainer Bob Anthony, who was my mentor at the time, would tell me: 'They're not all easy to ride; a lot of the great ones have quirks.'

"Linda had her share of quirks. But she also had more than her share of talent, and time has proven she could pass on that talent."

With Robin in the saddle, Doc Bar Linda made enough use of her temperamental talent to be named the 1972 AQHA Youth World Champion Hunter Under Saddle Horse. In addition, she earned Superiors in youth halter, showmanship, western horsemanship, and hunter under saddle. She was also a youth AQHA Champion and amassed 537 open and youth performance and halter points.

Given such exemplary breeding, and the fact that he had the looks to match, it didn't take Bob Loomis long to decide that Topsail should return to Nebraska with him. But originally, the stallion was slated to be sold to Loomis' brother.

"In 1978 my brother Ed was in the market

Mr. Fuller had. But generally they were sorrels, and they all looked alike.

"In 1978, while I was in Pennsylvania trying out Mr. Fuller's 2-year-olds, I happened by the yearling pasture. Sure enough, it was full of those little sorrel Joe Codys. Then, a taller, more-refined chestnut colt with a full blaze face came loping up to check me out. He was a different kind of Joe Cody, and the more I studied him, the more I liked him. He turned out to be Topsail Cody.

"He was sired by Joe, all right, but he was out of a mare named Doc Bar Linda. She was a daughter of Doc Bar — the only one ever bred to Joe — and she accounted for both Topsail's different look and, ultimately, his different type of athletic ability."

By the time she was purchased by Tom Fuller and added to Joe Cody's broodmare

PHOTO BY HUGHES, COURTESY ROBIN SEVERINSEN MERRILL

Here's another shot of Linda and Robin. The mare is universally credited with bequeathing her son Topsail Cody with a large portion of both his physical talent and genetic strength.

It was then that he realized he'd made a big mistake.

for a breeding stallion. He had lost his in a barn fire. I decided that Topsail would fill the bill, so I bought the colt for him.

"I broke him as a 2-year-old and then sent him home. Ed's daughter rode him all that summer. She put a lot of country miles on him, and even showed him some in western pleasure."

In the spring of 1980, Loomis took Topsail back for some additional training. It was then, he says, that he realized he'd made a big mistake.

The Perfect Pupil

"Once I started Topsail's reining training in earnest," he says, "it didn't take me but about 30 days to realize he was the best horse I'd ever ridden. He was super sensi-

tive in the ribs and so very 'light-faced.' And he had a bionic stop. So I called Ed and told him that. I also said I wanted to buy him back, and asked what he'd take for him. Ed priced him at four times what he'd paid for him. I didn't even blink. I just told him I'd be over that evening with a check."

With Topsail Cody back in his barn, Loomis learned that he still had one major obstacle to surmount. Oddly, it had nothing to do with the young stallion's talent or trainability. On the contrary, it was just the opposite.

In those years the NRHA Futurity was held in October during the Quarter Horse Congress (it's now held in early December in Oklahoma City).

Says Loomis, "By May of his 3-year-old year, Topsail was dead ready to go to the

67

Harold
Campton

After winning the junior reining class at the 1981 AQHA World Championship Show, Topsail Cody was retired and started on what would become a highly successful career at stud.

A pair of champions in the making—Topsail Cody, a future all-time leading reining horse sire, and Bobbi Jo Loomis, a future Miss Rodeo U.S.A.

PHOTO BY HAROLD CAMPTON, COURTESY BOB LOOMIS

Harold Campton

Topsail and Bob Loomis in the winner's circle after emerging victorious at the 1980 NRHA Futurity, held at the All-American Quarter Horse Congress in Columbus, Ohio.

COURTESY BOB LOOMIS

Here's a classic shot of Topsail and Bob, doing what they did best. The chestnut stallion's bionic stop was one of his greatest attributes.

Cee Blair Sailor, Topsail's top money-earning performer, earned more than $94,000 and was a 1995 inductee into the NRHA Hall of Fame.

Topsail the Sire

Bred lightly as a 2-year-old, Topsail Cody's first foal crop hit the ground in 1980. From it came the promising young sire's first world champion. Okleos Sail Win, a bay stallion out of Okleo's Mesqueet, by Okleo Skeet, was the 1984 AQHA World Champion Junior Reining Horse and a Superior reining horse as well.

With the age of Quarter Horse specialization dawning in the early 1980s, more of Topsail Cody's performing get earned their laurels in NRHA competition than in AQHA contests. Still, several fared exceptionally well in the latter events.

- Topsail Dude, a 1984 sorrel gelding out of Duchetta, by Blondy's Dude, was the 1991 and 1992 AQHA Youth World Champion Reining Horse; the 1993 AQHA Reserve World Champion Senior Reining Horse; and earned a Superior in open reining.
- Tugboat Cody, a 1985 sorrel gelding out of Farafield Okie, by Okie Leo, was the 1991 AQHA Reserve High-Point Reining Horse and the high-point reining gelding.
- Cash In Cody, a 1986 brown gelding out of Miss Alicia Cash, by Spool O Cash, was the 1991 AQHA World Champion Amateur Reining Horse.
- Sail Win Pistol, a 1989 bay gelding out of Charlotte Pistol, by Sugaro Pistol, was the 1994 Youth AQHA World Champion Team Penning Horse.

In addition, Checkmate Cody, El Dorado Sailor, Galapagos Cody, Cee Blair Sailor, Top Slider, Sailwin Chex, Sail To The North, and Topsail Cody Chex all earned a Superior in reining.

All told, in AQHA competition the get of Topsail Cody have earned 13 Superior performance awards, 172 performance ROMs, and 5,399 points in open, amateur, and youth competition as of June 2001.

But it is in big-money NRHA competition where the Topsail Codys excel. And they have made their sire one of the reining industry's all-time greats.

futurity. I'd never had a horse train up and be ready to show that quick. I didn't know what to do. So I just took it easy with him. I didn't really train hard on him. I didn't want him to peak too early and then drop off. We just concentrated on pleasure riding, with a little fine-tuning thrown in to keep his interest. By October we were still fresh and dead ready."

Prior to the 1980 NRHA Futurity, Loomis showed Topsail in two AQHA shows, winning both.

In the futurity's first go-round, the pair scored a 230—good enough to place on top. In the second round, they marked a 232.5, matching the score of a top reining mare named Miss Cee Blair. Then, in the third round, Bob and Topsail won handily with a score of 234 points, thereby securing the overall championship.

Next up for the duo was the 1981 AQHA World Show. There, Topsail won every go-round and the finals of the junior reining and was promptly retired. Undefeated in his short but brilliant reining career, he earned the futurity championship, $29,236 in NRHA contests, a world championship, and 24 performance points in AQHA competition.

All that was left now was to prove that he could live up to his family name as a sire.

PHOTO BY DICK WALTENBERRY, COURTESY NRHA

Freckles Top Prize, shown here with Shannon Raymond in the saddle, was a two-time NRHA non-pro world champion.

The Topsail Slide Show

Cee Blair Sailor would have to head the list of Topsail Cody's top NRHA-competing get. A 1988 sorrel stallion out of Miss Cee Blair — the mare who tied Topsail in the second go-round of the 1980 futurity — Cee Blair Sailor was the Reno Spectacular champion, the Lazy E Classic reserve champion, and an NRHA Futurity finalist. With Amanda Connor up, he was the 1993 NRHA Intermediate Non-Pro World Champion, and with Craig Schmersal in the saddle, he was the 1994 NRHA Open and Limited Open World Champion.

His NRHA earnings totaled $94,863, and in 1995 he was the youngest horse ever inducted into the NRHA Hall of Fame.

Other Topsails have done well in NRHA competition as well.

- Freckles Top Prize, a 1990 sorrel stallion out of Freckles Prize, by Colonel Freckles, was the 1994 Southwest Reining Horse Association Futurity champion and, ridden by Shannon Raymond, the 1996 and 1997 NRHA Non-Pro World Champion. His NRHA winnings total $61,304.
- Rest Stop, a 1985 buckskin mare out of

Villa Eddie, by Edmond Star, was the 1988 NRHA Futurity Reserve Champion with Doug Milholland up. She was also a non-pro reserve world champion and earned $56,072.
- Sail Win Sam, a 1984 sorrel stallion out of Elsie Cay, by Okie Leo, was ridden by Steve Schwartzenberger at the 1987 NRHA Futurity to the limited open championship. His NRHA earnings total $41,483.

Among the other top NRHA money winners by Topsail Cody: Topsail Skeets, earner of $39,227; Cool Change Cody, $28,317; and Sail On John, $26,255.

Topsail Whiz

With $49,865 to his credit, Topsail Whiz, a 1987 chestnut stallion out of Jeanie Whiz Bar, by Cee Red, also ranks high among his sire's money-earning get. More importantly, he is the horse Bob Loomis has hand-picked to serve as Topsail's replacement in the breeding shed.

"Just like Topsail," Loomis says, "Topsail Whiz has a great mother. The first time I

This head portrait of Topsail Whiz shows such hallmark Topsail Cody characteristics as a sorrel color and quiet, intelligent look.

Topsail Whiz, the 1987 son of Topsail Cody and Jeanie Whiz Bar, has been chosen by Loomis as Topsail's replacement in the breeding shed.

saw Jeanie Whiz Bar was in 1974 at the Dixie National in Jackson, Miss., one of the biggest shows in the country. The mare was just a 2-year-old and she was being shown in the junior reining by a youth rider named Tom McBeath, who was from Union, Mississippi. She'd never been with a professional trainer, but she won the class.

"Jeanie went on to be the 1977 Youth AQHA High-Point Reining Horse, and Tom put a couple hundred open and youth performance points on her. I tried to buy the mare, but Tom wouldn't sell. He did lease her to me, though, and I bred her to Topsail. Topsail Whiz was the result."

Just as he had with Topsail, Loomis let Whiz get away from him at the start.

"When Whiz was a yearling," he says, "I had a weak moment and sold him to a couple from Germany who were regular customers of mine. He stayed right here and I started getting him ready for the futurities as a 3-year-old.

"One day, I got a call from the German couple, asking how he was coming along.

" 'He's doing great!' I replied.

" 'Is he in your top three?'

" 'He's better than that — he's the best by a long shot. In fact, he's so good, I'd like to buy him back.'

"After a little negotiating, I got the deal done. This time around it cost me five times what I'd sold him for, so I can't say I'd gotten any smarter," Loomis grinned.

As he had with Topsail Cody, Loomis chose to campaign Topsail Whiz on a very limited basis. Still, the pair managed to slide to a championship at the 1991 Lazy E Classic in the open division, plus garnering wins at the 1991 Congress in the junior reining and open classes, and a third place at the 1990 NRHA Futurity.

As was also the case with Topsail Cody, Loomis feels that Whiz stands poised to become one of the industry's all-time leading sires.

"As much as Topsail Cody accomplished, I can truthfully say that the best thing he did for me was to sire Whiz. Whiz represents the next level to me. He's a popular sire who stands to a full book of mares every year, and his foals are consistent in their look and ability.

"He's still a young horse, but he's already sired the winners of more than $895,000. And a couple of his sons are beginning to make their own marks as sires. So I guess the line is destined to live on."

COURTESY NRHA

Here's Whizard Jac, a 1993 sorrel stallion by Topsail Whiz and out of Bees Honey Jac, by Hollywood Jac 86. Whizard Jac was ridden by Mike Flarida to victories at the 1996 NRHA Futurity and the 1999 USET Reining Championship. The talented performer had earned more than $155,000 as of early 2001.

California-Bound

In 1992, with his sights set on making Topsail Whiz the next supersire of the Joe Cody line, Loomis consented to sell Topsail Cody to Dick Randall of Cupertino, California. It was, according to the venerable reinsman, a hard decision to reach.

"Topsail was 15 at the time I sold him," he says. "He had been so good to me over the years. He had done everything I'd ever asked of him. He'd won the futurity and the AQHA World Show, and he'd become one of the reining industry's leading sires.

"But I had Topsail Whiz in place, and the true breeder's mentality is such that he's always looking for the next great breeding animal, and the emphasis is always on the next generation.

"I felt it was time to make a change. Dick and I had become acquainted several years earlier. He was very serious in his desire to breed and show top reining horses, so I thought the West Coast was where Topsail should go. Dick has done a real fine job with him. The first year Topsail stood out there, 73 mares were booked to him. So I still feel it was the correct decision to make."

In 1996 Topsail Cody was inducted into the NRHA Hall of Fame. Cee Blair Sailor

had been inducted the previous year, Bob Loomis was enshrined in 1992, and C.T. Fuller and Joe Cody were inducted in 1989, so the legacy of one of the reining industry's most famous families is secure.

In 1998 Topsail Cody added even more luster to his name by becoming the NRHA's third million-dollar sire. The chestnut stallion's offspring have earned $1,107,483, in officially sanctioned events, as of June 2001.

The Topsail Cody daughters are also proving their mettle as consistent producers of world-caliber reining horses. So well, in fact, that Topsail ranks as the NRHA's all-time leading maternal grandsire. To date, his daughters have produced the earners of $621,466.

With his 2000 maternal grandsire earnings accounting for $249,692 of the overall total, it seems a safe bet that the 24-year-old stallion will eventually become the industry's only million-dollar sire *and* million-dollar maternal grandsire. Just as it seems a sure thing that his son Topsail Whiz will become a million-dollar sire in the near future.

The Topsail Cody story is one of uncompromising success, and the final chapters have yet to be written.

PRETTY BUCK

By Frank Holmes

Although he stood in the shadow of Poco Bueno, Pretty Buck was perceived to be royalty as well.

ALTHOUGH HE spent the first half of his life in the shadow of Poco Bueno, Pretty Buck eventually took his rightful place as one of the breed's foundation sires.

Pretty Buck was foaled in 1942 on the Waggoner Ranch of Vernon, Texas. He was sired by Pretty Boy and was out of a Waggoner mare, by Buck Thomas.

Registered by his breeder-owner E. Paul Waggoner as a 3-year-old in 1945, Pretty Buck was listed as being brown. With his broad dorsal stripe and black points, he was probably a dark dun instead.

Pretty Boy, the sire of Pretty Buck, was a 1928 brown (or dun, depending on the account) stallion by Dodger and out of Little Maud. He was bred by Claude Collins of Sterling City, Tex., and purchased by the Waggoner Ranch in 1931.

Other than Pretty Buck, Pretty Boy's most notable male offspring were Monterrey and Talley Man. Monterrey, a 1940

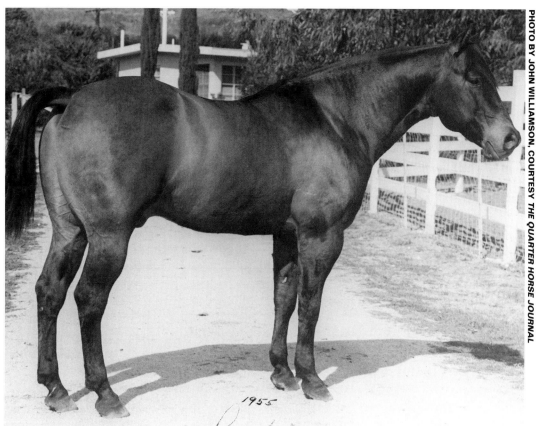

Pretty Buck, shown here as an aged stallion in California, was widely traveled and influenced the development of the Quarter Horse breed in several parts of the country.

PHOTO BY JOHN WILLIAMSON, COURTESY *THE QUARTER HORSE JOURNAL*

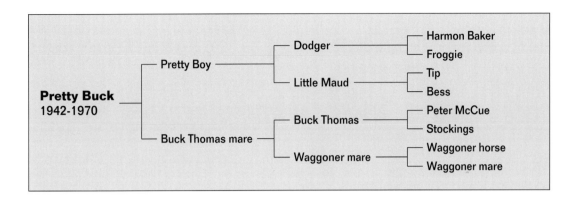

```
                                              ┌─ Harmon Baker
                              ┌─ Dodger ───────┤
              ┌─ Pretty Boy ──┤                └─ Froggie
              │               │                ┌─ Tip
              │               └─ Little Maud ───┤
Pretty Buck ──┤                                └─ Bess
1942-1970     │                                ┌─ Peter McCue
              │               ┌─ Buck Thomas ───┤
              └─ Buck Thomas  │                 └─ Stockings
                 mare      ───┤                 ┌─ Waggoner horse
                              └─ Waggoner mare ─┤
                                                └─ Waggoner mare
```

palomino stallion out of a Waggoner mare, by Waggoner's Rainy Day P-13, was a AAA and AQHA Champion sire. Talley Man, a 1946 dun stallion out of Lady Blackburn III, by Blackburn, was a Register Of Merit arena performer and a multiple AQHA Champion sire.

Pretty Boy's main contribution to the Waggoner Ranch breeding program was as a sire of broodmares. His daughters were a mainstay of the ranch's broodmare band throughout the 1940s and 1950s, and among the notable offspring they produced were Poco Tivio, Poco Lena, Poco Pine, Poco Stampede, Poco Champ, Pretty Pokey, Pretty Boy Pokey, and Poco Jane—the dam of King Fritz.

Pretty Buck's dam is listed simply as a Buck Thomas mare. Buck Thomas was a 1921 stallion sired by Peter McCue and out of Stockings, by Old Fred. Bred by the legendary Colorado horseman Coke Roberds, he was acquired by the Waggoner Ranch in 1927.

Although he, like Pretty Boy, was noted mostly as a broodmare sire, Buck Thomas was the sire of Red Buck and F&H Bill Thomas—two stallions who also made their mark on the breed.

At the time of Pretty Buck's birth, the Waggoner Ranch horse breeding program was in full swing and producing upwards of 300 foals a year.

Blackburn and Pretty Boy were the ranch's senior stallions. Aged 15 and 14 respectively, they were well established as sires of working and breeding stock. In their broodmare bands were own daughters of Waggoner's Rainy Day P-13 and Mid-

night. There were also some aged daughters of Cotton Eyed Joe and Joe Traveler—two sons of Little Joe, and a few even older daughters of Yellow Wolf and Yellow Bear—full brothers by Yellow Jacket and out of (Old) Mary. Rounding out the mare band were some half-breds by Royal Ford (TB) and Clover Leaf (TB).

Buck Thomas, while also in place as a Waggoner Ranch herd sire, was never accorded the level of respect that Blackburn and Pretty Boy enjoyed.

With his close-up Peter McCue and Old Fred breeding, Buck Thomas was taller and rangier than the other two stallions. Then too, as a sire of working cow ponies, he was somewhat controversial. Some Waggoner Ranch hands were known to have preferred his get as riding horses, while others were quoted as saying they would rather remain afoot than sit astride his offspring.

As the sire of one dun colt in particular, however, Buck Thomas did himself proud.

As noted earlier, Pretty Buck was foaled in 1942. He was an outstanding individual

A classic three-quarter front view of Pretty Buck taken by Stryker and reproduced here from the 1952 catalog for the third annual sale of Waggoner Three D Quarter Horses.

Poco Bueno was the immediate focal point of the Waggoner Ranch show string, and the acknowledged future head of the ranch's breeding program.

That's not to say that Pretty Buck was completely ignored. On the contrary, he was shown alongside Poco Bueno for a number of years, was broke to ride by Bob Burton (the same man who started Poco Bueno), and was heavily utilized as a breeding animal.

But Poco Bueno (*Legends 1*) was the Waggoner Ranch headliner. He was the indisputable star, and every other stallion in residence on the ranch had to be content with a spot on the supporting cast.

Still, as a show horse, Pretty Buck held his own.

A Pretty Good Show Horse

At the 1946 Southwestern Exposition and Fat Stock show, held in Fort Worth, Poco Bueno was the grand champion stallion and winner of the 2-year-old stallion class. Pretty Buck was the reserve champion stallion and winner of the aged stallion class.

Finishing behind Pretty Buck in his individual class at Fort Worth were Tar Baby, owned by R.L. Underwood of Wichita Falls, and Little Man, owned by the King Ranch of Kingsville, Texas.

At the 1947 National Western Stock Show in Denver, Poco Bueno was the grand champion stallion and winner of the 3-year-old stallion class, and Pretty Buck was the reserve champion stallion and winner of the aged stallion class.

At the 1948 National Western, Star Duster (*Legends 1*), owned by Quentin and Evelyn Semotan of Steamboat Springs, Colo., was the grand champion stallion and Pretty Buck once again had to be content with reserve champion honors.

At the same show, though, Pretty Buck did emerge victorious in the sire and get class. This class, which featured a stallion and two of his get shown as a group, was eventually replaced by the more popular, three-head get-of-sire class.

from the very beginning, and the decision was made to reserve him as a potential show horse and future sire.

New Kid in Town

At the time of Pretty Buck's birth, E. Paul Waggoner, the son of ranch founder W. T. Waggoner, was in charge of the horse breeding operation.

In the fall of 1945, E. Paul attended the annual Hankins Brothers horse sale at San Angelo, Texas. There he astounded the entire Quarter Horse world by giving the unheard of price of $5,700 for a yearling colt named Poco Bueno.

From that day forward, the die was cast.

This roping shot of Pretty Buck also appeared in Waggoner's 1952 sale catalog in which the dun was listed as a reference stallion. Part of the catalog information describes Pretty Buck as earning his keep "by siring consistently good colts on any and all kinds of mares and as a utility horse. You can take your rope down on him in pasture and ride up to anything you want to catch. He'll pull several times his weight by the saddle horn, haze broncs, and work quietly with green-broke colts. He's a pleasure to ride and an all-around good cow horse."

PHOTO BY JOHN A. STRYKER, COURTESY *THE QUARTER HORSE JOURNAL*

Although he was registered as being brown in color, this early photo of Pretty Buck clearly shows the broad dorsal stripe that branded him as a dun. Bob Burton, the Waggoner Ranch hand who broke Pretty Buck, Poco Bueno, and Jessie James to ride, holds the good-looking stallion in this rare photo.

This photo of Pretty Buck serves as testimony to the stallion's gentle nature. Waggoner Ranch foreman and trainer Pine Johnson's son, James Edward, sits atop Pretty Buck. The shot was taken at the Three D Stock Farm's Third Annual Quarter Horse Sale, held in Fort Worth, September 15, 1952.

By all accounts, he was a natural at roping.

Pretty Buck's last recorded ventures into halter competition occurred in Odessa, Tex., in 1951, and in San Antonio in 1952. AQHA records reveal that, at Odessa, he earned 1 halter point and, at San Antonio, he accumulated 4.

Throughout all of the 1940s and into the 1950s, the most promising of the Waggoner Ranch show and breeding prospects were housed at the Three D Stock Farm outside Arlington, Texas.

It was here that Bob Burton, the Waggoner Ranch cowboy who would later start Poco Bueno and Jessie James under saddle, broke Pretty Buck to ride as a 2-year-old. Burton also trained the young dun as a roping horse and, by all accounts he was a natural at it.

There are no recorded accounts of Pretty Buck being campaigned in roping—either in AQHA or rodeo competition.

Near the front of an early Waggoner Ranch production sale catalog, circa 1952, an alert Pretty Buck is shown working a tight rope with a calf being tied down on the other end. He is characterized on the facing page as being a horse that "you can take your rope down on ... in the pasture and ride up to anything you want to catch. He'll pull several times his weight by the saddle horn, haze broncs, quietly work with green broke colts, take you for a pleasure ride and, in general, make himself useful as an all-around good cow horse."

Pretty Buck's easygoing disposition is touted even more at the very back of the catalog. There, he is photographed with ranch foreman and head trainer Lewis "Pine" Johnson's four small children all riding bareback on him with just a halter for control.

The Waggoner Sire

Poco Bueno might have been the Waggoner Ranch king, but Pretty Buck was obviously perceived to be royalty as well.

One indication of how highly E. Paul

PHOTO BY ZINTGRAFF, COURTESY *THE QUARTER HORSE JOURNAL*

Snipper W., a 1946 dun gelding out of Snipette, was the first Pretty Buck get to excel in the show ring. A Superior halter horse, he is shown here standing grand at the San Antonio Livestock Exposition in the early 1950s. Pine Johnson holds Snipper; E. Paul Waggoner is the second man from the left.

Don Dodge, then living in Sacramento, Calif., acquired both Poco Tivio and Snipper W. from the Waggoner Ranch in the early 1950s. Here, he cuts on Tivio and an unknown rider turns back on Snipper.

Waggoner and his crew thought of Pretty Buck was the number and quality of mares bred to him.

From when he was first bred as a 2-year-old until he was sold as an 11-year-old, Pretty Buck was bred to some of the best mares the ranch had to offer. Included were daughters of Blackburn, Pretty Boy, King, Joe Traveler, Clover Leaf (TB), and Chubby. During his last years at the ranch he was bred to daughters of Poco Bueno and Pep Up as well.

PHOTO BY GRESSETT, COURTESY *THE QUARTER HORSE JOURNAL*

Clover Buck, a 1948 palomino stallion out of Belle Clover, was another early Pretty Buck champion. Shown almost exclusively in Palomino competition, he established one of the top show records of his day. The handler is not identified, but the woman is Natalie Carter.

The most consistent cross, both in terms of numbers and results, occurred when Pretty Buck was bred to the daughters of Blackburn. So successful was it from the very start that, of the 70 Waggoner-bred foals sired by Pretty Buck (whose maternal grandsires are known), 38 were out of Blackburn mares.

It didn't hurt the reputation of the cross that the first successful performer to come from it was Snipper W.

A 1946 dun gelding by Pretty Buck and out of Snipette, by Blackburn, Snipper W. was broke to ride and started in cutting by Pine Johnson.

In January of 1951, the duo won the open cutting at the Southwestern Exposition and Fat Stock Show in Fort Worth. It was the beginning of a highly successful yearlong campaign that would see Snipper W. finish as the number nine horse in the National Cutting Horse Association (NCHA) Top Ten.

In February of 1952, Don Dodge of Sacramento, Calif., purchased the talented gelding. Dodge, who would later return to the Waggoners to acquire Poco Tivio and Poco Lena as well, wasted no time in putting Snipper W. to work.

The pair ended the 1952 season as the NCHA Reserve World Champion Champion Cutting Horse. The following year, they improved their position by one notch, claiming the title of NCHA World Champion Cutting Horse and Champion Cutting Gelding.

In 1954 Dodge sold Snipper to Clyde Bauer of Victoria, Texas. Campaigned lightly over the course of the next two years, he ended the 1954 NCHA season as the twelfth high money-earner, and the 1956 season as eighth high money-earner.

In 1957, his final year of competition, Snipper W. once again proved that he had talent and natural cutting ability to burn. With Stanley Bush in the saddle, the 11-year-old gelding was again named NCHA Reserve World Champion Cutting Horse and Champion Cutting Gelding.

With Don Dodge in the saddle, Snipper W. was the 1953 NCHA World Champion Cutting Horse. The flashy gelding was also a member of the NCHA Hall of Fame and his sire's top point-earning performance offspring.

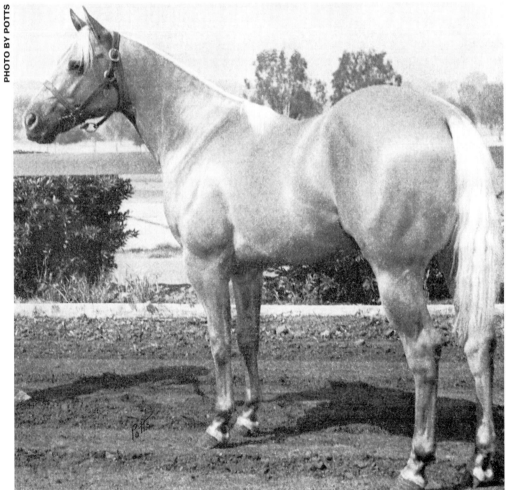

Handy Buck, a 1948 palomino stallion by Pretty Buck and out of Shielfly, won his class at the 1949 Southwestern Exposition and Fat Stock Show in Fort Worth. He went on to become a grand champion halter horse and a winner at cutting. He's shown here as a 2-year-old.

Here's a Waggoner Ranch-bred and Pretty Buck-sired diamond in the rough: Laddie Buck, a 1953 palomino stallion out of Poco Lassie, by Poco Bueno. Laddie grew up to earn 8 halter and 26 performance points, and $2,626 in NCHA competition.

Foxy Buck, a 1955 bay mare by Pretty Buck and out of Bonnie Fox, by The Rancher, produced five AQHA performers. She's shown here with her 1960 Poco Bob filly.

Kitty Buck, a 1953 bay filly by Pretty Buck and out of Miss Peppy D, by Pep Up, grew up to produce an NCHA Cutting Derby champion and a AAA-rated race horse.

He was retired in 1958 with $44,815 in earnings and awarded NCHA Hall of Fame Certificate No. 4 in recognition of his many accomplishments.

In addition to his NCHA feats, Snipper W. was also contested in AQHA-approved events. In 1951 he was one of the first eight AQHA Champions ever named. In 1953 he was awarded a Superior in cutting, and in 1957, a Superior in halter.

As Pretty Buck's first big-time show off-spring, the dun gelding more than did his part to enhance the reputation of his sire.

But there were other Pretty Buck stars as well.

Miss Bow Tie, a 1947 dun mare out of Shielfly, by Blackburn, earned 3 halter points and went on to become a top producer.

Clover Buck, a 1948 palomino stallion out of Belle Clover, by Clover Leaf (TB), had no official AQHA record, but was one of the greatest early champions in the history of the Palomino Horse Breeders Association.

Clover Buck was sold by the Waggoners

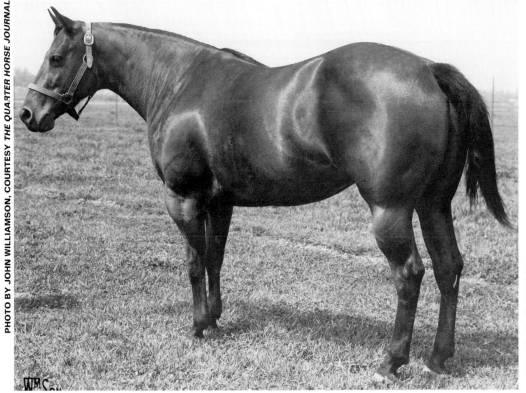

Strummer, a 1952 mare by Pretty Buck and out of Serenade Girl, by Blackburn, was an AQHA Champion. In this shot taken at the 1958 Fort Worth Cowtown Posse show, handler Jimmie Hobbs receives the grand champion mare trophy from Virginia Miller. Strummer was owned by I.M. Morgan, Smithfield, Texas.

Rita Buck, a 1952 bay mare by Pretty Buck and out of Rio Rita, by Chubby, was her sire's top halter point-earning get. The heavily muscled champion earned 105 halter points during her stellar show career.

Among Foxy Buck's best-known offspring was Two Eyed Fox, a 1969 chestnut stallion by Two Eyed Jack. An AQHA Champion and a Superior halter horse, Fox went on to become a top sire for Doug and Nancy Dear's Birdtail Ranch in Simms, Montana.

as a yearling in their 2nd Annual Quarter Horse sale. Purchased by Bob Lucas of Fort Worth for $1,500, he was shown in palomino competition 12 times as a 2-year-old. He won 11 firsts, 1 second, 6 grand championships, and 5 reserves.

It is interesting to note here that Pretty Buck was supposedly sold at the same sale. In the November 1949 issue of the Texas-based *Back In The Saddle* magazine, he was reported to have topped the 1949 sale—

commanding a final bid of $5,350 from G. W. Sams of Fort Worth.

There is no official AQHA record of his being transferred to Sams at that time, nor is there any sort of break in the scope and continuity of his siring record over the course of the next several years.

For all intrinsic purposes, he remained a Waggoner Ranch herd sire, turning out Three D Stock Farm-bred champions.

Champions such as Handy Buck, a 1948 palomino stallion out of Shielfly; Miss Snippy, a 1948 dun full sister to Snipper W.; Buck's Bay, a 1949 bay stallion out of Floppie, by Blackburn.

In fact, the years after he was reportedly sold turned out to be Pretty Buck's most productive as a Waggoner Ranch sire.

Buck Tommy, a 1950 dun stallion out of May Belle W, by Blackburn, was an AQHA Champion and earned a Superior at halter. Patsy Buck, a 1950 mare out of Patsy Clover, by Clover Leaf (TB), earned 21 halter points, and Buck Beam, a 1950 dun gelding out of Star Beam W., by Blackburn, amassed 11 halter and 7½ performance points.

In addition, Wonder Buck, a 1951 bay stallion out of Wonder Lady, by King, earned 8 halter and 9 performance points. Pretty Me, a dun mare out of Suits Me, by Pretty Boy—although not an AQHA point-earner—went on to become one of the greatest producers to ever come out of the Waggoner program.

Buck Deuce, Strummer, Poco Buck, and Rita Buck were the stars of Pretty Buck's 1952 foal crop.

Buck Deuce, a dun gelding out of Louetha D., by Blackburn, was an AQHA Champion, Superior halter and cutting horse, and the earner of $4,006 in NCHA competition. Strummer, a sorrel mare out of Serenade Girl, by Blackburn, was also an AQHA Champion with 44 halter and 12 performance points to her credit.

Poco Buck, a grulla stallion out of Cindy Bueno, by Poco Bueno, earned 28 performance points and was the 1966 AQHA High-Point Trail Horse Stallion.

Rita Buck, a bay mare out of Rio Rita, by Chubby, was her sire's top halter

PHOTO BY JAMES RAYNER, COURTESY THE QUARTER HORSE JOURNAL

Frank Buck, a 1956 grulla stallion by Pretty Buck and out of Wilson's Paper Doll, by Dan Waggoner, was an AQHA Champion. This photo was taken in the late 1960s after he had been sold by the E.R. Fowler estate of Naches, Wash., to Mr. and Mrs. Walter Shutts of Junction City, Oregon. That's Ken Thompson, Fowler Ranch manager on the left, the Shuttses in the middle, and their trainer, Mike Maynard, on the right.

PHOTO BY DALCO, COURTESY THE QUARTER HORSE JOURNAL

This cutting horse is Pretty Buck Gee, a 1961 dun gelding by Pretty Buck and out of Brenda Gee, by William Goodpasture. In addition to his prowess in the arena, Buck had enough looks to earn 19 halter points and an AQHA Championship.

PHOTO BY JIM KEELAND, COURTESY *THE QUARTER HORSE JOURNAL*

The cross of Poco Bueno and Miss Bow Tie produced three AQHA Champions, including Poco Bow Tie, a 1955 dun mare, shown here.

COURTESY *THE QUARTER HORSE JOURNAL*

Miss Bow Tie, a 1947 dun mare by Pretty Buck and out of Shielfly, by Blackburn, was a top show mare in her day. She is shown here earning reserve champion mare honors at the 1950 Stamford (Tex.) Cowboy Reunion show.

point-earning get. With 105 points to her credit, she more than qualified for a Superior in the event.

Also foaled in 1952 were Pretty Etta and Mabel Buck. Pretty Etta, a dun mare out of Etta's Birthday, by Joe Traveler, earned 10 halter and 6 performance points. Mabel Buck, a palomino full sister to Buck Tommy, earned 7 halter and 1 performance point, and earned $858 in NCHA contests.

Pretty Buck's last foal crop for the Waggoners hit the ground in 1953. From it came Laddie Buck, a palomino stallion out of Poco Lassie, by Poco Bueno. The earner of 8 halter and 26 performance points, Laddie Buck also had $2,626 in NCHA earnings.

Changing Hands

Citing a reduction in broodmare numbers and similarity of breeding as the reasons behind their decision, the Waggoners sold Pretty Buck in January of 1953 to Oscar Dodson of Chillicothe, Texas.

Pretty Buck's new owner kept him for two breeding seasons.

From an abbreviated 1954 foal crop numbering just 13, Pretty Buck sired only 2 point-earners — Rio Buck and Blazer Buck. From his 1955 foal crop, also numbering 13, Pretty Buck was able to muster up but two more point-earners — Buck Dividend and Buck Toriano.

In addition to the four point-earners, there were also two breeding horses of note foaled during the Dodson-Pretty Buck era.

Master Buck, a 1954 dun stallion out of Dolly D., by Blackburn, went on to become a sire of Register Of Merit race horses and arena performers, and Foxy Buck, a 1955 dun mare out of Bonnie Fox, by The Rancher, went on to become a multiple AQHA Champion producer.

In November of 1954, Pretty Buck changed hands once more.

California Dreamin'

This time he left the Lone Star State and headed for the West Coast under the ownership of John L. Taylor of La Habra Heights, California. Taylor was assembling a top Quarter Horse breeding operation at the time, and Pretty Buck was to be at its head.

For the next several years, everything went according to plan. Pretty Buck was bred to a variety of West Coast mares that included daughters of Blackburn, Poco Bueno, Ed Echols, Dan Waggoner, Lucky Taylor, and Topper.

Among the top horses he sired while in California were Frank Buck and Sir Buck.

Frank Buck, a 1956 grulla stallion out

PHOTO BY ALEXANDER, COURTESY THE QUARTER HORSE JOURNAL

Poco Bow, a 1957 dun mare by Poco Bueno and out of Miss Bow Tie, was an AQHA Champion and earned Superiors in halter and western pleasure as well.

of Wilson's Paper Doll, by Dan Waggoner, was an AQHA Champion and earned $1,597 in NCHA competition. Sir Buck, a 1959 dun gelding out of Clover Jacket, by Blackburn, earned 20 performance points.

Also foaled during the Taylor-Pretty Buck era were the AQHA point-earners Fred Buck, George Buck, Hilda Buck, Rudy Buck, and Pretty Buck 3.

With Taylor expanding his show and breeding operation to include a number of top Pretty Buck daughters, and such top young breeding stallions as Dividend AAA and Poco Pico, a rosy future for Pretty Buck seemed assured.

Then, in January of 1959, John Taylor was struck and killed while changing a

Among the top horses he sired while in California were Frank Buck and Sir Buck.

Like Miss Bow Tie, Pretty Me, by Pretty Buck, crossed well with Poco Bueno. One result was Poco Lon, a 1957 dun mare who earned an AQHA Championship and a Superior in halter.

PHOTO BY BERT BOLLINGER, COURTESY *THE QUARTER HORSE JOURNAL*

Pretty Me Too, a 1966 palomino mare by Bar's Choice and out of Pretty Me, was also an AQHA Champion and a Superior western pleasure horse.

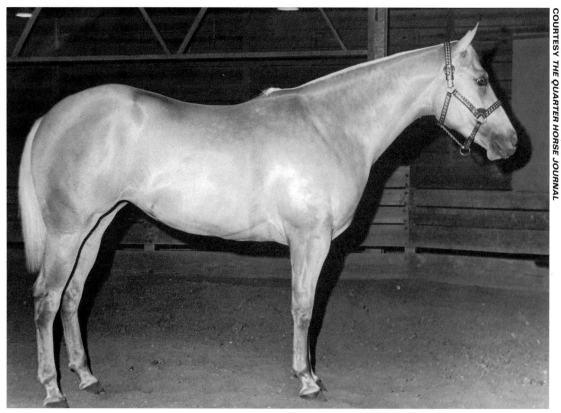

COURTESY *THE QUARTER HORSE JOURNAL*

flat tire en route to the National Western Stock Show. His horses were dispersed later the same year. In the watershed event, which was held August 12, 1959, at the Taylor Ranch near Chino, Calif., records fell like rain.

With the auctioning duties being handled by Hank and Ron Wiescamp of Alamosa, Colo., the sale established an all-time high average of $5,806 on 51 head. It easily eclipsed the previous high—set the fall before at the Pinehurst Ranch Sale in Houston—by $2,362.

So intense was the resolve on the part of the more than 3,000 Quarter Horse fanciers who attended the sale to acquire the Taylor stock that the record for a mare selling at auction was broken four times during the day.

Pretty Buck topped the Taylor dispersal, selling for $15,800 to G.W. "Glynn" Sams of Fort Worth—the same G.W. Sams who had supposedly purchased the stallion at the Waggoner Sale years earlier. In its coverage of the sale, *The Quarter Horse Journal* reported that the 17-year-old former Waggoner Ranch sire had "even been owned for a very brief period of time by Mr. Sams."

With Patsy Buck leading the way at $14,000, 13 Pretty Buck daughters averaged $6,031. Eleven Pretty Buck colts, including yearlings and weanlings, averaged $3,555. The $117,500 gross and $4,895 average that the 24 Pretty Buck get elicited at the event also established a record for the get of one sire.

Dividend and Poco Pico also sold that eventful day, with the former going to B.F. Phillips of Frisco, Tex., and the latter to Bob Norris of Colorado Springs, Colorado. Both stallions went on to enjoy hallmark breeding careers at their new homes.

Getting back to Pretty Buck, Sams kept the aging stallion for two years, and several of his top show get were born during that time.

Pretty Buck Gee, a 1961 dun gelding, and Pretty Boy Gee, a 1962 buckskin gelding, were both out of Brenda Gee, by William Goodpasture. Both were also AQHA Champions. And Miss Buda Buck, a 1962 dun

COURTESY THE QUARTER HORSE JOURNAL

After being sold by the Waggoners, Miss Bow Tie continued to produce well. Her daughter Miss Bar Tie (shown here), was a 1966 dun mare by Bar's Choice, and was an AQHA Champion and a Superior western pleasure horse.

mare out or Sorrelette, by Red Rattler, earned her AQHA Championship as well.

Northward Bound

In the fall of 1961, Sams sold Pretty Buck to the man who would be his last owner— Harold Schafer of Bismarck, North Dakota.

Schafer, whose Gold Seal Company manufactured such products as Snowy Bleach and Mr. Bubble, had recently formed his appropriately named Blackburn Ranch by acquiring 40 daughters of the

COURTESY *THE QUARTER HORSE JOURNAL*

Here's another top Pretty Buck granddaughter, Uniroyal. A 1971 chestnut mare by Ready Royal and out of Mindy Buck, she was an AQHA Champion, a Superior halter and western pleasure horse, and the earner of 348 halter and 82 performance points.

Even as an older stallion, Pretty Buck retained the good-looking head and intelligent expression that characterized him. It was a look and an attitude that he consistently transmitted to his offspring.

PHOTO BY JOHN WILLIAMSON. COURTESY *THE QUARTER HORSE JOURNAL*

famous old Waggoner sire — virtually all who were left alive that could be bought.

And what better horse could he have chosen than Pretty Buck to put at the head of such a broodmare band? Reunited with the Blackburn mares, the former Waggoner stallion closed out his long and illustrious breeding career in style.

Pretty Buck's first North Dakota foal crop, numbering 14, hit the ground in 1963. From it came such stars as Mr Blackburn 37, Mr Blackburn 40, Mr Blackburn 36, Mr Blackburn 35, and Mr Blackburn 42. All were out of daughters of Blackburn.

Mr Blackburn 37, a dun gelding out of Lady Black 82, and Mr Blackburn 40, a bay stallion out of Lady Cowan 5, went on to become AQHA Champions.

Mr Blackburn 36, a brown gelding out of Lady Cowan 2, earned 26 performance points, and Mr Blackburn 35, a dun stallion out of Lady Cowan 14, earned 2 halter points. Mr Blackburn 42, a palomino gelding out of Waggoner II, earned 1 halter point.

Over the course of the next two years, Schafer and his ranch manager Ted Ressler were only able to get four foals from Pretty Buck.

Pine Buck, a 1965 dun gelding out of Poco Pamelita, by Poco Pine, was a member of

Pretty Buck's final foal crop. By virtue of his 11 performance points, he was his sire's last point-earner as well.

Though his breeding days were now behind him, every attempt was made to keep Pretty Buck in good health, and to make his final days as comfortable as possible.

The Blackburn Ranch crew did their job well, to the extent that the famous sire lived another five years, until he quietly passed away in 1970.

A Lasting Impact

The final tally on Pretty Buck reveals him to be the sire of 274 horses. Of these, 103 were performers.

They earned nine AQHA Championships, four Superiors at halter, and two Superior performance awards. In addition, they achieved 29 ROMs and 1,260 total open and youth points. They earned $56,318 in NCHA-sanctioned cutting events.

As a maternal grandsire, Pretty Buck's record is just as sterling.

The daughters of the one-time Waggoner sire produced 183 performers who earned 11 AQHA Championships, 5 Superiors at halter, and 5 Superior performance awards. They achieved 37 ROMs and 3,348.5 open, amateur, and youth points. In NCHA competition, they earned $89,235.

Particularly noteworthy among the Pretty Buck producing daughters were Miss Bow Tie, Pretty Me, and Kitty Buck.

Miss Bow Tie, a 1947 dun mare out of Shielfly, was the dam of 10 performers. Five of these — Poco Bow Tie, Poco Bow, Poco Discount, Miss Bar Tie, and Bar Tie Two — were AQHA Champions. Poco Bow was also a Superior halter and western pleasure horse, and Miss Bar Tie and Bar Tie Two were Superior western pleasure horses.

Pretty Me, a 1950 dun mare out of Suits Me, was the dam of five performers including Poco Lon, a Superior halter horse, and Pretty Me Too, an AQHA Champion. She was also the dam of Poco Mos, the earner of 22 halter points, and E. Paul Waggoner's choice as the Poco Bueno son who would replace his sire.

This good-looking buckskin is Pretty Me, a 1950 mare by Pretty Buck and out of Suits Me, by Pretty Boy.

Kitty Buck, a 1953 bay mare out of Miss Peppy D, by Pep Up, was the dam of Doc's Kitty, winner of the 1970 NCHA Cutting Horse Derby, and Jay Jay Buck, a AAA-rated race horse.

Among the other top-producing daughters of Pretty Buck were the AQHA Champion producers Foxy Buck, Patsy Buck, Pretty Baby B, Little Bambino, and Mindy Buck. In addition, Pretty Doll was also a AAA producer.

As a group, the Pretty Buck mares did their part to enhance their sire's name.

Pretty Buck might have been unlucky to have been born just before, and be a stablemate to, one of the most legendary stallions in the history of the Quarter Horse breed.

Poco Bueno surely did cast a long shadow.

By the time it was all said and done, though, Pretty Buck had his moments in the sun, and he left the breed brighter for them.

8

PAT STAR JR.

By Frank Holmes

He put Howard Pitzer in the Quarter Horse breeding business.

IN THE annals of Quarter Horse history, the names Howard Pitzer and Two Eyed Jack are legendary. Pitzer stands alone as the all-time leading breeder of AQHA Champions (78), and Jack occupies a similar position as the all-time leading sire of AQHA Champions (119).

Because the two spent more than a quarter-century of their lives together, their names are virtually synonymous. To mention one is almost sure to conjure up images of the other.

Any in-depth discussion of Howard Pitzer and Two Eyed Jack and their rise to the top of the Quarter Horse world, however, should always include a third name: Pat Star Jr.

It was Pat Star Jr. who put Pitzer in the Quarter Horse breeding business to begin with, and he was Pitzer's first noteworthy sire. Through his potency as a broodmare sire, Pat Star Jr. paved the way for Jack to get off to his lightning-fast start in the breeding shed.

In other words, Pat Star Jr. set the table

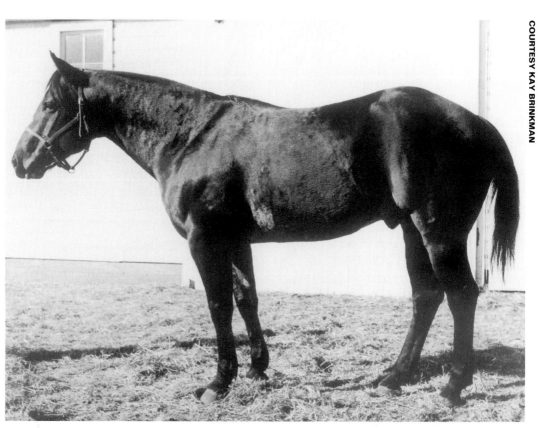

Pat Star Jr. was a superior ranch horse and a sire of superior ranch horses, show horses, and broodmares. He also still ranks as an all-time leading sire of AQHA Champions and as an all-time leading maternal grandsire of AQHA Champions.

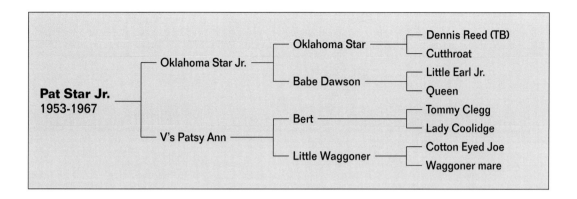

```
                                           ┌─ Dennis Reed (TB)
                          ┌─ Oklahoma Star ─┤
          ┌─ Oklahoma Star Jr. ─┤           └─ Cutthroat
          │               │                ┌─ Little Earl Jr.
          │               └─ Babe Dawson ───┤
Pat Star Jr. ─┤                             └─ Queen
1953-1967     │                             ┌─ Tommy Clegg
          │           ┌─ Bert ──────────────┤
          └─ V's Patsy Ann ─┤                └─ Lady Coolidge
                      │                      ┌─ Cotton Eyed Joe
                      └─ Little Waggoner ─────┤
                                             └─ Waggoner mare
```

for Howard Pitzer and Two Eyed Jack to serve up the meal. (Note: Two Eyed Jack is featured in *Legends 3*.)

Bred by John Kennedy of Okmulgee, Okla., and foaled in 1953, Pat Star Jr. was sired by Oklahoma Star Jr. (*Legends 2*) and was out of V's Patsy Ann, by Bert (*Legends 1*). At the time of the bay colt's birth, the Oklahoma Star Jr.-Bert cross was considered a golden one and had already produced such stellar performers as Willard Combs' great bulldogging mare Baby Doll and Jane Mayo's world champion barrel racing gelding V's Sandy.

By the early 1950s, Howard Pitzer was a well-established rancher in the Sandhills of central Nebraska. In support of his 28,000-acre cattle operation just north of Ericson, he had accumulated a band of 12 Quarter Horse mares. Their pedigrees included such well-known names as Red Dog, Nowata Star, Grey Badger II, Revenue, Bartender, and Joe Barrett. From them, Pitzer hoped to raise some good ranch horses. All he needed to put the plan into effect was a suitable herd sire. Pitzer accomplished that in the fall of 1956 when he purchased Pat Star Jr. from Gerald Sutton of Oklahoma City.

Dean Brinkman, who currently calls Corona, N.M., home, was connected with the Pitzer operation throughout the Pat Star Jr. era. Married to Howard's daughter, Kay, at the time, he remembers the day his father-in-law returned from the Sooner State with his new stallion.

"When Howard drove into the yard with Pat Star in tow," Brinkman recalls, "we all came out of the house to have a look at him.

Halter and Performance Record: None.

Progeny Record:

Foal Crops: 13	Performance Point-Earners: 86
Foals Registered: 348	Performance Points Earned: 1,728
AQHA Champions: 22	Performance Registers of Merit: 42
Youth Champions: 2	Superior Performance Awards: 3
Halter Point-Earners: 73	Race Starters: 2
Halter Points Earned: 1,805	Race Money Earned: $2,225
Superior Halter Awards: 11	Race Registers of Merit: 1
Leading Race Money-Earner: Rocket Pat Star ($1,935)	

As Howard was unloading him, he turned to his wife, Florence, and said, 'I just gave half the ranch for this horse.'

" 'My God, Howard, what did he cost?' Florence asked.

"I can't remember for sure what Howard's answer was, but it was in the neighborhood of $3,500. That was a lot of money to give for a horse back then."

For most of the years he spent there, Brinkman handled the Pitzer Ranch's cattle operation. As a result, he logged thousands of hours on the backs of Pat Star Jr. and his get. According to the Plainview, Neb., native, they were ideal ranch mounts.

"Pat Star and his get were the very best kind of horses," he says. "Pat Star himself was a little horse, standing maybe 14.3 hands. But he was tough, he was smart, and he was willing. All you had to do was ask, and he'd give. It didn't matter whether it was roping, sorting a cow, or loping across the prairie. He'd just do it.

"Another thing I remember about the

Dusty Pat Star, a 1958 mare out of Brown's Dusty, was the first AQHA Champion sired by Pat Star Jr. Although she looks brown in this photo, she was actually a gray. She is shown here with Pitzer Ranch trainer John Mullins after being named the grand champion mare at a 1960 Oshkosh, Neb., show.

horse," he continues, "is that he was so even-dispositioned. Howard always pasture-bred him, but we could go out to where he was running with his mares, put a halter on him, and ride him bareback to the barn. We'd work cattle on him all day, then turn him out with his mares at night. He just thought that was the way things were and accepted it without question."

In keeping with his original plan to raise top ranch horses, Pitzer was not bashful when it came to gelding the best of the Pat Star Jr. colts.

"Howard always felt it took a good stallion to make a good gelding," Brinkman says, "and Pat Star gave us some of the best geldings to ever look through a bridle.

"The Pat Star geldings were big and stout. They'd stand 15.2 to 15.3 hands and weigh 1,200 to 1,300 pounds. And, like their daddy, they were willing. I never had one turn me down when I asked him to do something.

"The best Pat Star I ever rode," he continues, "was Star Holt. He was a 1961 bay

gelding out of Madeline, by Texas Tom. We showed him enough to earn his AQHA Championship in 1967, but his main job was to be my No. 1 ranch horse.

"One winter day Star and I were chasing a stray cow across an irrigated hay meadow. Those meadows had a lot of moisture in them, even in the winter. We hit a slick spot and Star went down flat on his side. He slid 20 feet or so, hit the end of the patch, and then just got up and continued after the cow. I had managed to stay somewhere near the middle of the saddle through all the ruckus, and we collared that cow in short order and got her back to where she was supposed to be.

"That's the kind of horses those Pat Stars were."

John Mullins of Elba, N.Y., is another man who was well acquainted with Pitzer's foundation stud and his get. "I first went to work for Howard on July 4, 1952," Mullins says. "I was 17 years old at the time, and Dean Brinkman and I were first cousins.

Howard and my father were lifelong friends who grew up on farms in Antelope County between Plainview and Neligh, Nebraska. They went to school together and even after Howard moved to Ericson, our families stayed in touch.

"I was not at the ranch when Howard bought Pat Star. I was away, serving in the Army. But I sure got acquainted with him and his get a few years later, and Howard and I had many conversations about him.

"I know Howard liked Pat Star's conformation and disposition, because he said as much on more than one occasion. I also know that he first became interested in him because of all those top horses who were his three-quarter siblings. Howard always believed that bloodlines were important, and that horses from proven working lines would breed true more often than not."

Although Mullins was a relatively green horseman when he first went to work for Pitzer, by the time he returned from the service in 1960 he was a seasoned trainer.

"All the while I was in the Army," he recalls, "I trained and showed horses in the evenings and on the weekends. While stationed in Louisiana, I worked for pioneer breeders Hayes and Merle McDole. Then, when I was at Fort Sam Houston in San Antonio, I worked for another pioneer Appaloosa breeder, Gus Ottermann.

"I left the Army in the fall of 1958 and worked for a while for Wilson Trailers at Sioux City, Iowa. While there, I showed horses for yet another pioneer Appaloosa horseman, Don Imboden.

"In January of 1960, Howard made me an offer that I couldn't refuse—to come back to work for him as a full-time trainer and showman. I was really his first trainer, per se."

While Mullins was off serving his country, Howard Pitzer had been a busy man. In 1954 he began showing some of his original mares at halter, embarking on what would become one of the most storied show ring careers in the history of the American Quarter Horse Association.

Showing for a full four years before he won his first grand championship, Pitzer

COURTESY THE QUARTER HORSE JOURNAL

Jack Pat Star, a 1959 bay gelding by Pat Star Jr. and out of Patty's Queen, earned an AQHA Championship and a Superior in halter.

finally broke the ice in 1958 when he led Nancy Barrett to top honors at Burwell, Nebraska.

The Initial Pitzer Show String

The purchase of Pat Star Jr. in 1956 led to the production of what would become the first generation of Pitzer-bred show horses in 1957. To represent the ranch at the shows

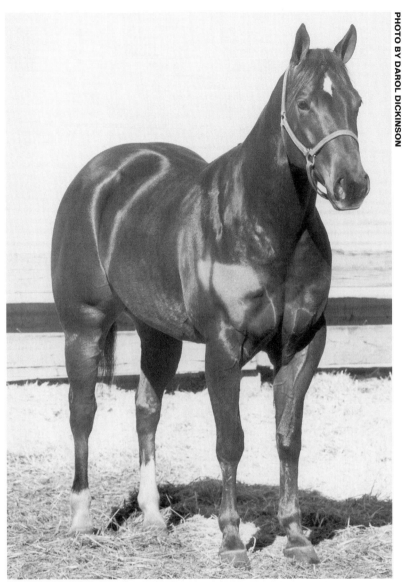

Dot Pat Star, a 1960 sorrel mare by Pat Star Jr. and out of My Tad, by Tadpole, earned 178 halter and 27.5 performance points en route to her AQHA Championship. She is shown here after being named the grand champion mare at the 1965 National Western Stock Show in Denver.

while the Pat Stars were coming of age, Pitzer acquired four top mares: Poco Sweetheart, Chubby Rachelle, Kay Mac Lee, and Lady Dondi. All four were eventually shown to their AQHA Championships.

By 1960 the first of the Pat Stars had reached riding age, and the stage was set for the return of John Mullins as trainer and exhibitor. Even with these two tasks as his main responsibilities, the then-26-year-old horseman still spent a little time on the "old man."

"Although 1960 through 1962 were big show years for Howard and me," Mullins says, "I still managed to log some hours on Pat Star, checking fences and working cattle. I remember him as a good-headed, good-necked horse; well built, with a powerful hip. He was as quick as a cat on his feet.

"Pat Star liked people and was a kind horse. Despite that, I think I would still have to classify him as a cowboy's horse. When it came to work, he was all business. Then, when the work was done, he didn't want to mess around. He wanted to get back to the barn.

"But far and away Pat Star's best trait was his prepotency. He had the look of eagles, and so did his foals. You could tell Pat Star offspring anywhere by their big, bright eyes."

Among Mullins' initial chores on his return to the Pitzer Ranch was training and showing Poco Sweetheart, Chubby Rachelle, Kay Mac Lee, and Lady Dondi. In addition, he selected and developed the first of the Pat Star Jr. show horses.

He chose Dusty Pat Star, a 1958 gray mare out of Brown's Dusty, and Jack Pat Star, a 1959 bay gelding out of Patty's Queen. Mullins showed both to their AQHA Championships in 1962, with Jack Pat Star tacking on a Superior in halter as well. They were the first of their sire's offspring to earn such honors.

By the fall of 1962, Mullins was once again ready to move on. He and his wife, Cleo, migrated east to Elba, N.Y., where they put down permanent roots and built highly successful careers as Appaloosa breeders and exhibitors. The couple took with them a striking black-and-white, blanket-hipped Appaloosa colt named Little Navajo Joe, who went on to become one of the breed's foundation show horses and sires and a 2000 inductee into the Appaloosa Horse Club's Hall of Fame.

Little Navajo Joe was bred by Mullins and was foaled on the Pitzer Ranch. Although he registered the colt himself, Mullins remains convinced to this day that his pedigree might be incorrect.

"Little Navajo Joe was foaled in 1962," he says. "His papers show him to be sired by

Little Fob, a Pitzer-owned Quarter Horse. His dam was Navajo Turquoise of AA, an Appaloosa show mare I purchased from Laura Boggio of Rapid City, South Dakota.

"When it came time to breed Turquoise, Howard and I turned her in with Pat Star Jr. The stud didn't like the mare and ran her off. He wouldn't accept her into his band. We bred her to Little Fob then, and he got her in foal—or so we thought.

"After Little Navajo Joe was foaled and got old enough for me to break and start riding, I always thought he favored Pat Star a lot more than he did Little Fob. He looked like a Pat Star, and he rode like one. And I should know—I rode a lot of them.

"Howard and I used to mull the situation over, and he always agreed with me. He thought that Joe was really by Pat Star.

"Recently, Dean Brinkman and I were discussing the same topic. He said to me, "I know who Little Navajo Joe's sire is; it's Pat Star Jr. I know because I saw Pat Star breed Joe's mother. It wasn't until after he bred her that he ran her off.'

"I asked him why he hadn't said anything about it before, and he replied, 'Because you never asked me.'

"I don't know if I'll ever do anything about straightening out Joe's pedigree. At this point, I'm not even sure I can. But, in my mind, he is a son of Pat Star Jr., and that makes him all the more special to me."

The Pat Star Jr. Influence

After Mullins' departure from the Pitzer Ranch in 1962, much of the training and showing of the Pat Star horses was turned over to Bill Keyser from Ord, Nebraska. Keyser is credited with developing four of the stallion's greatest daughters—Dot Pat Star, Georgia Pat Star, Kim Pat Star, and Babe Pat Star—and showed all four to their AQHA Championships in the mid-1960s.

By 1965 Pat Star Jr. was a fixture on virtually every AQHA Leading Sires list. Within the next two years, such show horses as Stumpy Star, Chubby Star Jr.,

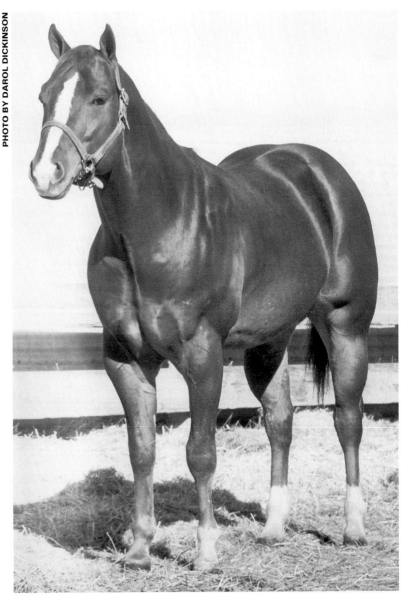

Two Eyed Jack, the Pitzer Ranch junior stallion at the time, made it a double major win for Pitzer when he was named grand champion stallion at the 1965 National Western.

Patty Pat Star, Sadie Pat Star, Star Holt, Bell Pat Star, Johnny Pat Star, Kippy Pat Star, and Poncho Pat Star would push the number of his AQHA Champion get well past the double-digit mark.

Then, in the fall of 1967, just as the Pitzer and Pat Star show machine was really cranking up into high gear, tragedy struck. Pat Star Jr., then only 14 years old, died.

"I can't remember exactly when Pat Star passed away," Kay Pitzer Brinkman says. "I do remember that it was after the kids— Jim and Jane—were back in school that

Georgia Pat Star, an AQHA Champion, topped the first annual Working Horse Sale at the 1965 National Western Stock Show in Denver. A 1960 bay mare by Pat Star Jr. and out of Georgia Star, Georgia Pat Star was consigned by Howard Pitzer and purchased for $3,400 by Margaret Stroud of Denver.

fall. And I remember it was after we'd taken him away from his mares.

"We used to run Pat Star with a bunch of the ranch geldings during the fall and winter, and that's where he died—in with them. Dad and Dean were with him when he passed away. They thought it was something like colic that took him, but they weren't sure. And they didn't 'post'

him. They hauled him to a pasture just west of the house and buried him.

"It was the pasture where Pat Star always ran with his mares. It has a small knoll where he liked to stand, and that's where they laid him to rest. And, from that point on, that's where all the great Pitzer stallions were buried. Two Eyed Jack is there, along with Watch Joe Jack, Jack Eyed, Baron Bell, and Red Baron Bell. Vickie Lee Pine, the first AQHA Superhorse, is the only mare buried there.

"We call it Pat Star's Cemetery. He was the first to go into it, and he started the tradition."

Ordinarily, the loss of a stallion of the stature of Pat Star Jr. would deal a devastating blow to any Quarter Horse program. To a certain extent, it did to the Pitzer program. But Howard had kept 30 Pat Star Jr. daughters as broodmares, and he had a promising young stallion to breed them to: Two Eyed Jack.

Even though Pat Star Jr. was gone, his influence—his legacy—was far from over.

For a decade to come the Pat Stars would continue to make their presence felt in the show ring. By the time the last one was retired, Pat Star's get had tallied in open, amateur, and youth classes 22 AQHA Championships, 11 Superiors at halter, 3 Superiors in performance, 42 ROMs, and 3,532 points in halter and performance.

Then, after their show days were over, the Pat Star daughters began to make their contributions as producers.

Pat Star Jr. Daughters

Crossed on Two Eyed Jack, the Pat Star mares started churning out show prospects the likes of which the Quarter Horse world had never seen.

Dot Pat Star, a 1961 sorrel mare out of My Tad, by Tadpole, became the dam of nine Two Eyed Jack performers. All nine— Denver Jack, Denver Dot, Mr Denver Jack, Miss Denver Dot, Two Eyed Denver, Denver Dotty, Denver Jackie, Denver Jax, and Denver Jack Two—were named to commemorate that both their parents had

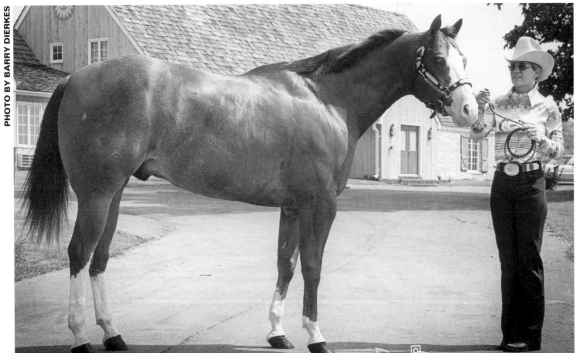

PHOTO BY BARRY DIERKES

PHOTO BY ALFRED JANSSEN III

Denver Jack (top) and Miss Denver Dot were both by Two Eyed Jack and out of Dot Pat Star. That cross produced a total of nine outstanding horses, who earned 2,023 open and youth points, 6 AQHA Championships, and 2 high-point halter awards. Denver Jack (965 points) and Miss Denver Dot (593 points) were the most prolific point-earners of that cross.

been named grand champions at the 1965 National Western Stock Show in Denver.

In the show ring those nine amassed 2,023 points in open and youth competition, 6 AQHA Championships, 8 Superiors, and 10 ROMs.

Other Pat Star daughters who produced well when bred to Jack included:

- Hilda Pat Star—the dam of three AQHA Champions: Hilda Jack, Two Eyed Dandy, and Jack's Hilda. She also pro-

PHOTO BY DAROL DICKINSON, COURTESY JOHN MULLINS

Babe Pat Star, a 1961 bay mare by Pat Star Jr. and out of Twinks, was one of her sire's most accomplished performers. Trained and shown by Bill Keyser, Babe was an AQHA Champion and also a Superior halter and cutting horse.

This is Little Navajo Joe, owned by John Mullins of Elba, New York. Although Joe is registered to the contrary, all evidence points to Pat Star Jr. as the real sire of this Appaloosa Horse Club Hall of Fame stallion. The colorful black-and-white stallion certainly has the patented Pat Star Jr. look.

Dixie Pat Star, a 1961 bay mare out of Star Again, was yet another of the Pat Star Jr. daughters versatile enough to earn both an AQHA Championship and a Superior at halter.

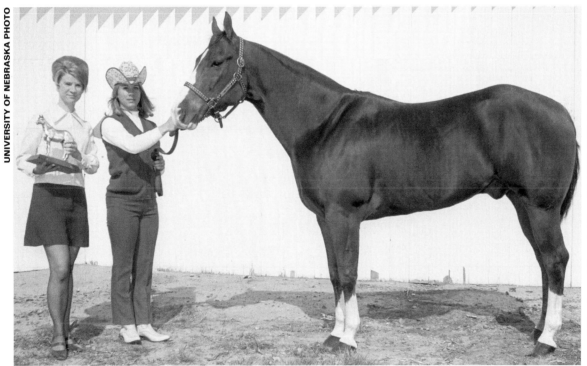

Johnny Pat Star, a 1962 sorrel gelding by Pat Star Jr. and out of Bay Mayme, won open and youth AQHA Championships, open and youth Superiors at halter, and a youth Superior in showmanship. The handler here is Debby Brehm of Lincoln, Nebraska. Karen Fenster, York, Neb., presents the trophy.

UNIVERSITY OF NEBRASKA PHOTO

duced a fourth foal, Two Eyed Hilda, who earned a Superior in open halter. In addition to his AQHA Championship, Two Eyed Dandy was the 1974 AQHA World Champion Aged Gelding.

- Dondi Pat Star—the dam of two AQHA Champions: Dondi Jo Jack and Two Eyed Lady Jack.
- Kim Pat Star—the dam of Two Eyed Kim, an AQHA Champion, and Kimmie Jack,

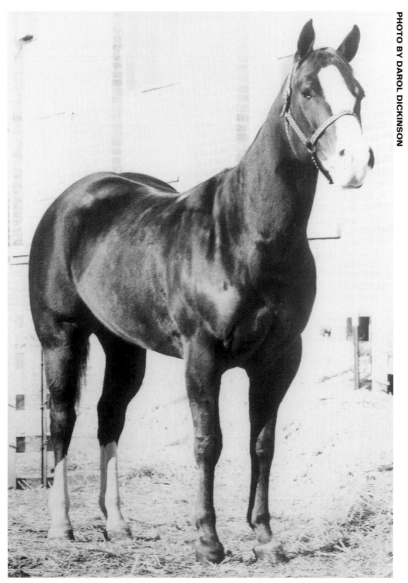

Harmon Pat Star, a 1963 sorrel gelding by Pat Star Jr. and out of Patty's Queen, was an AQHA Champion, won a Superior in halter, and earned 91 halter and 30.5 performance points. He is shown here after being named reserve champion gelding at the 1966 National Western.

a youth AQHA Champion and the 1976 Youth World Champion 2-Year-Old Mare.

- Kippy Pat Star — the dam of Aces High, an AQHA Champion, and Jack's Pants and Eye Jack, Superior-earning team roping horses.
- Dorothy Pat Star — the dam of Two Eyed Suzy Kay, an AQHA Champion, and Two Eyed Don, Jim Brinkman's great three-time world champion team roping gelding.
- Marj Pat Star — the dam of The Dallas

Cowboy, an AQHA Champion and the 1978 World Champion Aged Stallion; and Margie Star Jack, a Superior-earning halter horse.

All told, when bred to Two Eyed Jack, the Pat Star Jr. mares produced 18 open AQHA Champions, 6 youth AQHA Champions, and the earners of 40 Superior titles in open and youth competition.

Like the Oklahoma Star Jr.-Bert cross before it, the Two Eyed Jack-Pat Star Jr. cross was a golden one — and one that put the Pitzer Ranch on the map to stay.

And Pat Star was more than just a show and broodmare sire. Though not universally known as a sire of blazing straightaway speed, he managed to put his name in the AQHA speed record books. Rocket Pat Star, a 1967 Pat Star daughter out of Midnight Gold, by Revenue, earned her ROM in racing in 1970. She then went on to produce nine race starters and eight ROM earners. Two of them, Mr Double Rocket and Cottom Pat Star, achieved speed indexes of 101.

Finally, there was Barry Pat Star, a 1960 gray stallion and one of four AQHA Champions sired by Pat Star Jr. and out of Brown's Dusty. Though not as prolific a breeding horse as Pat Star, Barry did his part to carry on the family name by siring four AQHA Champions. Like Pat Star, Barry also made his mark as a broodmare sire. One of his daughters, Pat's Dusty Star, became the dam of Skipa Star, a Superior-earning halter horse and the 1975 World Champion 2-Year-Old Stallion.

Skipa Star, in turn, went on to become an all-time leading sire and maternal grandsire, and his profile also appears in this book.

All in all, Pat Star Jr., the little bay stallion that Howard Pitzer bought to raise some ranch horses with, did himself proud. Standing as he often did in the shadow of the legendary Two Eyed Jack, Pat Star Jr. seldom received the recognition he deserved. History should record him as one of the key contributors to not only the Pitzer Ranch, but the Quarter Horse breed as well. Pat Star Jr. was a superior ranch horse, and a superior ranch, show, and broodmare sire.

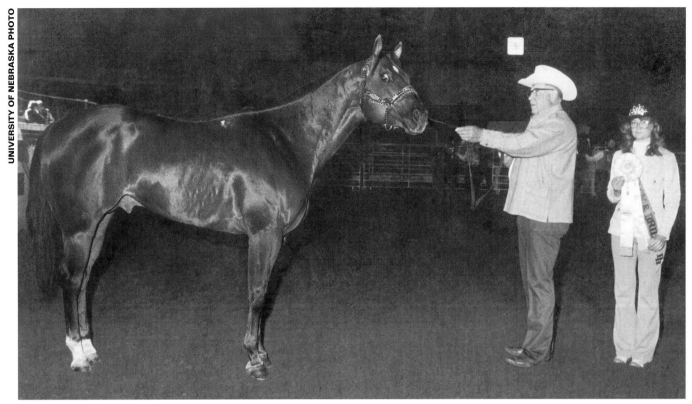

UNIVERSITY OF NEBRASKA PHOTO

Dondi Jo Jack, a 1973 stallion, was by Two Eyed Jack and out of Dondi Pat Star. The sorrel was an AQHA Champion and a long-time Pitzer herd sire. That's Howard Pitzer at the halter.

PHOTO BY HAROLD CAMPTON

The Dallas Cowboy was named the 1978 AQHA World Champion Aged Stallion. Foaled in 1974, he was by Two Eyed Jack and out of Marj Pat Star. The good-looking brown stallion was bred and owned by Kay Schleichardt (left) and shown by Tommy Manion.

103

9

SKIPA STAR

By Frank Holmes

He was one of the most classic halter horses of all time.

SKIPA STAR was the result of a rare blend of two of the most storied horse breeding programs in the history of the breed—the Hank Wiescamp operation of Alamosa, Colo., and Howard Pitzer's operation at Ericson, Nebraska.

It was a cross that, for some reason, was not often made. Maybe it should have been, for in Skipa Star's case it wound up producing one of the most classic halter horses of all time.

Skipa Star, a chestnut stallion foaled June 6, 1973, was bred by Jim Senkbeil of Chapman, Nebraska. He was sired by Skipper's Lad and was out of Pat's Dusty Star, by Barry Pat Star. Skipper's Lad was a direct son of the legendary Skipper W and was out Miss Helen, by Plaudit.

Skipper W—the horse whose name remains one of the most easily recognizable in all of Quarter Horse history—was featured in both *Legends 2* and *The Hank Wiescamp Story.*

Skipa Star, shown here as a 2-year-old in 1975, had the kind of timeless conformation and presence that enabled him to become one of the breed's all-time great halter horses and the fountainhead of an enduring family of champion halter and performance horses.

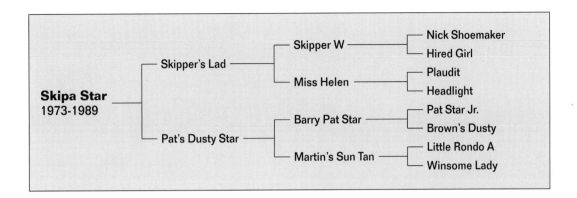

```
                                          ┌─ Nick Shoemaker
                         ┌─ Skipper W ─────┤
                         │                 └─ Hired Girl
        ┌─ Skipper's Lad ┤
        │                │                 ┌─ Plaudit
        │                └─ Miss Helen ────┤
Skipa Star                                └─ Headlight
1973-1989 ┤
        │                                  ┌─ Pat Star Jr.
        │                ┌─ Barry Pat Star ┤
        │                │                 └─ Brown's Dusty
        └─ Pat's Dusty Star ┤
                         │                 ┌─ Little Rondo A
                         └─ Martin's Sun Tan ┤
                                           └─ Winsome Lady
```

Miss Helen was a cornerstone mare in both the Warren Shoemaker breeding program at Watrous, N.M., and the Wiescamp program. To the former, she contributed the great palomino sire Gold Mount. For the latter, she produced such horses as Skipper's Lad, who earned 23 halter points and was a noted sire, and Skipadoo, who earned 44 halter points and who was widely recognized as one of the all-time classic Wiescamp mares.

Pat's Dusty Star, the dam of Skipa Star, came with her own impeccable set of genetic credentials. Barry Pat Star, her sire, was an AQHA Champion, Superior halter horse by Pat Star Jr. and out of Brown's Dusty, by Mr. Brown. Pat Star Jr., the first of the great Pitzer sires, is also featured in this volume.

Brown's Dusty produced four AQHA Champions—Dusty Pat Star, Barry Pat Star, Sadie Pat Star, and Dina Pat Star. All four were sired by Pat Star Jr.

So Skipa Star was bred to be good, and it was apparent from the very beginning that he was even better than just good.

"Skipa Star was a freaky kind of foal," Jim Senkbeil says. "By that I mean he was just so perfect. He had a little doll head, and the tiniest muzzle you could ever imagine. His neck was exceptional, as was his top line. And, structurally, he was very correct. He looked handmade.

"Skipa Star's mother, Pat's Dusty Star, was bred by Merlin Flessner of Burr, Nebraska. Merlin raised good horses and has never really been given the recognition he deserves. He owned Barry Pat Star when I was gathering up some of my first

Halter and Performance Record: Superior Halter Horse; 1975 AQHA World Champion 2-Year-Old Stallion.

Progeny Record: (As of June 2001)

Foal Crops: 14	Halter Points Earned: 5,840.5
Foals Registered: 915	Superior Halter Awards: 41
AQHA Champions: 15	Performance Point-Earners: 232
Amateur AQHA Champions: 2	Performance Points Earned: 5,170.5
Youth AQHA Champions: 3	Performance Registers of Merit: 99
World Champions: 5	Superior Performance Awards: 30
Halter Point-Earners: 304	

mares. I went to Merlin's place and saw Pat's Dusty Star and three of her full sisters. They were wonderful mares, and I wound up buying them all.

"Barry Pat Star and Pat's Dusty Star were both gray horses. They had beautiful heads and reminded me of the Wiescamp horses in that regard.

"Although all four of the mares I got from Merlin Flessner went on to be top producers for me," he continues, "Pat's Dusty Star did the best job. I owned Skipper's Lad at the time, and I bred Dusty Star to him four times. The first result of the cross was a 1972 sorrel gelding named Pitzcamp.

"Skipa Star was next.

"Then, in 1974, I raised a palomino mare named Skipa Starlet. I sold her and she went on to produce Mr Crowd Appeal—the 1982 AQHA World Champion Weanling Stallion.

"Skipa Prince, a 1975 chestnut stallion, came last.

"All four of the Skipper's Lad-Pat's

Here's Skipa Star as a yearling with owner Larry Sullivant of Gainesville, Texas.

Skipper's Lad, the sire of Skipa Star, sired the earners of five AQHA Championships, seven Superiors in halter and performance, twenty-two ROMs in performance, and 1,768.5 total points.

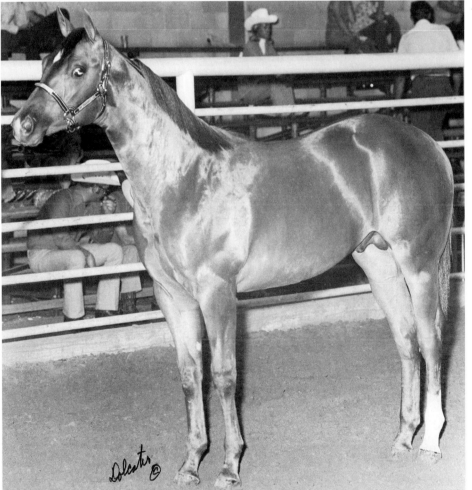

COURTESY JIM SENKBEIL

PHOTO BY DOLCATER, COURTESY THE QUARTER HORSE JOURNAL

Pat's Dusty Star produced an amazing 18 foals. In addition to Skipa Star, she produced Patty Baron, a 1971 palomino mare by Baron Bell who earned 10 halter and 21 performance points. The foal at her side in this picture is Skipa Prince, a full brother to Skipa Star.

At the 1974 Quarter Horse show in Amarillo, Skipa Star was named the grand champion stallion.

"Even though Skipa Star was small, he didn't have the characteristics of a small horse."
—Larry Sullivant

Skipa Star with Sam Wilson and C.B. Ames shortly after winning the 2-year-old stallion class at the 1975 AQHA World Championship Show.

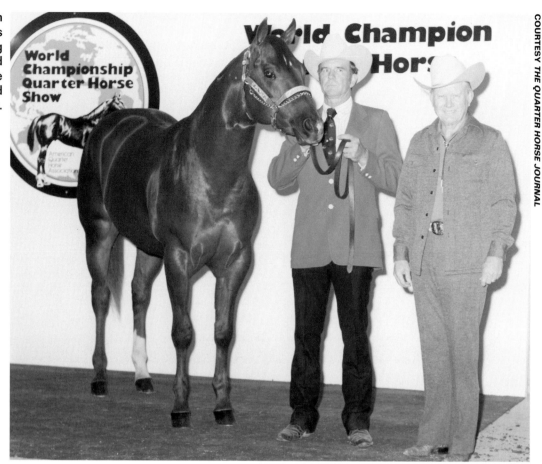

Dontcha Skip Me, a 1977 red dun mare by Skipa Star and out of Missy Skipper, by San Jacket, compiled a sterling halter record. Pictured here as a yearling, the elegant filly was shown 46 times and amassed 42 firsts, 11 grands, and 12 reserves.

Dusty Star horses were nice, but Skipa Star was in a league of his own."

Even though Senkbeil quickly recognized that in Skipa Star he had one of those rare individuals who only comes along once in a lifetime, he did not have the typey youngster for more than a few days.

"Skipa Star was only two or three days old when Willis Butler of Lafayette, Ind., came by to look at my Skipper's Lad foals," Senkbeil says. "I had eight of them, with Skipa Star being the youngest.

"I priced those foals at $3,500 each, and Butler bought all of them but one. I had raised an Appaloosa filly out of a daughter of Bright Eyes Brother. Butler didn't want her, so I kept her. I named her Skip's Brightette, and she went on to be a three-time national and world champion at halter and in performance.

"Butler had only given me a down payment on the foals—to hold them until they could be weaned," he continues. "As the summer wore on, I began to seriously regret agreeing to sell Skipa Star. I tried to talk Butler out of taking the colt, but he wouldn't have any part of it. He picked him and the other six foals up in January.

"But, I was fortunate to have bred Skipa Star, and to have seen him go on and accomplish such great things. I'm thankful for that."

As it turned out, Willis Butler would not own Skipa Star very long either. Within a few months, the colt sold again, and this time to the man who would take him to the top of the Quarter Horse halter world — Larry Sullivant of Gainesville, Texas.

Skipa Star Becomes a Star

"In 1974, I was a young lawyer and a relatively unknown entity in the Quarter Horse show ring," Sullivant says. "I was fortunate to have been mentored by one of the greatest horsemen of all time, George Tyler of Gainesville, and had even had my hands on a few top halter prospects.

"But I hadn't really gotten the chance to

PHOTO BY DAROL DICKINSON, COURTESY *THE QUARTER HORSE JOURNAL*

As a 3-year-old, Skipa Star stood 15.1 hands and weighed a well-balanced 1,150 pounds.

show a great one. I was young and green, and trying to make some money with halter horses, so I'd had to sell every good one I ever got my hands on — just to keep the whole thing going.

"In the spring of 1974, I went to Indiana to look at what was supposed to be a top yearling stallion show prospect. Jim Fuller, who now lives in Valley View, Tex., was with me on that trip.

"We went to see the colt and looked him over. I didn't like him very much, but then Jim said, 'I saw one the other day that you'd like.' So we wound up at Willis

Born As A Star, a 1977 sorrel stallion by Skipa Star and out of Azure Mikada, by Azure Te (TB), earned a Superior in halter and went on to sire the earners of 863 points.

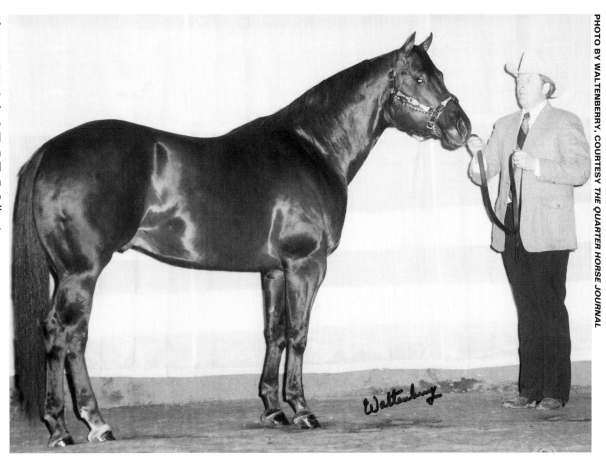

PHOTO BY WALTENBERRY, COURTESY *THE QUARTER HORSE JOURNAL*

Deck Of Stars, a 1977 sorrel stallion by Skipa Star and out of Opal Deck, by Bent Deck, earned a Superior halter award in 1982. A highly successful sire in his own right, Deck Of Stars had 241 performers. As of June 2001, they had earned 56 Superiors in performance and 3 in halter, 9 AQHA Championships, 1 youth Supreme Championship, and 12,018 total points. Also as of June 2001, Deck Of Stars had $84,631 in AQHA Incentive Fund earnings.

PHOTO BY WALTENBERRY, COURTESY JUDY PRYOR

Butler's and that's when I got my first glimpse of Skipa Star.

"This was in April or May, so the colt wasn't even a full year old yet. He was small, and hadn't ever been pushed so he was a tad underdeveloped. Several other halter horse people had looked at him before me and turned him down for those reasons.

"Even though Skipa Star was small," Sullivant continues, "he didn't have the characteristics of a small horse. I thought he was the greatest yearling stallion I'd ever seen, and I felt that he would get some size, and that he would catch up development-wise.

"I had a partner at the time, and we bought the colt on the spot for $12,500."

Sullivant took his new acquisition back to Texas and began prepping him for a career in the halter ring. Shown for the first time at Tulsa, then in Claremore, Okla., and Beaumont, Kan., in late May and early June, Skipa Star garnered three firsts and two reserve championships.

Next up for the promising youngster was the early June, four-day run at Des Moines, Iowa. Skipa Star quickly became the talk of the show — winning his class all four days and standing grand once — and it became apparent that he was destined to change hands again before the circuit was over.

"By this time," Sullivant says, "I had several partners on Skipa Star. I only had a 25 percent interest in him. All the big halter boys were at Des Moines, and they were all interested in Skipa Star. We had him priced at $40,000, and I wanted to retain some breedings as well.

"When it looked like someone was going to step up and buy him, I did some serious soul searching and came to the conclusion that this was the one horse — among all those I had been connected with to that point—that I shouldn't let go.

"I didn't have the kind of money it was going to take to buy out my partners, so in desperation I called George Tyler back in Gainesville. I explained my dilemma to him, and I can remember as clearly as if it were yesterday what his reply was.

Flaming Agnes, a 1977 chestnut mare by Skipa Star and out of Dana's Honey Bee, by Odom's Cochise, was her sire's first great all-around horse. The 1981 AQHA World Champion Junior Heeling Horse, Agnes also placed fourth in the aged mare class at the 1982 World Show, and was an AQHA Champion and Superior halter horse.

" 'Do you believe in this horse?' he asked.

" 'I really like him.'

" 'That's not what I asked,' George responded. 'I asked if you believed in him.'

" 'Yes, I do!'

" 'Write the check,' he said. 'This ol'

Skips Flaming Star, a 1977 sorrel mare out of Toy Hunt, by Brownie Hunt, was yet another sterling member of Skipa Star's first foal crop. Shown here with breeder Butch Hosmer after winning the 1978 Rocky Mountain Quarter Horse Association yearling filly halter futurity, Skips Flaming Star went on to become the 1982 Youth AQHA High-Point Halter Mare and an open and youth AQHA Superior halter horse.

broken-down horse trader has got the money to cover it.'

"So I did, and that's how I came to own Skipa Star outright."

After Sullivant and Skipa Star returned home from Iowa, George Tyler was quick to pay the pair a visit — to see what his loan had bought.

"It wasn't long after we got home," Sullivant says, "that George came over to see Skipa Star. I led him out and George walked around him one time and turned to me and said, 'Larry, you take care of this horse, and you won't ever have to worry about borrowing any more money from a broken-down ol' horse trader.

" 'This horse is worth more than a black-dirt farm.'

"I'll always be grateful to George for taking the time to teach me about horses and how to fit them, and for loaning me the money to buy Skipa Star. It was truly

what got me established in the Quarter Horse business."

A Record To Remember

After acquiring full ownership of Skipa Star, Sullivant continued to show him at halter. By year's end, the pair had attended 14 shows and amassed 13 firsts, 5 grands, and 3 reserves.

Skipa Star's sole defeat came at the 1974 All-American Quarter Horse Congress in Columbus, Ohio, where he placed fourth in the yearling stallion halter futurity. It would be the only time during his entire show career that he placed lower than second.

Skipa Star's 2-year-old halter campaign began in much the same manner as his yearling one had left off. Shown at the Gold Coast Circuit in West Palm Beach, Fla., in January, the chestnut stallion

Elle Skip A Star, a 1978 sorrel mare out of Azure Mikada, by Azure Te (TB), was Skipa Star's first youth AQHA Champion. Shown here with youth exhibitor Robyn Kaplow, the well-balanced mare also earned Superiors in open halter and western pleasure.

won two firsts, one second, one grand, and one reserve.

"I only showed Skipa Star at part of the Gold Coast show," Sullivant says. "My wife, Karon, and I were a young married couple, just starting our life together. In addition, I was building a career as a lawyer. We didn't have the money or the time to stay in Florida for the whole circuit, so we showed the first three days and then headed home.

"Karon deserves a lot of credit for Skipa Star's success," he continues. "She helped me fit him, helped me get him ready for the shows, and traveled with me to a lot of them. I couldn't have done any of it without her."

The Gold Coast circuit proved to be just the starting point for what would be an incredibly successful show year, and one that would firmly establish Skipa Star as one the most dominant halter horses of his era.

West Palm Beach was followed by an abbreviated stock show run that saw Skipa Star win his class and stand grand at

Amarillo, and place second at both Denver and San Antonio.

Over the course of the next 29 shows—beginning at Burkburnett, Tex., on March 2, and ending at Goodlettsville, Tenn., on July 15—Skipa Star was undefeated. During that time span, the classic stallion amassed 29 firsts, 25 grands, and 4 reserves.

After placing second in his class and being named reserve champion stallion at Goodlettsville, Skipa Star went on to earn an additional 10 firsts, 2 seconds, 8 grands, and 2 reserves during the rest of the year.

After placing second in a class of 15 2-year-old stallions at the 1975 All-American Quarter Horse Congress, he came back a few short weeks later to be named the AQHA World Champion 2-Year-Old Stallion at the AQHA World Championship Show held that November in Kentucky.

All in all, it had been a show season to remember.

"At the time I found Skipa Star and started showing him," Larry Sullivant says, "I was virtually unknown as a Quarter Horse halter exhibitor. He changed

Harold Campton

Skipastarsky, a 1979 gray stallion by Skipa Star and out of King Moore's Dora, by King Moore, was the 1983 AQHA High-Point Junior Heeling Horse. Shown here in the winner's circle at the 1983 All-American Quarter Horse Congress with Dan Harrison Jr. aboard, Skipastarsky earned 105 performance points and a Superior in heeling.

all of that. Skipa Star was as close to unbeatable as any halter horse I've ever had anything to do with, and I had him and Te N' Te in my barn at the same time.

Skipa Star was my first world champion, and I led 16 more after him.

"He was so pretty and so well-balanced that he could steal a halter class. He could go in a class and not be the heaviest-muscled horse in it. But he had such presence—such a 'look of eagles'—that it would seem he was the only horse in the ring. More than any horse I've ever been connected with, before or since, Skipa Star had the most positive impact on my life. He did more for me than I did for him."

In addition to his classic halter conformation, Skipa Star was bred to be a top-notch performance horse. Why then, the logical question might be, was he never given a chance to perform?

"I broke Skipa Star to ride as a 2-year-old," Sullivant says. "He always had a wonderful disposition and was easy to break. I still clearly remember the day I first climbed up on him. He had incredibly big, soft eyes, and I can distinctly remember sitting in the saddle and looking down at his head. His eyes were so big, and stuck out so far, that I could see them both almost in their entirety.

"Skipa Star was an athletic horse and a natural lead changer. But there's an easy answer as to why I never went on with him in performance: 'What did I have to gain?'

"Skipa Star was a dominant force in the halter ring, and that's how people came to view him. If I'd have taken him into performance, he would not have been as dominant. He would have won some and lost some. And every time he got beat, some people have said, 'See, he's not so great after all.'

"I was trying to build a name for both Skipa Star and myself, and I felt the best way to do it was strictly through halter competition. As it turned out I must have been right, because he got so popular I just couldn't hold on to him."

A Change of Partners

In November 1975, Sullivant did sell Skipa Star. It was, in his own words, not an

PHOTO BY DAROL DICKINSON, COURTESY THE QUARTER HORSE JOURNAL

Super Starlette, a 1978 sorrel mare by Skipa Star and out of Zusa Chance, by Sir Chance, earned 218 points and a Superior halter award. The good-looking mare also placed in the top six three times at the AQHA World Show.

easy decision to make, and one that had been several months in the making.

"In April 1975," he says, "I showed Skipa Star at the University of Nebraska's Block & Bridle show in Lincoln. Sam Wilson was the judge, and he made Skipa Star his grand champion stallion.

"I guess that was the first time Sam had ever seen the horse, and to make a long story short, he never forgot him and wound up partnering with C.B. Ames of Houston and buying him shortly before the 1975 AQHA World Show.

"Selling Skipa Star was a hard decision for Karon and me to make. He was our first super show horse and his success in the ring opened a lot of doors for us. On the other hand, we were young and just getting started. The money Sam and Mr. Ames offered us was just too tempting to turn down.

"I'm not going to say what the exact purchase price was, but I will say that it was more than $150,000. It was the most that I'd ever heard of a halter horse bringing up to that time, and it sure made a believer out of my banker. That made it easier for me to get money to invest in good horses from that point on.

"And I will add that Sam did well by the horse. He saw to it that some good mares were bred to him, and the results were what everyone who was ever connected with the horse probably hoped they would be."

"... it sure made a believer out of my banker."

115

PHOTO BY WILLIS, COURTESY THE QUARTER HORSE JOURNAL

Skipa Stars Buck, a 1980 sorrel stallion out of Little Brenda Bar, by Little Town, is yet another top-siring son of Skipa Star. As of June 2001 his get had won five AQHA world championships and eight reserves. In addition, they had earned four AQHA Championships, three Superiors and six ROMs at halter; twenty-one Superiors and twenty-six ROMs in performance; and 3,521 points.

As for Wilson, he, too, vividly remembers the day he got his first glimpse of Skipa Star.

"I'll never forget that day I saw Skipa Star at Lincoln," he says. "He was one of those horses who just hit me. I couldn't quit looking at him. And when I went back and looked at him for the second time, he just got better. I guess the most appropriate word I could use to describe him is 'elegant.'

"He was a nice-sized horse, but he moved like a little horse. And after Mr. Ames and I bought him and took him home to my place near Pattison, Tex., I rode him and worked cattle with him enough to know that I was going to breed some of my cutting mares to him. He had a lot of cow in him. He was easy to get along with, and so were his foals."

After purchasing Skipa Star, and seeing him shown by Sullivant to his world championship, Wilson continued to campaign the stallion on a limited basis. Shown seven more times as a 2- and 3-year-old, Skipa Star went undefeated in his class and notched six more grands and one reserve. The reserve came at his last show, the 1976 All-American Quarter Horse Congress, where he also won the 3-year-old stallion class.

Outside of the one time he placed fourth in the Congress yearling stallion futurity, Skipa Star's record reveals that he was shown 67 times, placing first 61 times and second 6 times. He was named grand champion stallion 46 times, and reserve champion 12 times. He was awarded his Superior in open halter in 1975 and finished his show career with 82 open halter points.

Now all he had to prove was that he could reproduce himself.

A Promising Sire

"One of the greatest things about Skipa Star as a sire," Sam Wilson says, "was that it didn't matter what kind of mare you bred to him. He'd throw you a halter horse out of a performance mare, and a performance horse out of a halter mare.

"We were fortunate to attract some good outside mares to Skipa Star during

Star On Call, a 1979 chestnut mare by Skipa Star and out of Panzy Bee, by Bee Play, earned her Superior at halter in 1982.

Ames and Wilson syndicated him for an amount reported to be in excess of $1 million.

COURTESY THE QUARTER HORSE JOURNAL

those first years we stood him at stud, and we had a few of our own. We just kind of took over with his foals where we had left off with him."

Shortly after acquiring Skipa Star, Ames and Wilson syndicated him for an amount reported to be in excess of $1 million. Under the joint efforts of the new owners, Skipa Star's career as a sire got off to a flying start.

From his first foal crop, which hit the ground in 1977, came such stellar performers as:

- Flaming Agnes, 1981 AQHA World Champion Junior Heeling Horse, AQHA Champion, and Superior halter horse.
- Skips Flaming Star, 1982 AQHA Youth High-Point Halter Mare, youth AQHA Champion, and open and youth Superior halter horse.
- Skipastar Moneyman, AQHA Champion.
- Texas Star Ship, Superior hunter under saddle.
- Gotta Bea Star, Superior western pleasure.
- Born As A Star and Deck Of Stars, both Superior halter horses.

Here is Skipa Stars Lace, a 1984 gray mare by Skipa Stars Buck and out of Scoots Lace, by Sierra Scoot. Shown here with Jill Pennau in the saddle, Skipa Stars Lace was a five-time AQHA world champion western riding horse and the earner of multiple AQHA Superiors, championships, versatility classes, and high-point awards.

Over the course of the next two years those horses were joined by such halter stars as:

- Skipa Lindy Streak, 1981 AQHA World Champion 2-Year-Old Stallion, 1981 AQHA High-Point Halter Stallion, and Superior halter horse.
- Matinee Star, 1981 AQHA Youth Reserve World Champion 2-Year-Old Mare and Superior halter horse.
- Sensational Star, 1978 AQHA Reserve World Champion Weanling Stallion.
- Astar From Heaven, April Five Star, Super Starlette, Mr All Star, Star Encounter, and Star On Call, all Superior halter horses.

In performance, there were stars such as:

- Skipastarsky, 1983 High-Point Junior Heeling Horse and Superior heeling horse.
- Brinks Lestar, open, amateur, and youth AQHA Champion.
- Mr Dun Skip and Star Bright Kay, AQHA Champions and Superior halter horses.
- Skip To My Star, AQHA Champion and Superior western pleasure horse.
- Star Edition and Lone Star Redneck, AQHA Champions.
- Ellie Skip A Star, youth AQHA Champion and Superior halter and western pleasure.
- Take A Star, Superior western pleasure and trail horse.

COURTESY THE QUARTER HORSE JOURNAL

Ima Cool Skip, a 1984 sorrel stallion out of Susie Impressive, by Impressive Image, was Skipa Star's only three-time world halter champion and his top-siring son. Through February 2001, Ima Cool Skip's get had won 33 AQHA world championships and 34 reserves. They had also earned a quartet of AQHA Championships, 85 Superiors and 330 ROMs at halter; and 4 Superiors and 21 ROMs in performance; and a grand total of 17,513 points.

- Shirley A Star, Kountry Kerri, Canis Major, Dolly Starton, Ingalill, and Skipas Party Time, all Superior in western pleasure.

With only three foal crops representing him in the show ring, Skipa Star had become one of the hottest sires in the country.

In February 1979 the popular young sire sold for a fourth and final time. Once again, it was to a group of investors, and this time the syndication figure bandied about was $2.2 million.

Heading the new cartel was Allen Faulkner of Edmond, Oklahoma. Faulkner would also acquire controlling interest in Impressive four years later, giving him arguably the best one-two punch at that time in the halter horse industry. Even through this was the era in Quarter Horse halter history when the Impressive horses began dominating the event, Skipa Star's reputation continued to grow, as did the list of champions he sired.

The Star Brightens

Without a doubt, Ima Cool Skip was the brightest member of the Skipa Star family to be born during the Faulkner era. The 1984 sorrel stallion was out of Susie Impressive, by Impressive Image. He was bred by Douglas Hollifield of Marion, N.C., and owned throughout his show career by RGV Quarter Horses of Purcell, Oklahoma. With Jerry Wells of Purcell at his lead shank, the powerful stallion was the 1984 AQHA World Champion Weanling Stallion, the 1985 AQHA World Champion Yearling Stallion, and the 1986 AQHA World Champion 2-Year-Old Stallion. When he

In February 1979 the popular young sire sold for a fourth and final time.

was retired to stud, he went on to become an all-time leading sire.

But there were other Skipa Star standouts during the Faulkner era as well.

- Kissin Cousins, a 1981 sorrel stallion out of Sheza Jag On, by Jag On, was the 1981 AQHA World Champion Weanling Stallion.
- JBL Wish Me Luck, a 1989 chestnut gelding out of Real Cool Jewel, by Real Luck, was the 1992 AQHA World Champion Junior Western Riding Horse and a five-time AQHA High-Point International Halter Horse (a title awarded to horses shown overseas). In addition, he was an AQHA Champion and a Superior open and amateur western pleasure horse.
- Skipadette, a 1987 sorrel mare out of Intimidette, by The Intimidator, was a three-time AQHA reserve world champion halter mare and a Superior halter horse.
- Mr Simon Says, a 1982 chestnut stallion out of Lassie Jackie, by Two Eyed Jack, was the 1982 AQHA Reserve World Champion Weanling Stallion and a Superior western pleasure horse.
- Skippa Pay Check, a 1982 sorrel gelding out of Dana's Honey Bee, by Odom's Cochise, was the 1986 and 1987 AQHA High-Point Trail Horse Stallion and a Superior western pleasure and trail horse.
- Ismays A Skipa Star was an AQHA Champion and an open and amateur Superior halter horse.
- SR Dorothies Star was an AQHA Champion and a Superior hunter-under-saddle horse.
- Bogie Star was an AQHA Champion and a Superior western pleasure horse.
- Feature A Star, Skipanimpressivestar, and Lovie Skipa Star were AQHA Champions.
- Shes Our Star, Starrific, A Treasured Star, Cant Be Skipped, A Single Star, Streaks Sister, Dovetail Star, Fiveisenough, Ismays Bright Star, Ms Impressible Dream, Skip My Party, SS Super Star, Skipa Pressive, SR Shining Star, JBL Southern Breeze, El Bees Skippa Star, and

Skips Pioneer all earned one or more Superiors in halter.

- Barbara Starwick, Les Glos Lad, Ms Flaming Star, Star Too Dee Too, Ima Winning Star, The Star Queen, Starman Impression, and Skips Devotion earned Superiors in performance.

As of June 2001, the get of Skipa Star had earned seven AQHA world championships and seven reserves. In open, amateur, and youth competition, they had accumulated 20 AQHA Championships; 41 Superiors and 19 ROMs at halter; 30 Superiors and 99 ROMs in performance; and 11,011 total points.

A Broodmare Sire

As of early 2001, Skipa Star daughters had produced 15 AQHA world champions and 8 reserves. In open, amateur, and youth competition, they had earned a pair of AQHA Championships, 42 Superiors and 155 ROMs at halter, 21 Superiors and 113 ROMs in performance, and 13,022.5 total points.

The daughters of Skipa Star proved to be an especially successful nick with the Impressives. Among the horses produced from such crosses:

- Conclusive Lace, the dam of Kid Clu, an all-time leading sire.
- Tashmere, 1994 AQHA World Champion Weanling Stallion.
- Excelebration, 1998 AQHA World Champion 2-Year-Old Stallion.
- The Wild Wild West and The Phenomenal — two of the top young sires in the country — are both out of Skipa Star daughters.
- Telusive, the 1998 AQHA Amateur World Champion Aged Stallion and the sire of eight AQHA world champions and five reserves, is a double-bred Skipa Star.

Those are just a few examples of the potency of the cross.

The Sons

Finally, there are the sons of Skipa Star. Led by Ima Cool Skip, such horses as

PHOTO BY DON TROUT, COURTESY *THE QUARTER HORSE JOURNAL*

Another of the early Skipa Star champions was Astar From Heaven, a 1980 sorrel mare out of Two Eyed Olive Oil, by Two Eyed Jack. Bred by the Wilson Ranch of Pattison, Tex., Astar From Heaven earned 123 points and a Superior at halter.

Skipa Stars Buck, Skipa Lindy Streak, Deck Of Stars, Kissin Cousins, Skipastarsky, Starrific, and SS Super Star have all done, and are continuing to do, their part to enhance the family name.

In the late 1980s, Skipa Star was moved from Edmond, Okla., to Poplarville, Miss., where he stood to outside mares at Caillouet Farm, under the management of Mark Faulkner.

By the fall of 1989, the then 16-year-old stallion had begun to succumb to a founder condition he had contracted several years earlier. The decision was made to euthanize him.

In retrospect, Skipa Star can stake a firm claim to being one of the most influential Quarter Horse sires of all time. He was the result of a cross between two of the greatest foundation families in the history of the breed. He achieved prominence, both as a show horse and a sire, at a time when the Quarter Horse industry was undergoing dramatic change. From that perspective,

Skipa Star qualifies as one of the last of the great all-around sires of world class halter and performance horses.

Larry Sullivant's assessment of the breathtaking stallion probably best defines where he belongs in Quarter Horse lore:

"Skipa Star was as close to perfect an individual as I have ever been privileged to lay my eyes on," Sullivant says. "I've seen and owned some horses who might have been a little better here, or a little better there, but when you put the whole horse together, there has never been one quite like Skipa Star.

"He gave me the standard by which I evaluated every horse that followed him. He allowed me to visualize what I considered to be a perfect Quarter Horse in my mind, and to use that image to choose what I judged to be champions or hoped would be future champions.

"That was the greatest gift that Skipa Star gave to me. And I don't believe for a moment that I was the only one to receive it."

10 HANK H

By Frank Holmes

Despite his early death, Hank H earned a prominent place in Quarter Horse history.

HANK H was one of the best sons of King P-234 and had plenty of speed, athletic ability, and a flawless pedigree to augment his good looks. By all rights, he should have been one of the breed's all-time leading sires. Fate intervened however, and he died at an early age.

But blood will tell. What Hank H could not accomplish in his lifetime, his sons and daughters did in theirs. As a result, the family he founded did, in fact, go on to become one of the breed's best.

Hank H was a 1942 sorrel stallion by King P-234 and out of Queen H. Bred by J.O. Hankins of Rocksprings, Tex., Hank was the middle member of a five-horse, full-sibling set largely responsible for establishing the King dynasty. The other four were Duchess H, a 1940 bay mare; Squaw H, a 1941 sorrel mare; Booger H, a 1945 sorrel stallion; and Your Highness, a 1952 chestnut mare.

With Squaw H achieving a AAA rating on the track, and Hank H, Booger H, and Your Highness grading out at AA, it was

Hank H was one of the first top sons of King and he did much to enhance the family name. This photo of him appeared in AQHA Stud Book, Vol. 4, printed in 1947.

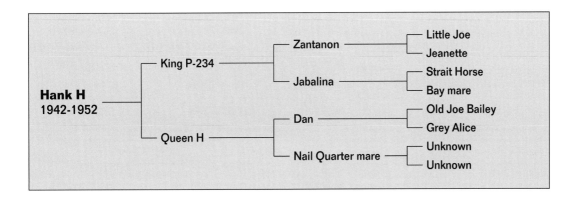

Hank H
1942-1952

King P-234
— Zantanon
— Little Joe
— Jeanette
— Jabalina
— Strait Horse
— Bay mare

Queen H
— Dan
— Old Joe Bailey
— Grey Alice
— Nail Quarter mare
— Unknown
— Unknown

one branch of the King family tree blessed with straightaway speed.

At the time of Hank H's birth, the King bloodline was just beginning to achieve national recognition. Royal King, Poco Bueno, and King's Pistol had not been foaled, and Squaw H was still a year away from the advent of her stellar race career. In short order, these four superstars and a host of their paternal brothers and sisters would advance their sire's reputation to the point where he could lay legitimate claim to being a cornerstone of an industry.

But in 1942, King was more of a regional phenomenon. His sons and daughters out of Queen H helped change that.

From the standpoint of breeding, there wasn't a lot about Queen H to indicate she would one day be one of the breed's premier matrons. Her sire, Dan, was an unregistered son of Old Joe Bailey (of Weatherford). Outside of Queen, Dan's only claim to fame was as the sire of one A-rated race horse, one arena ROM qualifier, and one additional producer. Queen's dam, who died shortly after foaling her, was a Nail Quarter mare of unknown breeding.

J.O. Hankins purchased Queen as a 3-year-old in 1938 from a man by the last name of Hay, who lived near Abilene, Texas. At the time, Hankins remembers her as "about as pretty a filly as I had ever seen."

Bred to King for the first time in 1939, Queen foaled Duchess H in 1940. Typified by her breeder as "the ugliest thing I have ever seen," Duchess H grew up and filled out so well that she was judged the grand champion mare as a yearling at the Stamford, Tex., horse

show. Retired to the broodmare band, she became an excellent producer.

Squaw H came next. She was named after Squaw, Coke Roberds' renowned, but unregistered, racing daughter of Peter McCue. A typey 1941 sorrel, Squaw H was picture-perfect from birth and measured up to her famous namesake in every way.

Like her older sister Duchess H, Squaw H was a grand champion halter mare. Unlike Duchess, she was also a race horse. In fact, over her six-year straightaway career—from 1944 through 1949—Squaw met and defeated such horses as Queenie, Piggin String (TB), Miss Panama, Miss South St. Marys, Leota W, and Wagon N. Retired to the broodmare band, she became a AAA producer.

Hank H was the next of the full siblings to be foaled, and the first colt. He was followed by Booger H, who went on to become a champion halter horse, ROM race horse, and top sire.

Your Highness, the last of the full siblings, was also an ROM runner and a AAA producer.

COURTESY THE QUARTER HORSE JOURNAL

Here's a rarely seen shot of King P-234, the sire of Hank H, in his prime. That's owner Jess Hankins of Rocksprings, Tex., holding the reins.

In 1944 at Fort Worth Hank H stood second in a 2-year-old stallion class remembered as one of the biggest and best ever held.

So Hank H, from the standpoint of his sire, dam, and performance-proven kinfolk, was bred to excel in the show ring, on the track, and in the breeding shed. He did not disappoint.

Shown by J.O. Hankins as a yearling, Hank took first place at San Angelo. At Fort Worth the following January he stood second in a 2-year-old stallion class remembered as one of the biggest and best ever held.

In early 1945 Hankins sold Hank H to Jack and Paul Smith, a pair of young ranchers and wheat farmers from Indiahoma, Oklahoma. The brothers wasted little time in preparing Hank for a racing career.

The 3-year-old stallion's initial training was handled by the boys' father, Tom G. Smith, and by George Ogle, who years earlier had been Joe Hancock's jockey in some of that legendary stallion's greatest races.

Hank began his straightaway career on July 4, 1945. On that day, he won a 440-yard event at Woodward, Okla., besting a local favorite named Red Elk in the process. Two weeks later, he took the measure of the top mare Black Bottom at Lawton with the same results.

In the fall of 1946, he competed at one of the absolute meccas of early Quarter Horse racing, Rillito Park in Tucson.

On November 17, 1946, Hank won a 330-yard sweepstakes at Rillito. That same year he won a 330-yard match race against a horse named Buster and finished second in a 300-yard feature to Miss Bank when she set a world's record of :17.4 at the distance. Finishing third and fourth behind Hank in the latter contest were the top mares Lady Lee and Prissy.

In yet another 330-yard speed stake at Rillito, Hank was beaten by a nose by Prissy and Senor Bill, who were given the identical time of :17.4 for the sprint — equalling Miss Bank's record mark. Hank's official time in the same race was given as :17.5 and that was enough for the American Quarter Racing Association to award him a AA track rating.

Raced lightly over the course of three seasons — from 1945 through 1947 — Hank's official AQHA record shows that he started six times with two wins, one second, and three thirds. It further lists his official speed index as 85.

Queen H, the dam of Hank H, was an early halter champion and one of the breed's premier producers.

Squaw H, Hank H's famous older sister, was a top speedster of her era.

As a mature stallion, Hank stood 14.3 hands and weighed 1,200 pounds in halter shape. In 1947, while in race condition, he placed third in the aged stallion class at the Tucson show. The winner of the class and subsequent grand champion stallion was the well-known California champion Geronimo. Standing behind Hank in the class were the top Arizona show and race horse Little Joe Jr. and the good California show and working horse Tip Top.

At the conclusion of the 1947 Rillito race meet, Hank H was retired from racing and returned to south-central Oklahoma to begin a full-time career as a breeding horse.

Superstar Offspring

The Smith-owned sorrel had actually been test-bred to a few mares as a 2-year-old. From his first small foal crop, which hit the ground in 1945, would come one of his biggest stars—Gold King Bailey.

A palomino stallion out of Beauty Bailey, by Old Joe Bailey, Gold King Bailey was sold as a young horse to Guy Ray Rutland of Pawhuska, Oklahoma. Campaigned on

Hank H's well-balanced conformation is apparent in this interesting reprint of a full-page ad that appeared in the 1947 edition of *The Quarter Running Horse*. That was the official yearbook and ROM listing of the old American Quarter Racing Association.

Retired to stud, Gold King Bailey became a leading performance sire.

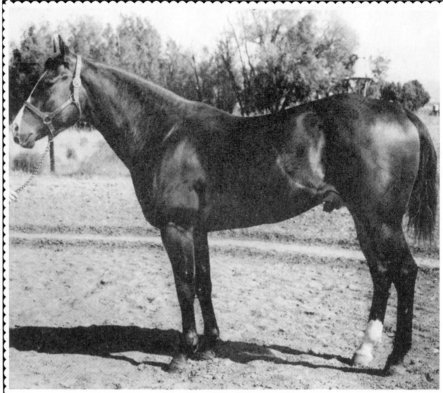

HANK H

AQHA #2154

Sire: King AQHA #234   Dam: Queen H AQHA #1372

Full Brother to **SQUAW H**

HANK H is now standing **AT STUD** four miles south and three-fourths of a mile west of Indiahoma, Oklahoma.

FEE—$50 at time of Service, with two returns.

No boarding privileges

Jack & Paul Smith

INDIAHOMA   **OKLA.**

HANK H Beating **Buster** in a Match Race—300-120-:16.5f.

the track by Rutland, who later moved to Independence, Kan., Gold King Bailey had three official starts that resulted in two wins and a AA race rating.

Retired to stud, the golden palomino became a leading performance sire with nine AQHA Champions and fourteen ROM performance horses to his credit. The latter included Pat Dawson, the 1961 and 1962 AQHA Honor Roll Barrel Racing Champion. As a race sire, Gold King Bailey had 32 ROM qualifiers.

To put the frosting on the cake, Gold King Bailey's daughters produced well enough to make him an all-time leading maternal grandsire of racing ROM qualifiers. His daughters also produced 37 show ROMs and 9 AQHA Champions.

PHOTO BY J. LEINENKUGEL, COURTESY THE QUARTER HORSE JOURNAL

In this December 1946 win photo of Hank H, taken at the Rillito track near Tucson, owner Jack Smith is at Hank's head and trainer Lyo Lee is to the far left. The boy and jockey are unidentified.

COURTESY THE QUARTER HORSE JOURNAL

Booger H, a full brother to Hank H and Squaw H, serves as living proof that the King-Queen H cross was golden. Sold to the West Coast, the big-hipped sorrel stallion went on to become a multiple AQHA Champion and AAA sire.

Pacific Bailey—by Gold Pacific, by Gold King Bailey, and out of Nell Bert McCue, by Wyatt McCue—was an outstanding great grandson of Hank H. He was AAAT on the track, an AQHA Champion, and became a great sire of racing and performance horses. He was owned by Guy Ray Rutland of Independence, Kansas.

Gold King Bailey was perhaps the best son of Hank H. He was rated AA on the track, sired nine AQHA Champions, and was a leading maternal grandsire of racing ROM qualifiers.

Hank H's next three superstars came from his 1951 foal crop. They were Harlan, Hanky Doodle, and Little Bay Lady.

• Harlan (*Legends 4*), a buckskin stallion out of Dixie Beach, by Beetch'syellowjacket, was the undisputed head of the class. Bred by the Smith Brothers, Harlan was like his sire inasmuch as he was royally bred on both sides of his pedigree. By the time Dixie Beach foaled him—her 13th and final foal—she was renowned for her ability as a producer.

Among her other foals were Little Jodie, a leading maternal grandsire of AQHA Champions; Little Dixie Beach, the dam of leading sire Paul A.; and Bailarina, the dam of Short Spark, an AQHA Champion and the 1960 AQHA Honor Roll Reining Horse.

In addition, two more Dixie Beach daughters—San Siemon's Dixie and Bay Pee Wee—were AQHA Champion-producers as well.

Harlan lived up to his genetic birthright by becoming the sire of 17 AQHA Champions, 5 Superior halter horses, 8 Superior performance horses, and the earners of 51 ROMs and 2,996 AQHA points.

Through such prominent male descendants as Firewater Flit in Oklahoma and Two Eyed Red Buck in Nebraska, the Harlan line remains prominent today in Quarter Horse performance circles.

• Hanky Doodle, a sorrel gelding out of Osage Jessie, by Osage Star, earned 12 halter points and 23.5 performance points to become his sire's sole AQHA Champion.

• Little Bay Lady, a bay mare out of Tom's Lady Gray, by Joe Reed II, achieved a speed index of 85 and her ROM rating on the track. From an amazing 98 lifetime starts, she managed 11 firsts, 16 seconds, 14 thirds, and earned $7,968 to become her sire's leading money-earner.

Hank's fifth and final superstar came from his ninth and final foal crop. This was Hank's Suc, a 1953 sorrel mare out of Patsy

WESTERN HORSEMAN PHOTO

Hank's Sue, a 1953 sorrel mare by Hank H and out of Patsy Sue, by Little Horace, was the 1957 AQHA High-Point Halter Horse. She's shown here with Matlock Rose after earning grand champion mare honors at the 1957 National Western Stock Show in Denver.

PHOTO BY RALPH MORGAN, COURTESY THE QUARTER HORSE JOURNAL

Regal Bar, a 1961 sorrel stallion by Barjo and out of Miss Hank, by Hank H, was a AAA AQHA Champion.

PHOTO BY ALFRED JANSSEN III, COURTESY *THE QUARTER HORSE JOURNAL*

PHOTO BY HINES PHOTO SERVICE, COURTESY *THE QUARTER HORSE JOURNAL*

Hank Bar also served as a classic example of the superior individuals who resulted when the sons of Three Bars (TB) were crossed on the daughters of Hank H. A 1961 sorrel stallion by Sugar Bars and out of Peggy Young, by Hank H, Hank Bar earned 19 halter and 3 performance points. Bred by pioneer South Dakota breeders, the De Jong Brothers of Kennebec, he was also an influential Northern Plains sire for years.

Here's an example of the Three Bars-Hank H cross. Duck Call, a 1964 sorrel stallion by Tonto Bars Gill and out of Sally Hank, by Hank H, was a Superior halter horse and also earned an ROM on the track.

COURTESY *THE QUARTER HORSE JOURNAL*

Hank H Bars, a 1960 sorrel stallion, was sired by Mr Bar None, and was out of Hanka Woka, by Hank H. Rated AAA on the track, he became a top speed sire.

Good Again, a 1970 sorrel stallion by Good and out of Hank's Nancy, by Hank H, was an AQHA Champion and a top sire.

Sue, by Little Horace. Bred by Campbell and Loftis of Frederick, Okla., Sue was sold to B.F. Phillips of Dallas.

Under his ownership, the strip-faced mare was the 1957 AQHA Honor Roll Halter Horse. Beginning the year with a grand championship at the National Western Stock Show in Denver, Hank's Sue was named grand champion five more times, reserve champion nine times, and never placed lower than second in the twenty-four shows from which she received points.

Shortly after the 1957 show season, she was sold to A.O. Howell, also of Dallas.

More Offspring

Hank H sired a number of race and show performers in addition to the five horses already mentioned.

On the track, Hank H Jr., Lady Hank, Hank's Snooper, Hanka, Beauty Bailey II, Whitcomb's Lady Hank, Hankryetta, Snow Baby, Billy Gray, Pale Brown, Sally Hank, and White Rose were all ROM qualifiers.

In the show ring, Stewart's Hank, Anthony's Miss H, Hank A Mae, Sledge's Hank, Little Apache Joe, Plow Lad, and Billy Gray earned performance ROMs.

In retrospect, Hank H's record as a sire was modest at best. But then, he really didn't have much time to make it anything more. In the fall of 1952, after servicing a full complement of mares the prior spring and summer, Hank died at age 10—a victim of dust pneumonia brought about by the drought conditions that held much of the Southern Plains in its grip at the time.

Hank H sired 137 registered foals from 9 foal crops. Of these, 28 were race starters. They earned 14 ROMs and $20,948.

In the show arena, 18 of Hank's get were entered in halter competition, earning a Superior and 132 points. Another 17 were shown in performance events, earning 1 AQHA Championship, 8 ROMs, and 77 points.

In NCHA competition, the get of Hank H earned $837.

Grandget

What Hank H didn't finish as a sire, however, his sons and daughters finished

Hank H died from dust pneumonia at age 10.

As his name implies, Double Hank was a double-bred grandson of Hank H. A 1958 sorrel stallion by Hank's Baldy and out of Sherry Ann, Double Hank was an AQHA Champion.

for him. Through them, the bloodline continued to flourish and exert a positive influence on the breed.

The sons of Hank H did their part, even though not many of them were used for breeding. Of Hank's 137 foals, only 30 of the colts were left as stallions. Had there only been two—Gold King Bailey and Harlan— it would have ensured the continuity of the line. But there were others as well.

Hank Parrish, Bottom River, and Midnight Hank sired AAA race horses, and Prince Hank and Pepper Royal sired race ROM qualifiers.

Whale Bone, Hank, Capital, Hank's Baldy, Wolf Hank, Jay Hank, and Last Hank sired AQHA Champions, and Mike

Beetch, Billy In Lowground, Colonel Pat, Plow Lady, Prince Hank, Toughie Hank, Kercino Silk, and Pepper Royal sired ROM performance qualifiers.

The daughters of Hank H did even better.

As race producers, they sent 133 starters to the gates. Of these, 48 were ROM qualifiers and they earned $259,514.

- Hanka, a 1948 chestnut mare by Hank H and out of Hi Baby, by King, was an ROM runner herself and a third-place finisher in the 1950 Oklahoma Futurity. Bred to Tonto Bars Gill in 1957, she produced Tonto Bars Hank, the legendary "Flying Boxcar" (*Legends 4*). A winner of 10 stakes and $133,919, Tonto Bars Hank was a three-time AQHA Champion Quarter Running Horse.

- Ginger Marie, a 1948 bay mare by Hank H and out of Randy B, by Joe Reed P-3, was unraced. Retired to the broodmare band, she produced Clabber's Barbie and Le Etta Chicks. Clabbers Barbie, a 1962 sorrel mare by Clabber Bar, achieved a speed index of 95 and won the 1965 Springfield Classic Derby. Le Etta Chicks, a 1966 bay mare by Three Chicks, had a speed index of 107 and was an 11-time stakes winner. An iron horse on the tracks, she started 52 times, winning 25, placing second 13 times, and third 5 times.

- Miss Sooner Hank, a 1951 bay mare by Hank H and out of Delene T, produced Miss Sooner Bars, SI 95; Sooner Bars Hank, SI 95; and Hanka Dial, SI 95.

- Rafter N Hanka, a 1951 sorrel mare by Hank H and out of a Waggoner mare, produced Sugar Bar's Hank, SI 95, and Miss Rafter None, SI 95.

- Hi Honey, a 1953 sorrel mare by Hank H and out of Hi Baby, produced Scooper Hank, SI 100, and Hank's Bid, SI 90.

- The Hank H daughters Hank's Van, Hanka Woka, Speed Belle, and Whitcomb's Lady Hank all produced runners with speed indexes of 90 or higher.

As good as they were at passing on their inherited speed, the Hank H mares were probably even better at passing on their good looks and athletic ability.

PHOTO BY JERRY MATACALE, COURTESY *THE QUARTER HORSE JOURNAL*

Silky Socks, a 1964 sorrel gelding by Coker's Trouble and out of Doty's Socks, by Hank H, was an outstanding flat-saddle competitor in his day. Shown here with youth rider Jan Thompson, Silky was the 1974 AQHA World Champion Hunter Under Saddle and a four-time AQHA high-point working hunter.

From 148 show performers, the daughters of Hank H produced 16 AQHA Champions, 6 Superior halter horses, 11 Superior performance horses, 42 ROM qualifiers, and the earners of 3,549 AQHA points.

White Rose, Flying May, and Hank's Bunch were the best of the show producers.

- White Rose, a 1952 sorrel mare by Hank H and out of White Angel, by Chief P-5, produced four top performers by Two Eyed Jack. Two Eyed Rosie, a 1969 sorrel mare, was an AQHA Champion and a Superior reining horse. Rosie Jack, a 1971 sorrel mare, was an AQHA Champion and a Superior western pleasure horse. Miss Rosy Jack, a 1972 sorrel mare, was the 1977 AQHA World Champion Senior Heading Horse and a Superior steer roping horse. Jack Henry, a 1973 sorrel stallion, was an AQHA Champion and a Superior western pleasure horse.
- Flying May, a 1951 sorrel mare by Hank H and out of Winnie Mae, by Fool's Gold, produced nine point-earners.
- Hank's Nancy, a 1952 sorrel mare by

Hank H and out of Lavera, by Hank H, produced two AQHA Champions — Hank's Kickapoo and Good Again.
- Coker's Troubles, a 1950 brown mare by Hank H and out of Troubles By blackjack, by Black Jack, was the dam of Silky Socks, an AQHA world champion hunter under saddle and four-time AQHA high-point working hunter under saddle.
- The Hank H daughters Beauty Bailey II, Miss Hank, Sally Hank, Sandy Punkin, and Sherry Anne produced either AQHA Champions or offspring who earned Superior titles.

One can only imagine what Hank H could have accomplished if he had lived a full, productive life. But, abbreviated or not, his efforts as a race horse, show horse, and sire were more than enough to secure a prominent place for him in the annals of Quarter Horse history.

He was born to be good, and he lived up to his calling.

CHUBBY

By Frank Holmes

Chubby's influence on the breed was positive and far-reaching.

ALTHOUGH HE came from a top line of ranch and race horses, and was a top-notch performer in his own right, Chubby never enjoyed widespread acceptance at the stud. As a result, few top mares found their way to his court.

Despite this, his impact on the breed was positive and far-reaching and serves as proof that, one way or another, genetic prepotency will have its way.

Chubby was foaled in 1924 on the famed Waggoner Ranch of Vernon, Texas. Midnight, his sire (*Legends 2*), was by Badger,

by Peter McCue, and out of Nellie Trammell, by Pid Hart. In addition to Chubby, Midnight also sired such notable stallions as Waggoner (usually referred to as One Eyed Waggoner) and Midnight Jr.

Fourth Of July 1, Chubby's dam, was by Bobby Lowe, by Eureka, and out of Old Mary, by Old Joe Bailey, according to AQHA records. However, some historians say Old Mary was by Ben Burton. In addition to Chubby, Fourth Of July 1 also produced the top sire, F&H Bill Thomas, by Buck Thomas. Old Mary, in addition to pro-

Foaled a decade and a half before the formation of the AQHA, Chubby founded a family of west Texas Quarter Horses known for their conformation and working ability.

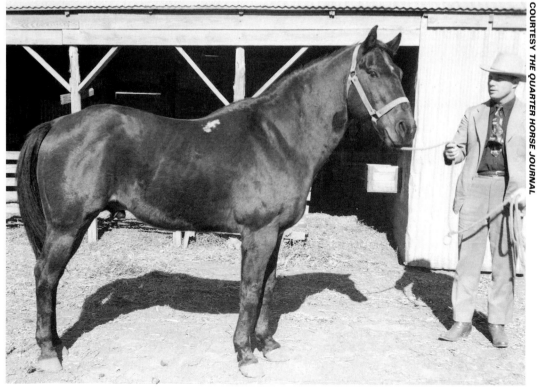

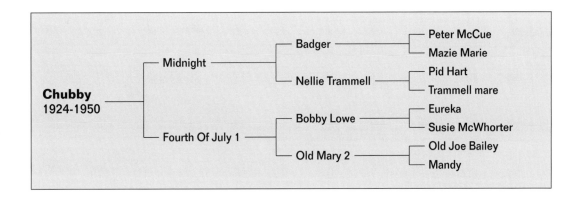

Chubby
1924-1950

Midnight
— Badger
  — Peter McCue
  — Mazie Marie
— Nellie Trammell
  — Pid Hart
  — Trammell mare

Fourth Of July 1
— Bobby Lowe
  — Eureka
  — Susie McWhorter
— Old Mary 2
  — Old Joe Bailey
  — Mandy

ducing Fourth Of July 1, was also the dam of the foundation Waggoner sires Yellow Wolf and Yellow Bear.

So, all things considered, Chubby was fashionably bred, with a pedigree chock-full of top turn-of-the-century Quarter Horses. The common denominator was speed.

Midnight, Chubby's sire, was a top sprinter in his heyday. Bred by Jess Cooper of Roosevelt, Okla., and foaled in 1916, he won several match races as a 2-, 3-, and 4-year-old against tough competition.

Among the horses he defeated were Roger Mills, the fleet daughter of Peter McCue and Nellie Trammell; A.D. Reed, the son of Peter McCue and Good Enough; and Article, a race horse imported from Cuba.

After he was purchased by the Waggoner Ranch in 1923, Midnight's racing career continued. Raced regularly for a number of years, he once set a mark of 33 seconds for three-eighths of a mile at Abilene.

Since Midnight, Badger, Nellie Trammell, and Peter McCue were all top sprinters in their prime, the top side of Chubby's pedigree was laced with speed. The same held true for the bottom.

Fourth Of July 1, his dam, was reported to be one of Waggoner's fastest race mares. Old Mary, the dam of Fourth Of July 1, had achieved such recognition as a runner that W.T. Waggoner paid the unheard of sum of $500 each for her and her weanling colt, Yellow Wolf, in 1915. (Robert M. Denhardt, in his book, *Foundation Sires of the American Quarter Horse*, lists the foaling dates for Yellow Wolf and his full brother, Yellow Bear, as 1912 and 1913. But a photo of Old Mary in racing shape, circa

1912 or 1913, makes Denhardt's foaling dates unlikely.)

So, however you care to dissect his pedigree, Chubby was bred to be fleet of foot. All he needed was the chance to prove it.

Early accounts of Chubby's life are sketchy at best. At maturity, he has been described as a blood bay, standing 14.2 and weighing 1,100. He was branded 5 inside a D on his left forearm and 4 on his left hindquarter.

It is also known that the Waggoners sold him as a young horse, probably in the late 1920s, to a man named Scott, who lived in the "Panhandle country." Scott then sold him to Bill Bryan of Plainview, Texas.

It was in 1932, while owned by Bryan, that Chubby received what would be his first two documented tests as a runner. The events took place while Bryan was riding the stallion on a horse drive from Plainview to Dimmitt—a distance of 40 miles. On the return trip Chubby was matched against a local country boy's horse. The winner's purse was $35 and Chubby claimed it.

Here's a photo of Chubby taken when he was registered with the AQHA. Although past his prime, the 16-year-old stallion still had the strong hindquarters and strong, low hocks that stood him in such good stead as a race horse.

The purse was a sack of oats, and Chubby again emerged victorious.

Later that same day, he was matched again. This time the competition was a race mare being trained by R.E. "Shorty" Warren of Plainview. The purse was a sack of oats, and Chubby again emerged victorious.

Warren was known as one of the top race trainers in the Texas Panhandle, and it wasn't long after the horse drive that Chubby wound up in his hands to be seriously conditioned for the track.

Over the course of the next several years, Warren matched Chubby 21 times. The bay stallion won 20 of the contests, with his sole defeat coming in his last race. Matched for 220 yards against a mare from Oklahoma and, by Warren's own account, out of shape and with a strange jockey aboard, Chubby was narrowly defeated.

During his short but highly succcssful racing career, Chubby met and defeated such horses as Barney Owens, Joker Joe, and Driftwood—at such locations as Olton, Odessa, Fort Stockton, Lubbock, Abilene, and San Angelo.

On one day in Abilene, Chubby was entered in and won two 440-yard races. Entered in a third race—a 330-yard event—he broke to an 8-length lead, and held on to win by a narrow margin.

Throughout his career, he was known as a savvy "lap-and-tap" starter whose powerful getaway was considered the secret to his long string of victories.

By 1933 Chubby's race career was over, and he was sold to J.C. Hooper and sons of Plainview. In 1940 Hooper registered the then-16-year-old stallion with the newly formed AQHA, and he was assigned number 656.

Midnight, Chubby's sire, is shown here on the famed JA Ranch near Palo Duro, Tex., in the late 1920s. A top race horse in his prime, the big gray stallion passed his speed on to his get and grandget.

Maudie Williams, a 1946 brown mare by Billy Anson and out of Miss Chubby, by Chubby, was a Register of Merit runner who once held the 220-yard track record at Pawhuska, Oklahoma.

Joe Fax, a 1963 dun stallion by Fairfax Joe and out of Maudie Williams, was a double-bred Chubby. He was an AQHA Supreme Champion.

"JOE FAX"

LA MESA PARK, N.M.   AUG. 6, 1965   W. LOVELL, UP
SWEET'N LOVELY (2nd)   400 Yds 20:58   BOLD BAR LADY (3)
LESTER E. WILLIAMS, OWNER   JOSEPH E. NEFF, TR.

Unfortunately for Chubby, the Hooper family was more oriented to raising and using good ranch horses than to showing, rodeoing, or racing. As a result, for much of the rest of his life, Chubby headed a band of largely nondescript ranch and draft mares.

This doesn't imply that Hooper didn't value Chubby and his offspring. By all accounts he did. He was just not interested in breeding for competition. As a result, Chubby was not heavily promoted, and went unnoticed for years by much of the Quarter Horse world.

COURTESY THE QUARTER HORSE JOURNAL

Leo Maudie, a 1961 bay stallion by Leo and out of Maudie Williams, a Chubby granddaughter, was an AQHA Supreme Champion.

COURTESY THE QUARTER HORSE JOURNAL

Lady Fairfax, a 1949 sorrel mare by Leo and out of Miss Chubby, earned an ROM race rating and placed second in the 1951 Oklahoma Futurity. She is shown here with owner Lester Williams of Fairfax, Okla., after being named grand champion mare at the 1954 Osage County Fair.

Fairbars, a 1961 sorrel stallion by Three Bars (TB) and out of Lady Fairfax, earned his AQHA Supreme Championship in 1968. The epitome of the highly successful Three Bars-Leo cross, Fairbars went on to sire several high-point and Superior halter and performance horses.

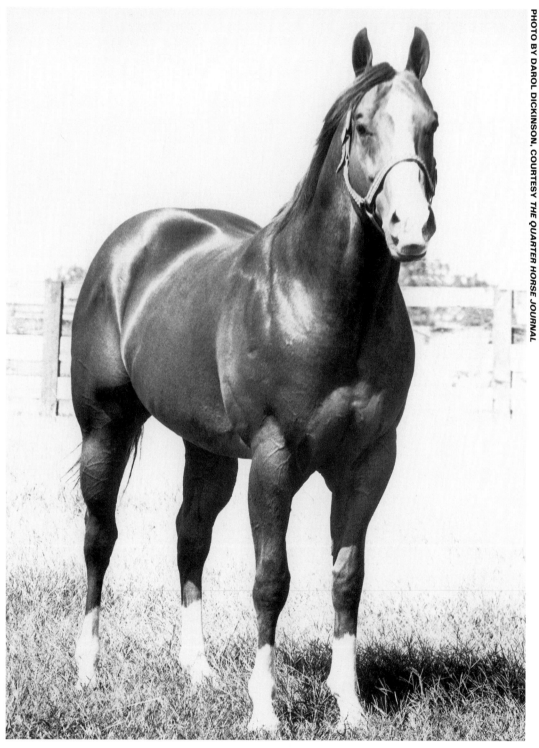

PHOTO BY DAROL DICKINSON, COURTESY *THE QUARTER HORSE JOURNAL*

Shorty Wheeler was one of the first to bring a top mare to Chubby's court.

A Few Good Mares

Luckily for the stallion, however, there were a number of local horsemen who did enjoy competing, and they were quick to use the blood of Hooper's bay stallion. Shorty Wheeler was one of the first to bring a top mare to Chubby's court. Her name was Ruth, and she was a product of the famed J. Frank Norfleet horse program of Hale Center, Texas.

The first result of the Chubby-Ruth cross was a mare named Little Ruth. Although the year she was foaled is unclear,

PHOTO BY SHIRER, MANN & LYNN, COURTESY *THE QUARTER HORSE JOURNAL*

After being purchased by Ed Honnen, who owned Quincy Farms in Denver, Lady Fairfax became every bit as prolific a producer as Maudie Williams. Shown here is Quincy Lady, a 1958 dun mare by Joak and out of Lady Fairfax, who was an AQHA Champion and Superior halter horse. Quincy Farms manager Leonard Milligan showed Lady Fairfax to grand champion mare honors at the 1961 National Western Livestock Show in Denver.

it is known that she won 19 successive starts as a 2-year-old before succumbing to blood poisoning.

In 1935 Manitobian, a full brother to Little Ruth, was foaled. Eventually sold to Eldon Fancher of Paicines, Calif., this breedy-looking sorrel stallion became a top rope horse and runner who could go up to five-eighths of a mile.

Before he left west Texas, Manitobian sired Bartender—the horse who would be most responsible for seeing that Chubby's blood was perpetuated. (See the following chapter for more on Bartender.)

After Shorty Warren, the next local breeder to jump on the Chubby bandwagon was S.B. Barnes of Tulia, Texas. The breeder of Bartender, Barnes assured himself a permanent spot in the annals of Quarter Horse history when, in 1936, he bred Bartender's mother, The Old Vaughn Mare, to Chubby.

Miss Chubby, the resulting foal, was sold to Lester "Pete" Williams of Fairfax, Okla., under whose ownership she went on to become one of the breed's premier matrons. Two of her most accomplished foals were the Register of Merit runners Maudie Williams and Lady Fairfax.

PHOTO BY ALEXANDER, COURTESY *THE QUARTER HORSE JOURNAL*

This is Poco Sail, a 1957 bay mare by Poco Bueno and out of Rio Rita, by Chubby. She is shown here with G. W. Hastings after being named grand champion mare at an early 1960s Frederick, Okla., show.

Maudie Williams was a 1946 brown mare sired by Billy Anson, who produced seven ROM race horses and two AQHA Supreme Champions: Leo Maudie and Joe Fax.

Lady Fairfax, a 1949 sorrel mare by Leo, produced Fairfax Joe AAA; Quincy Lady, an AQHA Champion and Superior halter horse; and Fairbars, also an AQHA Supreme Champion. As if that weren't enough, Fairfax Joe went on to sire two AQHA Supreme Champions—Joe Fax and Goodbye Sam.

A Supreme Champion family to be sure; and two out of four horses were double-bred descendants of Chubby.

Curly Daugherty

After Wheeler and Barnes, Frank "Curly" Daugherty of Olney, Tex., began making judicious use of the Chubby blood. Beginning in the 1930s, Daugherty was one of the most respected horsemen in west Texas. Like Wheeler, his broodmare band was steeped in the blood of the J. Frank and Bob Norfleet horses and included daughters of such famous Norfleet horses as Jim Trammell, by Barney Owens; Red Bird, by Jim Trammell; Spark Plug, by Jack McCue; and Panzarita, by Spark Plug.

At one time, Daugherty even owned the

COURTESY J. FRANK DAUGHERTY

Here's Rio Rita, a 1948 sorrel mare by Chubby and out of Panzarita Daugherty, who was another top-producing Chubby daughter. Shown here with breeder Curly Daugherty of Olney, Tex., Rio Rita was sold as a 4-year-old to E. Paul Waggoner of Vernon, Texas. She produced three Superior halter horses for Waggoner.

PHOTO BY HARVEY CAPLIN, COURTESY THE QUARTER HORSE JOURNAL

Poco Dana, a 1956 sorrel mare by Poco Dell and out of Dutchie Chub, earned her AQHA Championship in 1960. With 93 open halter points to her credit, she was also a Superior halter horse.

PHOTO BY SQUIRE HASKINS, COURTESY THE QUARTER HORSE JOURNAL

Chucker Vee was a 1953 bay stallion by Chuck Wagon W., by Chubby, and out of Miss Wardlaw 50. Chucker Vee was an AQHA Champion and a Superior halter horse. Emmett Dalton of Dallas holds the stallion after he had been named the reserve champion stallion of the 1958 State Fair of Texas.

legendary Panzarita, whom early day AQHA inspector Jim Minnick once described as the most perfect mare he had ever laid eyes on.

Such cornerstone matrons as Patsy Daugherty, Panzarita Daugherty, Peaches Daugherty, and Mayflower Daugherty came from the Curly Daugherty program, and it was mares of this quality that the intuitive horse breeder took to the court of Chubby.

Jim Dandy, a 1939 bay stallion out of Panzarita, was the first of the Daugherty-bred Chubbys to make a name for himself. Sold to Elmer Hepler of Carlsbad, N.M., in utero, Jim Dandy was shown by Hepler at the 1940 Southwestern Livestock Exposition in Fort Worth. After topping the class of 22 2-year-old stallions, he sold to August Busch of St. Louis for $3,000.

Patsy Daugherty, a famed performer, was the next Daugherty mare bred to Chubby. A 1932 sorrel mare by Spark Plug

and out of Puss, by Red Bird, Patsy was one of the great reining and roping mares of her day. In 1948, at the age of 16, she was the all-around champion at the Stamford Cowboy Reunion Horse Show and was awarded the first trophy saddle ever presented by the AQHA.

Patsy had three foals by Chubby:

• Diamond Ring, a 1941 sorrel mare was the first. Sold to the Diamond 2 Cattle Company of Kirkland, Ariz., she became the cornerstone mare of their race breeding program. Bred to Little Joe Jr., the Diamond 2's top show and race stallion, Diamond Ring produced the ROM runners Diamond Tongs, Diamond Too, Diamond Tiara, Diamond Match, and Diamond Pin.

Diamond Tiara and Diamond Match, in turn, became top producers with such AAA speedsters as Boy's Ranch, Come Across, Diamond 2 Bar, Burning Match,

PHOTO BY C. H. & EVA POTTS, COURTESY THE QUARTER HORSE JOURNAL

Hijo Blaze, Shes A Jewel, and Well Lit to their credit.

- Billy The Kid Edwards was the second foal from the Chubby-Patsy Daugherty cross. A 1944 bay stallion, Billy sired two daughters who produced AQHA Champions.

- Peaches, the third foal to result from the cross, was a 1946 sorrel mare and the dam of two performers.

Panzarita Daugherty was the final mare that Curly Daugherty took to Chubby. A 1942 bay mare by Little Joe The Wrangler and out of Panzarita, Panzarita Daugherty was a model mare who won a number of grand championships at halter. Bred to Chubby in 1947, she foaled Rio Rita the following spring. Like her dam, Rio Rita had excellent conformation and was shown successfully at halter.

Sold to E. Paul Waggoner in January 1951, Rio Rita produced three Superior halter horses: Rita Buck, a 1952 bay mare by Pretty Buck; Poco Sail, a 1957 bay mare by Poco Bueno; and Poco Rico, a 1959 bay mare by Poco Bueno.

More Outstanding Offspring

If there had been any doubts up to this time in anyone's mind about Chubby's ability as a sire when bred to good mares, the results obtained by such breeders as Wheeler, Barnes, and Daugherty erased those doubts forever. By the mid- to late 1940s, interest in the Hooper stallion had, indeed, picked up. Standing to a full book of outside mares during those years, Chubby responded by siring some of his most notable show offspring.

- Chubby III, a 1940 bay stallion out of

Dutch Boy, a 1946 bay stallion by Chubby and out of Dutch Lady, was a California halter champion. He is shown here with owner Wild Bill Elliott after winning the 2-year-old stallion class at the 1948 Pacific Coast Quarter Horse Association's annual show.

Jole Blon S, a 1947 dun mare out of Dundee S, was Chubby's sole Superior halter award-winning daughter. Exhibited at 52 shows, she won 44 firsts and 25 grand championships. Doyle Saul, the mare's breeder, showed Jole to many of her early wins and is pictured with her after she went grand champion at the 1949 Paducah, Tex., show.

FH Chili Bean, was the grand champion stallion and winner of the get-of-sire class at the 1945 Amarillo Quarter Horse show.

- Chubby W, a 1942 chestnut stallion out of Miss Wade, was a champion as well.
- Dutchie Chub, a 1944 sorrel mare out of Dutch Lady, was the grand champion mare at the 1947 New Mexico State Fair in Albuquerque.
- Dutch Boy, a 1946 bay full brother to Dutchie, was sold to western movie star

Wild Bill Elliott and won the 2-year-old stallion class at the 1948 Pacific Coast Quarter Horse Association show.

- Chuck Wagon W, a 1946 bay stallion out of Miss Nubbin, became a Superior halter horse and a good sire.
- Jole Blon S, a 1947 dun mare out of Dundee S, also won a Superior at halter and became a good producer.
- Betty Lou Q, a 1947 sorrel mare out of Pocahontas II, was Chubby's top runner. AAA-rated, she earned a Superior in

The influence of Chubby continued long after his death and was instrumental in the development of some of the industry's top show and breeding programs. Here's a photo of a paternal great-granddaughter, Chubby Rachelle, when owned by Howard Pitzer, Ericson, Neb., after she won a Burwell, Neb., show. A 1957 sorrel mare by Chubby W. II and out of Rachel Girl, Chubby Rachelle was one of Pitzer's first three show horses and the forerunner of a program that would one day lead the nation.

racing and went on to become a AAA producer.

- Alchereta, a 1948 bay mare out of Cupie Doll, earned an ROM in racing.
- Jess Shurbet, a 1950 bay stallion out of Fleeta S, also earned an ROM in racing.

AQHA records reveal that Chubby sired 237 foals, of which 29 were performers. In racing, nine of his get earned three ROMs and one Superior.

In halter, 11 performers earned 2 Superiors and 165 total points.

In performance, three horses tallied two ROMs and five points.

Living as he did before the AQHA point system really took hold, Chubby did not rack up very impressive numbers as a sire, but fared somewhat better as a broodmare sire.

Forty-nine of Chubby's maternal grand-get went to the track. They earned 13 ROMs, 1 Superior in racing, and $59,146.

As show horses, 71 second-generation Chubbys earned 8 AQHA Championships, 13 Superior halter and performance awards, 34 ROMs, and 2,095 points. And they also accounted for $12,747 in NCHA earnings.

Chubby passed away on the J. C. Hooper Ranch estate in June 1950, at the age of 26. His influence on the breed continued for years to come.

12 BARTENDER

By Frank Holmes

He gained fame as a working ranch horse and sire.

DURING THE formative years of the AQHA—from the early 1940s through the mid-1950s—few horses did more to enhance the Chubby line than Bartender. And he did so not as a show horse, but as a working ranch horse and sire.

Bartender was a 1940 sorrel stallion sired by Manitobian and out of the Old Vaughn Mare. Manitobian was a 1935 sorrel stallion by Chubby and out of Ruth, by Brettenham (TB). With a Waggoner Ranch-bred stallion for a sire and a Frank Norfleet-bred mare for a dam, Manitobian was as well-bred as any west Texas horse could be.

The Old Vaughn Mare was a different story. A 1918 brown mare, she was bred by Tom Ivey of Hereford, Tex., and is listed as being by a John Ellard Quarter Horse and out of a Tom Ivey Quarter mare, by Ivey Roan. Whatever else was behind her pedigree is officially unknown.

But there must have been something

Bartender, as shown here in an early 1950s photograph, was a well-balanced working horse who developed into a top sire.

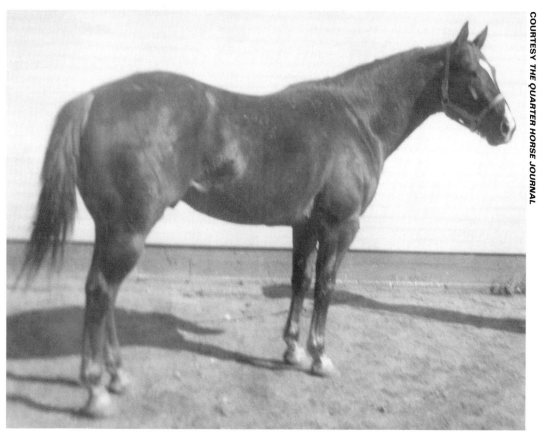

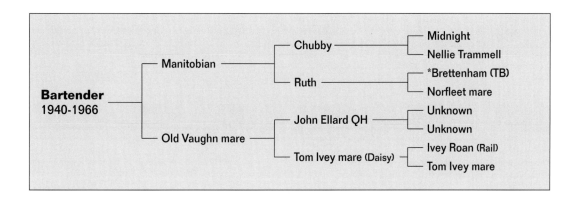

```
                                      ┌─ Chubby ──────────┬─ Midnight
                    ┌─ Manitobian ────┤                   └─ Nellie Trammell
                    │                 │
                    │                 └─ Ruth ────────────┬─ *Brettenham (TB)
Bartender ──────────┤                                     └─ Norfleet mare
1940-1966           │
                    │                 ┌─ John Ellard QH ──┬─ Unknown
                    └─ Old Vaughn mare ┤                  └─ Unknown
                                      │
                                      └─ Tom Ivey mare (Daisy) ┬─ Ivey Roan (Rail)
                                                               └─ Tom Ivey mare
```

good back there because, in addition to Bartender, the Old Vaughn Mare was the dam of two other noteworthy horses. Miss Chubby, a 1937 bay mare by Chubby, was one of the breed's great matriarchs and the cornerstone mare of the famed Lester Williams family of AQHA Supreme Champions. Chester B., a 1938 bay stallion by Chubby, was a noted Arizona show horse and sire.

Miss Chubby, Chester B., and Bartender were all bred by S.B. Barnes of Tulia, Tex., and owned in partnership by him and his son-in-law, Roland Moore. Moore, who also hailed from Tulia, was a highly respected AQHA judge and a top hand.

In 1942 Barnes wanted to dissolve the partnership and sell all three horses. Moore apparently had no qualms about getting rid of Miss Chubby and Chester B., but balked at selling Bartender. He had just started riding him and was high on his ability. The older man was adamant that all three should go, so that fall Moore took Bartender to a sale at Lubbock.

Clyde Miller of Fluvanna, Tex., was at the sale and wound up acquiring Bartender. Art Reeves of Mobridge, S.D., was working for Miller at the time and remembers how the transaction took place.

"Clyde and I went to Lubbock specifically to find a young stallion," he recalls. "There was a stallion entered in the sale that Clyde was interested in. As we were headed toward the sale barn, I noticed Roland riding a good-looking colt around. He didn't have him in the sale. He just had him there to see if he could generate any interest in him. I stopped

Clyde and told him, 'There's the horse you're looking for.'

"We went over and took a real close look at him. Roland was riding him with a hackamore, and that colt had an unbelievable handle on him. Clyde liked him and bought him on the spot for $1,000. And that was Bartender."

The Miller Years

The Clyde Miller Ranch was a working cattle outfit located in the harsh west Texas caprock country halfway between Abilene and Lubbock.

The ranch had been founded by Clyde's father, Rich Miller, in 1900. Its horse program was designed solely to produce working ranch horses, and that's the role that Bartender was slated to fill. Riley Miller, Clyde's son, is still on the ranch and recalls that his father's choice of stallions was a good one.

"Prior to getting Bartender," he says, "we

Manitobian, a 1935 son of Chubby, sired Bartender.

Bar Nothing Springer was one of the first sons of Bartender to establish his own reputation as a sire. Under the ownership of pioneer Quarter Horse breeder Arthur Reeves, who is shown with him here, the 1944 sorrel stallion founded an enduring line of South Dakota ranch and show horses.

PHOTO BY RODDEN STUDIO, COURTESY *THE QUARTER HORSE JOURNAL*

Here's another shot of Bartender as an aged horse. That's the brand of his second owner, Clyde Miller, on his left stifle.

were using a horse named Texas Miller as our main herd sire. He was a 1926 dun stallion by Sim's Yellow Boy and out of an OXO mare by Dr. Mack. He was a close-up Yellow Jacket- and Abe Frank (TB)-bred horse, which we liked. Yellow Jacket was the famous Waggoner Ranch sire, and Abe Frank was the sire of the great race horse Pan Zareta (who raced in the early 1900s and is not to be confused with later horses of the same or similar name).

"We had also used several government remount horses, such as Despot (TB), Lawyer (TB), and Ross Green (TB), so our broodmare band was full of the type of rangy, free-moving horses that were necessary to get the job done in our kind of country. Bartender crossed exceptionally well with our mares."

As a mature horse, Bartender stood 15 hands and weighed 1,170 pounds. In addition to his duties as a Miller Ranch sire, he was also expected to carry his share of the load as a working cow

horse. He proved adept at this as well.

"Roland Moore was a top horseman," Riley Miller says, "and he had really started Bartender right. I was 13 years old when Dad bought him, and I got to ride him quite a lot. He was one of the fastest, quickest horses I ever rode.

"It was usually my job to rustle in the remuda horses every morning. I'd use Bartender for that, and it was just like riding one of the geldings. He was all business and would never raise any ruckus. We also used him to rope and doctor cattle out in the open—branding, castrating, and treating for screwworm. He was a natural at it."

When he wasn't working for a living as a cow horse, Bartender was kept busy as a Miller Ranch herd sire. And from his first full foal crop came three of his greatest sons—Bar Nothing Springer, Little Bartender, and Preacher G.

Bar Nothing Springer, a 1944 sorrel stallion out of Deslena, by Despot (TB), was

When he wasn't working for a living as a cow horse, Bartender was kept busy as a Miller Ranch herd sire.

Little Bartender, a 1944 sorrel stallion by Bartender and out of Etta Mae, by Lawyer (TB), was a champion show horse and the sire of AAA race horses and AQHA Champions. Riley Miller is at the stud's halter in this shot taken at a late-1940s Texas Quarter Horse show.

Preacher G., a sorrel stallion out of Josephene, by Ross Green (TB), was the third member of Bartender's 1944 foal crop to gain fame as a sire.

PHOTO BY LESTER WILLIAMS, COURTESY *THE QUARTER HORSE JOURNAL*

sold to Art Reeves as a weanling. When Reeves migrated to South Dakota in 1949, he took Bar Nothing Springer with him and used him to establish the well-known Reeves "Roan Bar" family of horses.

Little Bartender, a 1944 sorrel stallion out of Etta Mae, by Lawyer (TB), was kept by the ranch and went on to sire such top performers as Gil's Bartender, a AAA-rated race horse, and Little Bar Blue, an AQHA Champion.

Preacher G., a 1944 sorrel stallion out of Josephene, by Ross Green (TB), was sold to George Gillham of Jerico, Texas. A moderately successful sire, he did his part to add luster to the Bartender line as the paternal grandsire of the NCHA cutting legend Senor George.

Senor George, a 1954 bay stallion, was sired by Claude, by Preacher G., and was out of Miss Bartender, by Bartender. Owned by Sig Jernigan of Goldthwaite, Tex., and ridden by Sonny Perry, Senor George was the 1961 NCHA World Champion Cutting Horse and amassed $61,253 in NCHA earnings. In AQHA competition, he was the 1961 and 1968 AQHA High-Point Cutting Horse, an AQHA Champion, and a Superior cutting horse.

From Bartender's second Miller-based foal crop came Dee Gee, his greatest daughter.

"Dee Gee was bred by Lewis Nance, a neighbor of ours," Riley Miller says. "He lived seven or eight miles from us, and rode in one day in the spring of 1944 leading a mare named Scarlett. She was by Little Fort, and he wanted to breed her to Bartender.

"Mr. Nance's son, L. E. 'Sonny' Nance, was away fighting in the war, and he wanted to have a foal for him to work with when he got home. Dee Gee was the result of that cross.

"Sonny Nance was a top hand, and when he came back home, he broke Dee Gee to ride and started her right. Then he sold her to Wanda Harper of Mason, Tex., and Wanda made her famous."

Wanda Harper (Bush) and Dee Gee did indeed go on to become one of the AQHA's first top show pairs. With Wanda as both trainer and rider, the 1945 bay mare championed most of the big shows in Texas at halter and in performance throughout the 1950s.

At halter, she was named grand champion mare at the 1952 and 1953 Southwestern Livestock Exposition & Stock Show — the industry's biggest event at the time. The 1955 AQHA High-Point Halter Horse, she is officially credited with a Superior and 64 points in the event.

In performance, the Bartender daughter

Here's a winning get-of-sire entry for Bartender, probably taken at a west Texas show in the early 1950s. From left, the horses are Toddy, Preacher G., and Sand Bowl. The handlers are unidentified.

PHOTO BY DALCO, COURTESY *THE QUARTER HORSE JOURNAL*

Senor George, a 1954 bay stallion by Claude, by Preacher G., was one of the first great representatives of the Bartender line. In this photo, taken in the late 1960s, Mrs. Rusty Belt is up.

So famous was Dee Gee that Harper was reported to have turned down a $25,000 offer for her.

was just as accomplished. Shown in barrel racing, roping, cutting, and reining, she was the 1955 AQHA High-Point Reining Horse and earned her Superior in that event.

Finally, as a broodmare, she was the dam of seven performers including Dee's Image, earner of 43 performance points and a third place at the 1977 AQHA World Show in senior reining; Dee Gee's King and Eternal Dee Gee, performance ROM-earners; Sunshine Echols, racing ROM; and Dee Gee's King, Dee Gee's Royal, and Dee Gee's Chess, NCHA money-earners.

So famous was Dee Gee that Harper was reported to have turned down a $25,000 offer for her.

As it turned out, the Bartender foal crop that produced Dee Gee would be the last one he would sire for Clyde Miller. In the spring of 1945, rather abruptly, he changed hands.

"Clyde and I were working on a windmill," Art Reeves remembers, "when a couple of fellows dressed in bib overalls drove up to visit. Clyde was up on the windmill when they approached us, and one of them hollered up to him, 'We're here to buy Bartender. What would you take for him?' I don't think Clyde ever intended to sell the horse. And those boys weren't exactly prosperous-looking, so he said, 'It would take $3,500 to get him bought.'

"Well, one of those guys darn near popped the buttons on his overalls, reaching for his wallet. He pulled out $3,500 in cash, handed it to Clyde, and went to load up the horse.

"Clyde was a man of his word and, as far as he was concerned, the deal was done. But he told me later that he thought the price would just blow those guys out of the water, and that would be the end of it."

Like his father, Riley Miller could not believe that Bartender was gone.

"When Dad told me he'd sold Bartender," he says, "I was sick. I was only 15 at the

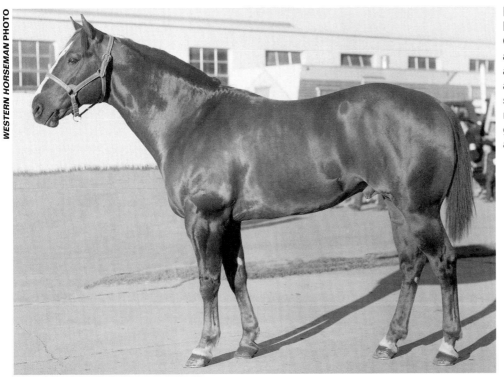

WESTERN HORSEMAN PHOTO

Lucky Bar was one of Bartender's best sons. Out of Ada Adair, he was an AQHA Champion and a Superior halter horse, and became a very good sire. This photo was taken right after he was named grand champion stallion at Fort Worth in 1960.

Here's another picture of Senor George with Sonny Perry in the saddle. Sonny, who stood 6'4", rode the 14.1-hand stallion to the title of 1961 NCHA World Champion Cutting Horse.

WESTERN HORSEMAN PHOTO

time, and that stud was 'it' to me. Once we got him, I thought we were really on our way as horse breeders. I know Dad felt just as poorly about the deal as I did.

"When it came to horse trading, one of his favorite expressions was, 'Once you give your word, you stay hooked, even if it takes your hide off.' It hurt him to sell Bartender, but he stood behind his word."

The McGehee Years

Despite how they were dressed at the time, the two men who had so skillfully relieved Clyde Miller of Bartender were quite prosperous. As two-thirds of "M.L. McGehee and Sons" of Wayside, Tex., they were highly successful wheat farmers and Quarter Horse breeders.

Prior to acquiring Bartender, they had also tracked down and purchased his aged dam. After registering her with the AQHA, they took immaculate care of her—going so far as to cook her feed into a palatable mash—and were able to get two more foals from her.

Billy Barnes, a 1943 sorrel stallion by Sergeant, went on to enjoy moderate suc-

PHOTO BY DICK HARMAN, COURTESY *THE QUARTER HORSE JOURNAL*

King Lucky Bar, a 1961 sorrel stallion by Lucky Bar, was a paternal grandson of Bartender. Out of King's Madam, by King P-234, he was an AQHA Champion.

cess as a sire. Duck Hunter McCue, a 1945 sorrel gelding by Reed McCue, earned a racing ROM.

But it was Bartender whom the McGehees intended to build their horse breeding program around, and their strategy proved sound.

Before he left the Miller Ranch in 1945, Bartender was bred to a number of the family's mares. Included among them was Edna, a daughter of Texas Miller owned by Clyde's brother Bill. In 1946 Edna foaled a sorrel mare named Kay's Bar Maid. Sold to J. W. Hastings of Windthorst, Tex., Bar Maid went on to become a top cutting mare, earning $10,570 in NCHA competition and a Superior and 59 performance points in AQHA contests.

Martini Girl was the first of the McGehees' Bartender offspring to make a splash. A 1947 sorrel mare out of Princess Adair, by Will Stead, Martini Girl was AAA-rated, a Superior race horse, and the earner of $5,465. She placed second in the 1952 Buttons and Bows Stakes and 1953 Bright Eyes Stakes, and third in the 1951 Raton Handicap, 1951 Button and Bows

Stakes, and 1952 Raton Handicap. As a producer, she was the dam of eight racing ROM-earners including Barteen, SI 100; Three Martinis, SI 96; and Martinis Folly and Mr. Bartini, each SI 95.

By the late 1940s Bartender's fame as a sire was beginning to spread, and horsemen from throughout west Texas began taking their mares to his court.

In 1950 Bill Hitson of Fort Sumner, N.M., bred Hitson's Queenie, a good granddaughter of Jack McCue, to Bartender. In 1951 she foaled Lee's Pride, a sorrel gelding who went on to earn $4,558 in NCHA competition and a Superior and 57 points in AQHA-sanctioned cuttings.

The McGehees were breeding their own mares to Bartender as well, and in 1955 they came up with two of his greatest sons.

Lucky Bar, a 1955 sorrel stallion out of Ada Adair, by Yellow Boy P-18, was eventually acquired by J. W. Hastings. He became an AQHA Champion and a Superior halter horse. From a total of 150 AQHA-registered foals, he sired 2 AAA-rated race horses, 5 AQHA Champions, and the earners of 5 Superiors in halter,

WESTERN HORSEMAN PHOTO

Toots Mansfield, a 1951 dun stallion by Preacher G. and out of Cynthia Ann Gillham, by Yellow Boy P-18, was another good representative of the Bartender line. Named after the famous R.C.A. calf roper, Toots is shown after being named reserve champion stallion at the July 1955 Weatherford, Tex., horse show. That's owner Bob Collins of Brownwood, Tex., at the halter.

WESTERN HORSEMAN PHOTO

Dee Gee, a 1945 bay mare by Bartender and out of Scarlett, by Little Fort, was one of her sire's greatest performers. A two-time AQHA high-point horse, Dee Gee is shown here with owner Wanda Harper of Mason, Tex., after winning the aged mare class at the July 1955 Weatherford, Tex., show.

1 Superior and 10 ROMs in performance, and 1,045.5 points.

Tender Boy, a 1955 sorrel stallion out of La Nita, by Buck, was sold to Sunny Jim Orr of Pueblo, Colorado. Trained and shown by Sunny Jim, he was the 1961 AQHA High-Point Calf Roping Horse, the 1961 AQHA High-Point Working Cow Horse, and an AQHA Champion. From only 33 registered foals, Tender Boy sired 3 AQHA high-point horses, 1 AQHA reserve world champion, 3 AQHA Champions, and the earners of 1 Superior in halter, 3 Superiors and 6 ROMs in performance, and 753.5 points.

Kay's Bar Maid was one of Bartender's greatest performing offspring. A 1946 sorrel mare out of Edna, by Texas Miller, Bar Maid is shown here with Hoot Walker after winning the senior cutting at the September 1959 Frederick, Okla., show. The mare was owned by J.W. Hastings.

Four of the best Bartender get foals during this era were bred by the Stroles.

In 1955, Bartender sold for the third and final time. His new owners, Dr. and Mrs. D. G. Strole of Abilene, Tex., were well-known Quarter Horse breeders and exhibitors, and the move served to bring the then-15-year-old stallion even closer to the limelight.

The Strole Years

By this point in his life, Bartender's reputation as a sire was secure. His outside book filled rapidly each spring, and the net result was an ever-increasing list of Bartender-sired champions.

Bartender Duke, a 1956 sorrel stallion out of Balmola, by Balmy L., earned $7,343 in NCHA contests and a Superior in AQHA cutting events. Allen's Star, a 1957 chestnut mare out of Wishing Star, by Hughes Horse, was the 1969 and 1970 AQHA High-Point Pole Bending Mare, a Superior barrel racing horse, and the earner of 101.5 performance points.

Four of the best Bartender get foals during this era were bred by the Stroles.

Gatita Lady, a 1958 sorrel mare out of Bandido's Gold, by Bandido, and Texas Fizz, a 1958 sorrel mare out of Susie Lue, by Top Flight, were AQHA Champions.

Rum Saffire, a 1960 bay mare out of Queen Needles, by King, and Tequilla Hombre, a 1961 sorrel gelding out of Midnight Roper, by Roper Boy, earned Superiors in cutting.

In his last five foal crops—1962 through 1967 (there were no foals born in 1966)—Bartender sired thirty horses. Among these were his last two significant performers.

King Barkeep, a 1963 palomino gelding out of Gold Shasta, by Cuellar, earned a performance ROM, and Santender, a 1965 sorrel Strole-bred mare out of Bandido's Ultima, by El Bandido, earned $10,612 in NCHA cutting events and a performance ROM in AQHA competition.

Bartender passed away in 1966, at the age

PHOTO BY GERALD KEOWN, COURTESY THE QUARTER HORSE JOURNAL

Lottie Bar was another of Lucky Bar's AQHA Champion get. A 1963 sorrel mare out of Poco Lottie, by Poco Pine, Lottie is shown here with owner J.W. Hastings and ribbon girl Cheryl Hoelscher after earning reserve champion mare honors at the October 1965 Robstown, Tex., show.

PHOTO BY BOBBI, COURTESY THE QUARTER HORSE JOURNAL

Here's Lucky Bar Lass, yet another AQHA Champion by Lucky Bar. A 1964 mare out of Erine Murphy, by Lee Moore, the trim mare is held by Mary Anne Parris.

Texas Fizz, a 1958 sorrel mare by Bartender and out of Susie Lue, by Top Flight, was also bred by the Stroles. In this photo, the AQHA Champion had just won grand champion mare honors at the Pennsylvania National Horse Show in Harrisburg. Owner Patricia Dunnuck of Cassopolis, Mich., is at the halter.

PHOTO BY ABERNATHY, COURTESY THE QUARTER HORSE JOURNAL

Contributing to his record as a maternal grandsire, Bartender's daughters accounted for 803 registered foals.

of 26. His final foal, a brown stallion appropriately named Last Round, was born the following spring.

The Final Tally

From 25 foal crops, Bartender sired 218 AQHA-registered horses; of these, 71 competed in the arena. In racing, he sired 13 starters who earned 2 ROMs and $6,338.

In halter and performance, Bartender sired 71 performers who earned 5 AQHA Championships, 2 Superior halter awards, 7 Superior performance awards, 25 performance ROMs, and 369 halter and 895.5 performance points.

Contributing to his record as a maternal grandsire, Bartender's daughters accounted for 803 registered foals.

In racing, led by Martini Girl—the dam of eight ROM runners—and Spear Seven Sue—the dam of three ROM runners—the Bartender daughters produced 29 winners. They won 133 races and $129,392. They were also the dams of two Superior race horses and earners of twenty-eight racing ROMs.

In halter and performance, the Bartender daughters produced 171 performers who

earned 1 AQHA high-point title, 7 AQHA Championships, 1 Superior halter award, 4 Superior performance awards, 32 performance ROMs, and 666 halter and 2,570.5 performance points. In addition, they earned $84,848 in NCHA competition.

Of special note in evaluating the historical impact of Bartender and his descendants is the Roan Bar line of horses founded by Art Reeves of Mobridge, S.D., and carried on by his sons and grandchildren.

Beginning with Bar Nothing Springer, and continuing with such horses as Roan Bar, Fancy Roan Bar, Roan Bar Country, and a host of other trademarked roan stallions, the Reeves family has crafted one of the most influential Quarter Horse lines on the Northern Plains.

Like most people ever connected with the Bartender line, the Reeves have stayed with it. And that might just be the most fitting tribute to the horse who started it all.

Bartender was never a show horse, and he never headed up a high-dollar, white-fence kind of breeding operation. From the day Roland Moore broke him, he was a working man's horse, as his descendants are today.

Gatita Lady, a 1958 sorrel mare by Bartender and out of Bandido's Gato, by El Bandido, was bred by Bartender's last owners—Dr. and Mrs. D.G. Strole of Abilene, Texas. She is shown here after earning reserve champion mare honors at the 1959 San Saba, Tex., show. That's Jack Lawrence at the halter and Dick Brown holding the trophy.

Here's Tender Boy and Sunny Jim Orr right after Tender Boy had been named grand champion stallion at the August 1961, Calhan, Colo., show. Sunny and Tender Boy also won the reining at that show. A 1955 sorrel stallion by Bartender and out of La Nita, by Buck, Tender Boy established a top line of performance horses in the Rocky Mountain region.

LEO SAN

By Sally Harrison

Leo San was the progenitor of an outstanding line of performance horses.

IN 1949, when Leo San was foaled, the AQHA registry was in its infancy and Quarter Horse breeders relied on phenotype as much as genotype to produce the smart and handy horses they preferred to race and ride.

For example, H.H. Darks, the breeder of Leo San, preferred a compact, muscular horse, built for short bursts of speed, and who also had a good disposition. Darks, who lived in central Oklahoma, bred versatile horses who were popular with ranchers and rodeo cowboys. His stallions included Bert, Billy Van, and San Siemon. The latter was a son of the famed Quarter Horse foundation sire Zantanon (*Legends 4*).

Leo San was out of the San Siemon daughter San Sue Darks. Except for her breeding, not much information is available on San Sue Darks.

While Darks was raising cow horses at

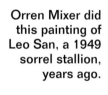

Orren Mixer did this painting of Leo San, a 1949 sorrel stallion, years ago.

COURTESY ORREN MIXER

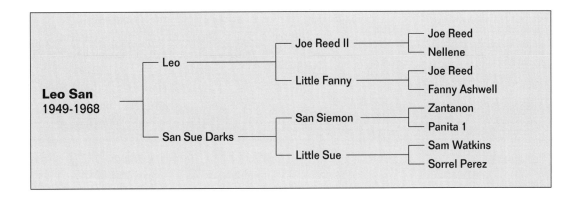

```
                                            ┌─ Joe Reed
                            ┌─ Joe Reed II ──┤
                            │                └─ Nellene
              ┌─ Leo ───────┤
              │             │                ┌─ Joe Reed
              │             └─ Little Fanny ──┤
Leo San       │                              └─ Fanny Ashwell
1949-1968 ────┤
              │                              ┌─ Zantanon
              │             ┌─ San Siemon ───┤
              │             │                └─ Panita 1
              └─ San Sue Darks ──┤
                            │                ┌─ Sam Watkins
                            └─ Little Sue ───┤
                                             └─ Sorrel Perez
```

his farm in Wetumka, Bud Warren, of Perry, an hour north of Oklahoma City, was building a race stable and breeding farm centered on Leo, a pretty darn good match race horse he had purchased in 1947. In appearance, Leo (*Legends 1*) fit Darks' model for a good Quarter Horse. At 14.3 hands and 1,200 pounds, he was heavily muscled with good bone, short cannons, and a pretty head.

Gene Moore, Leo's previous owner, had even used him to work cattle on his ranch near Fairfax, Oklahoma. "He was one of the best cow horses I have ever thrown a saddle on," said Moore, in an article published in the *Thoroughbred Record*. "His disposition was truly wonderful—my little 8-year-old girl used to ride him."

Leo's docile disposition, cow sense, and athletic ability can be attributed to his breeding. Sired by Joe Reed II out of Little Fanny, he was inbred to Joe Reed (his paternal and maternal grandsire).

"One thing about line breeding or inbreeding, it intensifies points, whether they're good points or bad points," said Dorothy Wood, who with her husband, Bert, owned Joe Reed II and Little Fanny. "I think Joe Reed was so strong and had so many good qualities, that they overcame things that in a weaker horse might have shown up."

Quarter Horse historian Nelson Nye concurred. "The Joe Reeds are noted for beautiful heads, top conformation, versatile performance, and terrific early speed," Nye wrote in 1951. "Many a successful Quarter Horse breeder has founded his operation with mares from this line. They are good breeders and long producers, sound as granite and tough as they come."

Halter and Performance Record: None.

Progeny Record:

Foal Crops: 17	Superior Halter Awards: 13
Foals Registered: 404	Performance Point-Earners: 64
AQHA Champions: 9	Performance Points Earned: 1,497
NCHA World Champions: 2	Performance Registers of Merit: 35
AQHA World Champions: 1	Superior Performance Awards: 8
Halter Point-Earners: 77	Race Starters: 27
Halter Points Earned: 1,671	Race Money Earned: $14,329
Total NCHA Earnings: $209,153	Race Registers of Merit: 5
Leading Race Money-Earner: Leo San Bar ($8,253)	

Joe Reed II (*Legends 1*) is best known for his race record (1942-43 World Champion Quarter Running Stallion) and his race progeny, but the Wood family loved him for other qualities as well. "We used him for working cattle on the ranch," said Dorothy Wood. "They all (Joe Reed II offspring) would follow cattle. Back then horsemen used to talk about the bulldog type for working cattle and then the racing type; but to me, Joe personified all in one. He could run, and he was equally as good with cattle."

Joe Reed II had a short racing career because of an injury to a hoof while he and Bert Wood were chasing a cow near Tucson. This happened before Joe had ever set foot on a track. He had stepped on a glass bottle and cut his coronet band, which affected the growth of the hoof. After he raced just a few times, Wood had to retire him from the track. By that time, however, he had built a reputation both as a race horse and a pet with the Wood household.

PHOTO COURTESY *THE QUARTER HORSE JOURNAL*

It's not known when this photo of Leo San was taken, but it shows his short cannon bones and good hip. Matlock Rose once said that "Leo San has more hip than Leo."

"He was very gentle," said Dorothy, who confirmed that they had once turned down an offer of $40,000 for the stallion. "Our kids used to ride him bareback and crawl over him and under him. He was easy to breed too. In fact, lots of times it was easier for me to handle him than to handle the mares."

With Joe Reed II's cow sense and tractable disposition, it is not surprising that Leo also sired good cow horses, although it was his racing offspring who made him famous. There were a few breeders, however, who recognized the potential benefits of crossing race horses with cow and show horses. Among these astute horsemen was oil field tycoon Gordon Howell of Dallas. It was Howell who purchased Leo San as a 2-year-old from H.H. Darks.

"I've always been a connoisseur of the Joe Reed horses and Leo bloodlines, and this horse (Leo San) had sure-'nuff top breeding," said Howell, in an article published in the May 1984 issue of *The Quarter Horse Journal*. "I'm inclined to think that Leo San was the most consistent stallion I ever saw, in the sense that anybody who was a good horseman could go among a group of horses and pick out his foals. He marked his offspring like a fine Hereford bull."

Matlock Rose, who worked for Howell during the early 1960s, showed many of Leo San's offspring in the cutting arena and at halter in the show ring. "He was a breeding horse," said Rose, who won four of his five NCHA world championships on Leo San offspring and grand-offspring: once on Peppy San, by Leo San; twice on Peponita, by Peppy San; and once on Peppy's Desire, by Peppy San. "You could tell his foals just by looking at them. And they were natural cow horses. They wanted to work cattle."

Rose, a stickler when it came to conformation, especially liked Leo San's masculine good looks and the makeup of his foals. "He had more hip than Leo, and he had the shortest cannon bones and prettiest head that I ever saw on a horse," Rose once noted. "He had some scale to him too. He probably weighed 1,300 pounds and stood 14.3."

Howell, too, insisted on good conformation. "I don't consider any horse to be a good horse unless he has a tremendous amount of conformation," he said. "I don't care if he is a race horse or whatever. If he doesn't have any muscling or balance, he can't go to the top of the class." In addition to owning Leo San, Howell was also noted as the breeder of 440-yard record-setter and racing champion Truckle Feature.

Offspring

From 1959 through 1963, Howell campaigned Leo San sons and daughters, and a summary of their show records is included on the previous page. As a side note: In those days get-of-sire classes, in which three offspring of a stallion constituted an entry, were popular. In 66 of those classes, Leo San never placed lower than third.

PHOTO COURTESY SALLY HARRISON

Peppy San, shown here with Matlock Rose aboard, was one of Leo San's two greatest sons. Foaled in 1959, he was out of Peppy Belle. Among many other honors, he was the 1967 NCHA World Champion Cutting Horse and an AQHA Champion.

Just a few of his better-known offspring during that period included:

- Bert Leo, AQHA Champion with Superiors in cutting and halter.
- Leo San Van, AQHA Champion, 1961 AQHA high-point halter gelding, 1961 and 1962 AQHA high-point cutting gelding, and Superiors in halter and cutting.
- Wimpy Leo San, 1961 Honor Roll halter horse.
- Leo San Susie, Leo's Lady San, Leo's Baby, Busy San, Joe Hild Man, Leo San Siemon, Cutter Smokey, Hilda San, all Superior halter horses.
- Calhoun's Lasan, Star Leo Bert, Flying San, Sana Brian, all AQHA Champions.

Leo San also sired horses who could run. Among his 19 race winners was Tabor's Leo, a 1957 stallion out of Little Taggie, by Question Mark (*Legends 3*). In 1961 the chestnut earned his ROM in racing. In 1962 he not only won his ROM in performance, but was AQHA's high-point barrel-racing stallion. Then in 1964, according to AQHA records, Tabor's Leo went back to racing and set a track record.

Bert Leo was one of Leo San's first successful sons. "He wasn't the best halter horse I've ever seen," admitted Matlock Rose, who showed the stallion extensively for Howell. "But he was good enough to beat what was there at the time. He also had a lot of speed and could hold a bad cow. I roped calves and team roped on him, and I even showed him in reining."

The bay had been used as a rope horse before Howell purchased him, but Matlock decided to expand Bert Leo's portfolio. At his first show with Rose, Bert Leo won the

Leo San also sired horses who could run.

165

PHOTO COURTESY NCHA

Buster Welch cutting on Mr San Peppy, the other of Leo San's two greatest sons. He was owned by the King Ranch, Kingsville, Texas.

TRACK MAGAZINE PHOTO BY BEN HUDSON

Gordon Howell purchased Leo San as a 2-year-old from H.H. Darks and campaigned many of the horse's sons and daughters.

cutting, the reining, and the calf roping, and was named grand champion at halter.

"I don't know of one horse like that today," noted prominent farrier Doyle Blagg, who shod many of Rose's mounts. "With cutting you want a horse to sit back and watch a cow. He'll take the offensive when he has to, but he knows how to wait and fade back. In calf roping, you want the horse to run as fast as he can right behind the cow and then wait for the jerk on the rope. And in team roping, you want the horse to run and stop or run and turn off and drag the steer. It takes a tremendous amount of talent and ability for a horse to do all those things and do them well."

Stanley Bush, an early cutting champion, was confounded by Rose's success with Bert Leo. Bush remembers one show, in particular, held in Johnson City, Tex., in an outdoor arena next to the Pedernales River. "Bert Leo was so terrible in the first round that Matlock threatened to load him up and go home," Bush recalled.

"But we all told him that he needed to stay and turn back for us. Later we heard a commotion coming from the Pedernales, and it turned out to be Matlock down there working with Bert Leo. He came back and beat us all that night. Afterwards someone said we would have been smart to have let him go home."

The Two Greatest Sons

Like Bert Leo, many of Leo San's successful performers were out of daughters of Bert or Bert Jr. But the most successful Leo San cross was with Peppy Belle, a Pep Up daughter Howell had purchased on the advice of Matlock Rose.

Peppy Belle's first foal by Leo San was Peppy San, trained by Rose and campaigned to the 1967 NCHA World Championship plus many other major titles and honors, including AQHA Champion and induction into the AQHA Hall of Fame. It was Rose who recognized potential in the

PHOTO COURTESY SALLY HARRISON

Mr San Peppy was foaled in 1968 and was the 1974 and 1976 NCHA World Champion Cutting Horse.

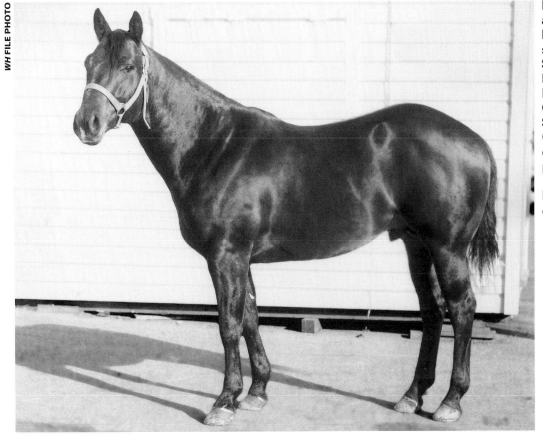

WH FILE PHOTO

Bert Leo, by Leo San and out of Trixie Blake, by Bert, typified the successful cross of Leo San on Bert daughters. Foaled in 1955, Bert Leo was an AQHA Champion and earned Superiors in halter (with 74 points) and cutting (69 points). This picture was taken in 1958 at Amarillo, where he was named grand champion stallion.

A successful contemporary descendant of Leo San is Riosmysister. With owner-rider Kevin Arnold of Kermit, Tex., in the saddle, the 1997 sorrel stallion won the non-pro championship at the 2001 NCHA Super Stakes. (However, this picture was taken at the 2000 NCHA Futurity.) Riosmysister was sired by King of Clarks, who was by Clarks Doc Bar and out of Rubio San, by Leo San.

pretty sorrel colt from the time he took his first wobbly steps in 1959.

"Peppy San looked like a stud prospect when he was just a young colt," said Rose. "While just standing still he looked like he could do something."

Gordon Howell favored Old Sorrel bloodlines in his broodmares, and it was Old Sorrel breeding that had attracted him to Peppy Belle. She traced to Old Sorrel through her sire, Pep Up, a grandson of the famous King Ranch horse.

Peppy Belle produced six more foals by Leo San after Peppy San. But it was Mr San Peppy, foaled in 1968, who drew the attention of the cutting world once again to Peppy Belle and Leo San.

Mr San Peppy became the NCHA world champion in 1974 and 1976 and won the NCHA Derby in 1972 plus many other titles. He was owned by the King Ranch and was trained and ridden by the legendary Buster Welch.

Like Peppy San, Mr San Peppy went on to enjoy a long and successful breeding career. In fact, the influence of these full brothers on the performance horse industry, and especially the sport of cutting, is overwhelming.

In the category of all-time leading cutting sires, through 1999, Mr San Peppy's son Peppy San Badger ("Little Peppy") topped the list with more than $22 million in progeny earnings.

Smart Little Lena, by Doc O'Lena and out of the Peppy San daughter Smart Peppy, was ranked second with $20 million. Dual Pep and Haidas Little Pep, both Peppy San Badger sons, also ranked among the top 10 with $7.7 million and $6 million, respectively.

Among the top 10 paternal sires, Mr San Peppy, Peppy San Badger, Peppy San, and Leo San were ranked fourth through seventh as of 1999.

In 1963, Howell had a dispersal sale and Leo San sold to James Kemp, who kept the horse until Howell bought him back in 1968. Leo San then was kept on Rebecca Tyler's ranch at Gainesville, Tex.. where he died in February 1968. But his legacy lives on today through many of descendants.

Here's a picture of the Leo San daughter Sanleo and her 1957 foal, Leo Zero, by Johnny Zero. Leo Zero grew up to become an AQHA Champion with 44 halter and 14 performance points. This photo was taken at the 1957 Tulsa State Fair where the pair won the Quarter Horse mare and foal class. The two handlers are not identified, but one might be W.E. Spencer, the breeder of Leo Zero.

Leo San's influence is still felt today through horses such as Smart Chic Olena, one of the greatest contemporary sires of reining horses. Smart Chic Olena was by Smart Little Lena, who was out of Smart Peppy, by Peppy San, by Leo San. This photo was taken at the 1990 AQHA World Show where Smart Chic Olena, ridden by Dell Bell, won the senior cutting.

CUSTUS RASTUS (TB)

By Frank Holmes

A royally bred Thoroughbred, he became a great sire of Quarter Horses.

HE MIGHT have had an unusual name, but when it came to his ability as a sire, there was nothing funny about Custus Rastus (TB). Beginning in the early 1950s and continuing through the mid-1970s, he forged a family of triple-threat Quarter Horses that were renowned for their ability to run fast, look good, and work hard.

A dark brown stallion foaled in 1948, Custus Rastus was bred by Mrs. Vera S. Bragg. He was sired by Requested and was out of Slim Rosie, by Tryster.

Requested, a son of noted speed sire Questionnaire, was an eight-time stakes winner of $116,595. Slim Rosie, the dam of Custus Rastus, was a solid handicap mare with 12 wins to her credit. Tryster, her sire, was the unbeaten 2-year-old champion of his year. So, from a genetic standpoint, Custus Rastus was no fluke. He was bred to be great.

In 1949 Mrs. Bragg thought enough of her yearling colt's potential to consign him

As an aged stallion, Custus Rastus stood 16 hands and weighed a well-proportioned 1,300 pounds. The big Thoroughbred consistently transmitted both his size and good looks to his get, resulting in a great family of all-around Quarter Horses.

COURTESY LOU AND LIBBY TUCK

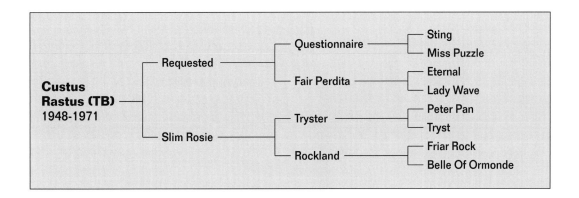

				Sting
		Questionnaire		Miss Puzzle
	Requested			Eternal
		Fair Perdita		Lady Wave
Custus Rastus (TB) 1948-1971				Peter Pan
		Tryster		Tryst
	Slim Rosie			Friar Rock
		Rockland		Belle Of Ormonde

to the prestigious Keeneland Thoroughbred Sale held in Lexington, Kentucky. There he was purchased for $16,000 by W.H. Ingerton, who shipped him to Hot Springs, Ark., and put him in race training.

As a 2-year-old, Custus Rastus was reported to have shown promising speed. Then a broken sesamoid bone ended his career before it could get started, and he was taken out of training and sold to Lewis Blackwell of Amarillo, Texas.

Blackwell was one of the Southwest's top Quarter race-horse men at the time, having already been connected with such champion sprinters as Hard Twist, Monita, and Miss Panama. In Custus Rastus, the savvy horseman obviously looked past the injury to the potential as a sire.

Custus Rastus' first foal crop for Blackwell hit the ground in 1952. From it came the stallion's first two straightaway performers. One was Gold Note, a sorrel mare out of Blackwell's Tic Tac, by Jack Dempsey. Gold Note hit the track as a 2-year-old, and she went on to become a consistent AAA-rated race horse—her sire's first. She was also stakes-placed and the winner of eight races. Retired from the track, she produced four AAA runners including Golden Note, the 1961 Co-Champion Quarter Running 2-Year-Old Filly, and Palleo's Note, a AAA AQHA Champion.

It is interesting to note that Blackwell's Tic Tac, the dam of Gold Note, was once owned by an unsung hero of early Quarter racing lore—Johnny Alonzo of Laguna Pueblo, New Mexico. In addition to raising Tic Tac, Alonzo also bred the following horses:

Halter and Performance Record: None.

Progeny Record:

Foal Crops: 21	Performance Point-Earners: 22
Foals Registered: 167	Performance Points Earned: 479
AQHA Champions: 14	Performance Registers of Merit: 17
Supreme Champions: 1	Race Starters: 107
Halter Point-Earners: 34	Race Money Earned: $275,002
Halter Points Earned: 661	Race Registers of Merit: 59
Superior Halter Awards: 3	Superior Race Awards: 1
Leading Race Money-Earner: Bull Rastus ($49,430)	

- Miss Revenue, who would eventually figure prominently in the Custus Rastus story.
- Blackwell's Red Wing, the dam of Bar B Twist AAA and Kay's Roan, an AQHA Champion.
- Bullet, whose daughter Annette Kay produced five AAA runners and one AQHA Supreme Champion.

And, as if that weren't enough, Alonzo also owned the controversial "Paint-aloosa" mare Plaudette at the time she was carrying the legendary sprinter Maddon's Bright Eyes (*Legends 3*) in her belly.

Getting back to Custus Rastus, his next noteworthy get from his first foal crop, and his first AAA AQHA Champion, was Jaguar. A bay stallion out of Mame Taylor, by Jack Dempsey, Jaguar was an honest but unspectacular race horse. However, he achieved his AAA rating in 1955 and his AQHA Championship in 1957.

Like his sire, Jaguar's main contribution

COURTESY THE QUARTER HORSE JOURNAL

A 1955 picture of the AAA-rated Gold Note, by Custus Rastus, after she won a 549-yard race at Los Alamitos Race Course.

to the Quarter Horse breed would come as a breeding animal (see following chapter).

Over the course of the next half-dozen years—from 1953 through 1958—Custus Rastus was lightly bred. Despite this, he managed to turn out such AAA speedsters as Chicadoo, King Rastus, Rufus Rastus, and Raz Miss Taz.

During this period, Custus also added two more AAA AQHA Champions to his list—Ricky Taylor, a 1954 chestnut stallion out of Mame Taylor, and Custus Sandy, a 1958 bay stallion out of Sandia Sue, by Sandy Man.

In addition, Ima Pixie, a 1958 bay mare out of Ima You, by Revenue, achieved a AA rating on the track, won the 1960 New Mexico Futurity, was a state high-point halter mare, and produced Ima Pixie Too, AAA, and Silky Fox, AQHA Champion.

In the fall of 1958, Custus Rastus changed hands for a third and final time. Although his new owner, L. L. "Lou" Tuck of Littleton, Colo., was a relative newcomer to the Quarter Horse racing industry, he was no stranger to horses in general. He was born and raised in southern Illinois where his

father had raced Thoroughbreds locally. As a fighter pilot during World War II, Tuck was stationed in south Texas near Kingsville. While there, he struck up friendships with King Ranch luminaries Robert Kleberg and Dr. J.K. Northway. Both acquaintances piqued the young aviator's interest in the fledgling Quarter Horse registry.

After the war Tuck married Elizabeth "Libby" Lewis of Houston and relocated to Littleton. There he combined his childhood exposure to running horses with his newfound interest in Quarter Horses and began building a Quarter race and show horse breeding program.

"In the early 1950s," Tuck says, "I struck up friendships with Bud Warren of Perry, Okla., who owned Leo, and Sid Vail of Douglas, Ariz., who owned Three Bars (TB). I was able to incorporate horses bred by both of these great horsemen into my own program and this sure got me off on the right foot."

Among the first horses that Tuck purchased from Warren were Boom Town, a 1952 bay stallion by Pondie and out of Flit, by Leo; Sweet Leilani, a 1951 sorrel mare by Leo and out of Jezebell W., by Jess

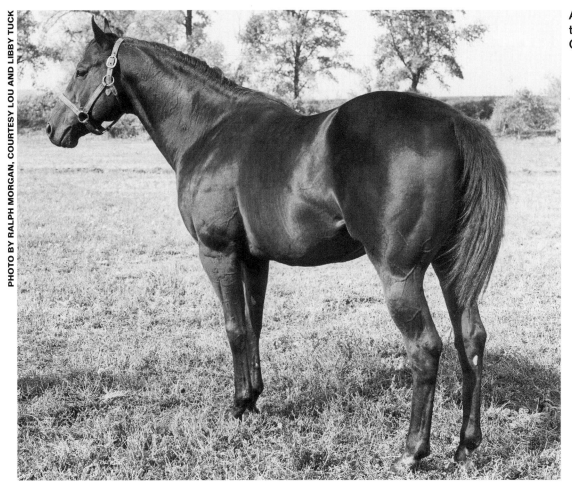

PHOTO BY RALPH MORGAN, COURTESY LOU AND LIBBY TUCK

Another view of the royally bred Custus Rastus.

COURTESY *THE QUARTER HORSE JOURNAL*

Here's a seldom-seen picture of Custus Rastus, circa early 1950s, when he was owned by Lewis Blackwell of Amarillo.

PHOTO BY JOE MURPHY, COURTESY THE QUARTER HORSE JOURNAL

Custus Sandy, a 1958 bay stallion out of Sandia Sue, by Sandy Man, was among the first in Custus Rastus' long line of AAA and AQHA Champions.

Hankins; and Leolib, a 1952 chestnut full sister to Sweet Leilani.

Although he became a AA-rated race horse and a halter point-earner, Boom Town did not have any lasting effect on the Tuck program. But Sweet Leilani and Leolib did.

"I acquired Boom Town and Leolib without too much trouble," Tuck says, "but I had to work pretty hard to get Leilani. Bud sent her to me as a 2-year-old to train and race. I took her knowing all the while that what I really wanted was to own her.

"Bud wasn't too keen about selling her though. You could always tell when he didn't want to sell a horse because he'd say, 'That's Reba's horse; I don't guess I better price it.' Reba was Bud's wife and, when he opened negotiations with that line, you knew two things for sure. Number one was that he didn't want to sell the horse. Number two was, if you did manage to get it bought, it was going to cost you. It took me over a year to get

Sweet Leilani bought, but I finally got the job done."

The wait, as it turned out, was worth it. Trained for racing by Tuck, Sweet Leilani earned a Register of Merit rating. Shown at halter by the Tucks, she earned an AQHA Championship. Turned into a broodmare, she produced five AAA runners and one AQHA Champion.

Leolib, although not as accomplished a race or show mare as Leilani, proved to be almost as good a producer with two AAA runners, two AQHA Champions, and one AQHA Supreme Champion to her credit.

Several years after acquiring his pair of cornerstone Leo mares, Tuck looked to further expand his breeding operation by visiting Lewis Blackwell. "Through my racing interests," Tuck explains, "I knew of Blackwell and his horses. In 1957 I made a trip to one of Lewis' ranches near Logan, N.M., to see what he might have for sale. I took Jay Chambers, a neighbor of mine, with me.

"Jay would later own and race the great Jet Deck, but that trip was his first real exposure to Quarter racing stock. And he wound up buying some horses from Lewis, either outright or in partnership with me.

"As for myself, I bought a couple of top race producers named Mabel Crawford and Billie M., but the most important thing to come out of the whole experience was that I got my first look at Custus Rastus. I liked him right from the very beginning and tried to buy him. But Lewis wasn't ready to sell at that time, so I had to return home without him.

"A year later, though, I made a second trip south, and this time I came back with both Custus and a mare named Miss Revenue. She was by Teddy and out of Blackwell's Tick Tac, the dam of Gold Note. We bred her back to Custus a number of times, and she became one of our more consistent producers."

Custus Rastus' Colorado Foals

After settling in at his new Rocky Mountain home, Custus Rastus wasted little

Southern Sea,
a 1963 bay mare
by Custus
Rastus and
out of Sweet
Leilani W.,
earned a AAA
rating on
the track
and an AQHA
Championship
in the show ring.

Toujours Moi,
a 1965 brown
mare, was one
of three AAA
runners by
Custus Rastus
and out of
Heavenly Flower.
The 1965 brown
mare was named
after one of Libby
Tuck's favorite
perfumes.

Printer's Devil was a member of Custus Rastus' first Colorado foal crop. The 1959 bay stallion, who was out of Miss Print, by Red Man, was a AAA-rated AQHA Champion and the sire of 27 AAA race horses and 1 AQHA Champion.

Milk River and Net Profit were the acknowledged superstars of Custus Rastus' third Colorado foal crop.

time in proving to the Quarter Horse world that he was, indeed, a sire to be reckoned with.

From his first Colorado foal crop—born in 1959—came the likes of Printer's Devil and Custus Belle. Printer's Devil, a bay stallion out of Miss Print, by Red Man, was a AAA AQHA Champion and a three-times stakes winner. Custus Belle, a gray mare out of Jezebel Twist, by Hard Twist, was an AQHA Champion, a Superior Halter Horse, and the grand champion mare of the 1964 National Western Livestock Show in Denver.

Also foaled in 1959 were the AAA runners Custus Rain, Lady Custes, My Lady Sheron, and Slim Rosie.

From Custus Rastus' 1960 foal crop, Baby Rastus, Capital Gain, and Silver Rastus were tops. Baby Rastus, a bay stallion out of Baby String, by Piggin String (TB), was a AAA-rated, two-time stakes winner. Capital Gain, a bay stallion out of the Johnny Alonzo-bred Miss Revenue, was an AQHA Champion and Superior halter horse. Silver Rastus, a bay gelded full brother to Custus Belle, was a AAA runner with 12 wins, 11 places, and

14 shows from 87 lifetime starts.

Also foaled in 1960 was Solid Sada, a chestnut Thoroughbred son of Custus Rastus, out of Coosada. Home-bred by the Tucks on their Wild Plum Canyon Farms and trained for racing by Lou, Solid Sada won the 1962 Colorado Breeders Stake by five lengths, the 1963 Colorado Derby and Mayflower Handicap, and the 1964 Las Cruces Handicap.

Milk River and Net Profit were the acknowledged superstars of Custus Rastus' third Colorado foal crop. Milk River, a chestnut stallion out of Leolib, was an AQHA Supreme Champion, a three-time stakes-placed race horse, and the earner of 26 halter and 33 performance points in five events. Net Profit, a bay stallion out of Miss Revenue, was an AQHA Champion and Superior halter horse.

From Custus Rastus' 1962 foal crop came the AQHA Champion Custus Mist, a palomino mare out of Heels' Paula, by Gold Heels. Also foaled that year were the AAA-rated Custus Maiden, Rawhide Rastus, and Stormy Custus.

PHOTO BY ORREN MIXER, COURTESY *THE QUARTER HORSE JOURNAL*

Capital Gain was a 1960 bay stallion by Custus Rastus and out of Miss Revenue. Last owned by Pamela Turin of Kiron, Iowa, Capital Gain was an AQHA Champion and a Superior halter horse. As a sire, he is credited with 14 Superior halter and performance horses, 7 AQHA Champions, and horses earning 5,209.5 points.

PHOTO BY ORREN MIXER, COURTESY *THE QUARTER HORSE JOURNAL*

This beautiful gray Custus Rastus daughter, Custus Belle, was foaled in 1959. Sold to Bob Sutherland of Kansas City, Mo., Belle became an AQHA Champion. She was also a Superior halter horse with 190 open halter points.

Custus Mist, a 1962 palomino mare by Custus Rastus and out of Heel's Paula, earned an AQHA Championship. When retired to the broodmare band and bred to Three Wars, the palomino produced Three Timer AAA.

Two AAA AQHA Champions—Southern Sea, a bay mare out of Sweet Leilani W., and Times Two, a chestnut stallion out of This Time, by J. B. King—were the cream of the 1963 crop. Mr. Moose, a chestnut stallion out of Fanny Leo, by Leo, also qualified for his AAA rating.

Bull Rastus, arguably the greatest 870-yard runner in the history of Quarter Horse racing, was the marquee star of Custus Rastus' 1964 foal crop. A bay stallion out of Raza, by Spotted Bull (TB), Bull Rastus raced sound for five years at distances from 330 to 870 yards. He was the first horse to win at Sunland Park carrying 130 pounds, and he set world or track records for 870 yards at 3, 4, 5, and 6 years of age. From 95 lifetime starts, he garnered 40 wins, 18 places, and 6 shows, and earned $49,430.

Yankee Rob, a 1964 chestnut gelding by Custus Rastus and out of Heavenly Flower, by Three Bars, also did his part to enhance his sire's reputation. A three-times stakes winner, he won 15 races and earned $27,492 during his 6-year straightaway career. In addition, Unprintable, a 1964 bay full brother to Printer's Devil, and White River, a 1964 chestnut full sister to Milk River, also earned AAA ratings.

The theme for the 1965 Custus Rastus foal crop could easily have been "sibling rivalry." From that offering, Double Entry, a bay mare, became the third AQHA Champion to come from the Custus Rastus-Miss Revenue cross.

Likewise, Five Star Final, a bay stallion, became the third AAA runner from the Custus Rastus-Miss Print cross. Northern Sea became the second AAA runner from the Custus Rastus-Sweet Leilani mating; and Toujours Moi became the second AAA racer from the Custus Rastus-Heavenly Flower pairing.

Yankee Dolla, a 1968 brown stallion, was the third AAA-rated race horse to be sired by Custus Rastus and out of Heavenly Flower. And he would be the last, due to the terrible tragedy that struck Wild Plum Canyon Farms in the fall of the year Dolla was foaled.

Thieves Cause Heartbreak

"In October of 1968," Lou Tuck says, "four horses were stolen from our pasture: Heavenly Flower, a 10-year-old mare by Three Bars and out of Sweet Leilani; Lovely Lani, a 7-year-old mare by Custus and out of Leilani; Royal Doulton, a yearling filly by Buzz Bar and out of Custus Liz; and an unnamed weanling filly by Buzz Bar and out of Lovely Lani.

"After receiving what I deemed to be less-than-acceptable cooperation from local law enforcement agencies, and acting on information passed on to me by friends, I took up the search for the missing horses on my own. I rented a plane and flew to Roundup, Mont., where I enlisted the aid of a conscientious young sheriff named Vern

PHOTO BY ORREN MIXER, COURTESY LOU AND LIBBY TUCK

Milk River, a 1961 chestnut stallion by Custus Rastus and out of Leolib, was a AAA race horse and an AQHA Supreme Champion. Even though he was lightly bred, he sired top performers such as Cream Creek AAA; Rastus River AAA; Tivio River, an AQHA Champion; and Tru Nessen Quality, who won Superiors in western riding, western pleasure, and hunter under saddle.

Fogle. Together we located and retrieved Royal Doulton. It seems the rustlers had opted to hide her out on a local ranch, with the probable intention of putting false papers on her and racing her.

"We weren't so lucky with the others. Heavenly Flower and Lovely Lani had been killed, and their bodies dumped in a nearby lake. Lani's filly had also been destroyed, and her body had been stuffed in a rocky crevice four miles from the lake.

"The responsible people were tried and convicted," he continues. "They received varying sentences and fines, but no amount of time or money could ever replace the heartbreak surrounding the loss of those horses.

"The loss of Heavenly Flower was especially hard to take. We had hauled Sweet Leilani all the way to California to breed her to Three Bars. 'Flower' was the result; she grew into a beautiful AAA race mare who won both the Rocky Mountain Quarter Horse Association's Futurity and Derby.

"But, more than all of that, she was a very personal part of what we were trying to accomplish in the Quarter Horse business. To

PHOTO BY DAROL DICKINSON, COURTESY THE QUARTER HORSE JOURNAL

A 1961 bay stallion, Net Profit was a son of Custus Rastus and Miss Revenue and also an AQHA Champion and a Superior halter horse. When shown together, Capital Gain and Net Profit won the produce of dam class for Miss Revenue at the 1964 Southwestern Exposition and Livestock Show in Fort Worth.

Bull Rastus, a 1964 bay stallion by Custus Rastus and out of Raza, was a terrific 870-yard runner. A former world record-holder at the distance, he tallied 40 wins, 18 places, and 6 shows in 95 starts.

After going to the post as a 35-to-1 longshot, Solid Sada, a 1960 Thoroughbred son of Custus Rastus and Coosada, won the 1962 Colorado Breeders Stake in wire-to-wire fashion by 5 lengths. As consistent as he was speedy, the good-looking chestnut also notched three stakes victories at 2, 3, and 4 years of age.

have her taken from us the way she was, was difficult to overcome."

But, as hard as it was to do, overcome it the Tucks did. And they continued with a family operation—and one that by now included the active participation of sons Buzz and Robert and daughters Mary Lou and Jane. Their operation was generally recognized to be one of the industry's best.

Custus Rastus' Twilight Years

By 1970 Custus Rastus was at the end of his breeding career. In fact, Mis Custus Candy, a 1969 bay mare out of Elegant Sue, and Aguila Baron, her 1971 bay full brother, were the last of Custus' get to make a splash as AQHA performers. Both earned AQHA Championships, with Candy receiving hers in 1972, and Baron getting his in 1976.

The final tally for Custus Rastus, whose last crop was foaled in 1971, was impressive.

As a speed sire, Custus sent 107 horses to the tracks. They earned 33 AAA race ratings, 59 Register of Merits, and accounted for 262 wins and $275,002, racing mostly in the era of small purses.

As a show horse sire, Custus sired 1 AQHA Supreme Champion, 14 AQHA Champions, 3 Superior halter horses, and the earners of 17 performance ROMs and 1,140 total AQHA points.

And then there was the next generation.

Taken as a whole, the sons of Custus Rastus proved to be an exceptional set of sires. Jaguar was a top breeding horse for Ed Honnen of Denver, as was Printer's Devil for Marie Monroe of Cutbank, Montana. Ricky Taylor became a top sire for Ray and Edna Guthrie of Prineville, Oregon. In addition, Chicadoo, Custus Sandy, Capital Gain, Milk River, Net Profit, and Bull Rastus all held up their part of the deal.

So did the Custus Rastus daughters. Take Custus Liz for example.

"Liz, a 1960 bay mare out of Leolib, was one of our favorites," Libby Tuck says. "When she was just a couple of months old,

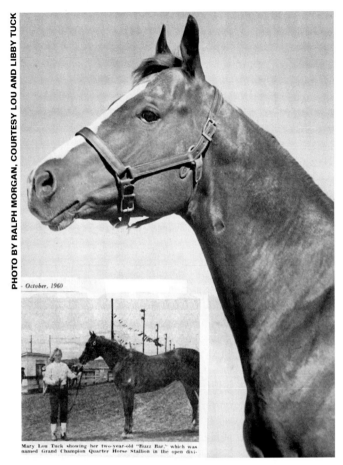

PHOTO BY RALPH MORGAN, COURTESY LOU AND LIBBY TUCK

- October, 1960

Mary Lou Tuck showing her two-year-old "Buzz Bar," which was named Grand Champion Quarter Horse Stallion in the open divi-

Lou Tuck acquired Buzz Bar in 1962 to cross on his outstanding set of Custus Rastus daughters. A 1961 sorrel stallion by Three Bars (TB) and out of Bar Annie, by Three Bars (TB), Buzz Bar was trained by Tuck to his AAA speed rating and shown by the Tuck family to several grand champion halter titles. During his lifetime, Buzz Bar sired AAA race horses, an AQHA Supreme Champion, AQHA Champions, and many other horses who won halter and performance points. That's Mary Lou Tuck in the inset photo showing Buzz Bar as a 2-year-old to a grand champion halter award at a Colorado show.

she suffered such a severe blow to her head in a freak barnyard accident that we had to go out every few hours for weeks and physically help her nurse. She recovered after a fashion, but it took years before she got any kind of true mobility back."

Unable to race, Liz was bred as a 3-year-old to Buzz Bar, the son of Three Bars the Tucks had purchased from Sid Vail specifically to breed to their Custus daughters. Safe in foal to him, the crippled mare was sold.

Then the new owner begged out of the deal and Liz was returned to Wild Plum Canyon Farms.

Silky Fox, a 1965 chestnut stallion by Rapid Bar and out of Ima Pixie, by Custus Rastus, was owned by Frank Dickinson of Calhan, Colorado. An AQHA Champion, Silky Fox sired 3 AQHA Champions and the earners of 16 Superior halter and performance awards and 5,242 AQHA points. This photo was shot by Darol Dickinson, Frank's son.

The next spring she foaled a chestnut colt named Little Town, who became a AAA-rated Superior race horse, an AQHA Supreme Champion, and a leading sire in his own right.

Bred back to Buzz Bar eight more times, Custus Liz produced six additional AAA runners — Dresden, Royal Doulton, Spode, North Slope, South Slope, and Delft. Of these, Royal Doulton and North Slope were the most accomplished.

Royal Doulton, a 1967 mare and the sole survivor of the 1968 horse theft catastrophe, achieved a speed index of 100, and won eight stakes and $91,211. North Slope, a 1969 chestnut stallion, earned a speed index of 97 and was an AQHA Champion.

In 1975 Custus Liz was sold again, and this time the new owner did not ask to return her. Bred to Shecky Greene (TB), she produced Sheckys Custus Leo SI 90. Bred to Easy Jet three times, she produced Easy Custus SI 95, Easy Jet Liz SI 98, and Custus Jet Lizzie SI 103.

And the other daughters of Custus Rastus proved just as talented as their sister when it came to producing speed and good looks.

Miss Rastus, a 1957 black mare out of Miss Sedadle, produced six AAA runners sired by six stallions. Likewise, Mame Kirk, a 1956 bay mare out of Mame Taylor, produced five AAA offspring sired by five stallions. French Riviera, a 1967 bay mare out of the ill-fated Heavenly Flower, also produced five AAAs. Gold Note and Dancing Sea, a 1967 bay mare out of Sweet Leilani W., contributed four each.

Custus Princess, Custus River, Estella Baby, My Lady Cheron, Sally Rastus, Slim Rosie, and Southern Sea each produced three AAA runners.

Like their sire, the Custus Rastus mares were also consistent producers of show horses. Gold Note, Ima Pixe, and Custus Liz together contributed one AQHA Supreme Champion and four AQHA Champions. Heaven Sent and Skedadle Miss were AQHA Champion producers as well.

Lindita, a straight-Thoroughbred daughter of Custus Rastus, produced Go Lindy Go, a Superior halter horse, and Lindy Hank, a Superior western pleasure horse. Oh Anna Oh, another Custus daughter, produced Charge It AAA and Sharp Dancer Leo, an open and youth Superior barrel racing horse.

All told, the daughters of Custus Rastus produced 306 race starters who earned 163 Register of Merits, 83 race ratings of 90 or higher, 8 Superior race awards, and $966,446.

As show ring producers, they produced 335 performers who earned 1 Supreme Championship, 7 AQHA Championships, 2 Superior halter awards, 3 Superior perfor-

COURTESY LOU AND LIBBY TUCK

Royal Doulton, a 1967 chestnut mare by Buzz Bar and out of Custus Liz, was her sire's top sprinter. The sole survivor of the 1968 horse theft tragedy, Royal Doulton won eight stakes, placed in six more, and earned $91,211.

Go Lindy Go, a 1964 red roan stallion, was the only AQHA Superior halter horse ever sired by Go Man Go. The colorful stallion, who also earned a racing ROM, was out of Lindita (TB), by Custus Rastus.

mance awards, 22 performance ROMs, and 1,650 total AQHA points.

Custus Rastus passed away in the spring of 1971 at the age of 23.

Known by all of those connected with him as an even-dispositioned horse who required very little special attention, the big brown Thoroughbred seemed to pass from the scene in much the same way as he had been a part of it—quietly, without a lot of fanfare.

"In all the years he spent with us," Libby Tuck says, "Custus never asked for a lot. He liked to spend his days outside, but he wanted to come in at night. In the fall of each year, after we had weaned the foals, we turned Custus in with them. He was a kind horse and never offered to hurt them. In fact, he seemed to enjoy their company.

"After he passed away, we buried him right here on the farm, in a paddock not too far from where he used to do his babysitting. It just seemed like the right thing to do."

From a Kentucky-bred youngster with unlimited potential to the founder of one of the Quarter Horse breed's most enduring families of all-around horses, Custus Rastus led an interesting life.

Name notwithstanding, he was one serious sire.

PHOTO BY MARGIE SPENCE, COURTESY THE QUARTER HORSE JOURNAL

marge

JAGUAR

By Frank Holmes

As one of the earliest AAA AQHA Champions, Jaguar was the epitome of the all-around Quarter Horse.

LIKE THE car and the cat that share his name, Jaguar was a sleek customer, with looks and speed to burn. As one of the first AAA AQHA Champions, he was also a poster child for that era in Quarter Horse evolution that put a premium on the all-around athlete.

A 1952 bay stallion by Custus Rastus

(TB) and out of Mame Taylor, Jaguar was bred by Lewis M. Blackwell of Amarillo, Texas. Mame Taylor was bred by Louis Kirk of Farmington, New Mexico. Custus Rastus, as detailed in the previous chapter, was an impeccably bred Thoroughbred and the founder of a great family of horses. As also mentioned, Lewis Blackwell was one of

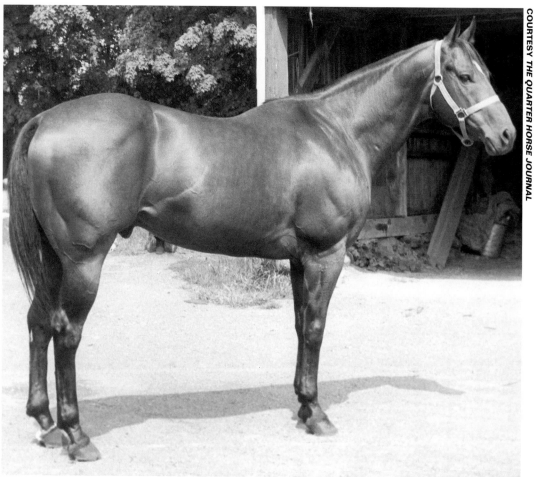

COURTESY THE QUARTER HORSE JOURNAL

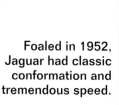

Foaled in 1952, Jaguar had classic conformation and tremendous speed.

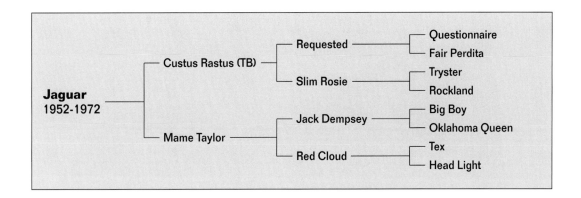

```
                                           ┌─ Questionnaire
                        ┌─ Requested ───────┤
                        │                   └─ Fair Perdita
       ┌─ Custus Rastus (TB) ─┤
       │                │                   ┌─ Tryster
       │                └─ Slim Rosie ──────┤
Jaguar ┤                                    └─ Rockland
1952-1972                                   ┌─ Big Boy
       │                ┌─ Jack Dempsey ────┤
       │                │                   └─ Oklahoma Queen
       └─ Mame Taylor ──┤
                        │                   ┌─ Tex
                        └─ Red Cloud ───────┤
                                            └─ Head Light
```

the Southwest's top Quarter Horse breeders and race-horse men. Mame Taylor and Louis Kirk were just as accomplished.

Mame was a sorrel mare foaled in 1934, sired by Jack Dempsey and out of Red Cloud. Kirk had purchased her sire several years earlier in Arizona, and had bred both her dam and her granddam. In addition, Mame's great granddam, Little Pet, by Traveler, had been Kirk's original mare, purchased in 1911.

Jack Dempsey, a 1921 stallion by Big Boy and out of Oklahoma Queen, by A.D. Reed, by Peter McCue, was an accomplished race horse in his own right. Campaigned on the brush tracks throughout the Four Corners region of New Mexico, Colorado, Utah, and Arizona for seven years, he was matched at distances up to ½ mile, for purses up to $2,500. He retired undefeated in 1930 at age 9.

Like her sire, Mame Taylor was blessed with speed. And, like him, she proved her mettle on the brush tracks of the Four Corners region. She was gentle and even-dispositioned as a rule, but Mame could turn temperamental when she knew a race was imminent.

Purses were small when Mame was in her racing prime. Running as she did from the mid- to late 1930s, with the country in the grip of the Great Depression, the Kirk mare consistently vied for purses in the $25 to $50 range. One notable exception occurred in August 1937 when she ran a match race in Gallup, N.M., for $1,500 against a local speedster named Hoover. She won by daylight.

At the classic quarter-mile distance, and from a standing start, she was reportedly

Halter and Performance Record: Race Register of Merit.

Progeny Record:

Foal Crops: 18	Performance Points Earned: 1,228.5
Foals Registered: 184	Performance Registers of Merit: 30
AQHA Champions: 12	Superior Performance Awards: 7
Halter Point-Earners: 47	Race Starters: 84
Halter Points Earned: 867	Race Money Earned: $101,892
Superior Halter Awards: 5	Race Registers of Merit: 49
Performance Point-Earners: 42	
Leading Race Money-Earner: Jag ($11,936)	

Here is the only known photo of Jaguar's dam, Mame Taylor, with George McNeece up. The celebrated sprinter did all of her running before the days of organized racing. She proved her speed was no fluke by producing such top-notch speedsters as Hard Twist, Jaguar, and Ricky Taylor.

clocked on more than one occasion in :22.5. Retired from racing in the late 1930s, Mame gained further fame through her prowess as a producer. In 1942, she produced Hard Twist, by Cowboy P-12.

185

PHOTO BY FRASCA, COURTESY *THE QUARTER HORSE JOURNAL*

Even at the age of 20, Jaguar still retained the elegance and style that prompted two of the Quarter Horse industry's hallmark breeders to build programs around him.

Honnen was looking for a young race-bred stallion to head his breeding program.

Bred by Kirk and eventually acquired by Lewis Blackwell, Hard Twist was the 1946-47 Champion Quarter Running Stallion and the 1951 Co-Champion Quarter Running Stallion (*Legends 1*).

Mame's next foals never distinguished themselves except for one who earned an ROM in racing. But in 1952, she foaled Jaguar. As a member of the inaugural crop of Lewis Blackwell's Custus Rastus foals, Jaguar became a standard-bearer for that great family of race and show horses.

At the time of Jaguar's foaling on a ranch Blackwell owned near Tucumcari, N.M., another great family of horses was being assembled at Quincy Farms, located in Denver, Colo., and owned by construction mogul Ed Honnen.

In 1952 Honnen had just begun accumulating what would eventually be a star-studded broodmare band that included 34 daughters of Leo.

At that same time, Honnen was looking for a young race-bred stallion to head his breeding program. His search took him to Blackwell's ranch, where he purchased Jaguar. He also leased Jaguar's maternal half-brother, Hard Twist, to service his mares until the younger colt could prove himself in performance.

Jaguar was broke to ride as a 2-year-old and conditioned for a career on the straightaway as a 3-year-old. Unlike his half-brother Hard Twist, who was reputed to be difficult to handle, Jaguar was noted for his even disposition. In Honnen's own words, he "trained well, stayed sound, and gave his all when asked."

Unlike his dam and maternal grandsire, Jaguar's racing career was brief and relatively uneventful. He went to the post only 12 times in 1955 and 1956. He won once, placed second twice, and third twice. His total track earnings were a modest $6,703.

Jaguar's most impressive race occurred on April 23, 1955. The place was the Los Alamitos track in California, and the occasion was the Pacific Coast Quarter Racing Association Derby.

Ridge Butler, who became the 1955 Champion Quarter Running 3-Year-Colt, won the 440-yard event in :22.3. Jaguar finished second, a scant neck behind Ridge Butler, and about the same distance ahead of Rocket Bar (TB) and Joe Queen, who dead-heated for third. Also in the beaten field was Palleo Pete, 1954 Champion Quarter Running Stallion and 2-Year-Old Colt.

Jaguar's earnings for the race amounted to $4,500, far and away the fattest check he received during his two-year straight-away career.

The sole highlight of his sophomore year of racing was his third-place finish in the Rocky Mountain Quarter Horse Association Stallion Stakes held at Centennial in Denver.

Jaguar was retired from the track at the conclusion of the 1957 racing season and readied for a career at halter. As was the case during his racing career, the bay stallion was shown but lightly at halter. AQHA records revealed that, from August of 1954 through January of 1960, he was led in to the show arena only eight times.

In 1957 he stood grand at Cheyenne, Wyo., and Scottsbluff, Nebraska. At the 1957 Colorado State Fair in Pueblo, he placed second in a class of 16 aged stallions.

Jaguar was shown at the National Western Stock Show in Denver four times. In 1955, as a 3-year-old, he placed second to Hank Wiescamp's Skipper's Lad

PHOTO BY ORREN MIXER, COURTESY THE QUARTER HORSE JOURNAL

At the time he purchased Jaguar from Lewis Blackwell, Ed Honnen leased the colt's half-brother Hard Twist. The two-time champion Quarter running stallion was known as the "Comeback King of the Quarter" because he came out of retirement to claim his second championship title.

in a class of 14. In 1956 he placed fourth, and in 1958 he placed third. The 1960 Stock Show marked Jaguar's last venture into a halter ring. In it, he placed second to Skipper's Smoke, earning his final five halter points.

The former race horse earned his AQHA Championship in 1957 with 32 racing and 8 halter points to his credit. He later got an additional eight halter points, bringing his total in that event to sixteen.

Sire Record

Like his sire Custus Rastus, Jaguar's greatest contribution to the breed was not

PHOTO BY ORREN MIXER, COURTESY *THE QUARTER HORSE JOURNAL*.

Coy's Bonanza was not as well known as a race horse as his siblings were, but the 1959 stallion became the 1963 AQHA High-Point Halter Stallion, earned a total of 154 halter points, and became an all-time leading sire of show horses. The sorrel was by Jaguar and out of Sparky JoAnn, by Little Joe The Wrangler.

as a race or show horse, but as a sire. And Ed Honnen had very emphatically stacked the deck in the young stallion's favor.

As stated earlier, Honnen at one time owned 34 direct daughters of Leo. And they weren't just any daughters. They were mares such as Leolita and Leola, both AAA AQHA Champions; Mona Leta and Oleo, both AAA world-record holders; and Etta Leo, who was AA and the dam of seven AAAs.

Complementing this outstanding set of mares were other top performers such as Baby Girl Bunting AAA; Amber's Star

AAA, by Top Deck (TB); and Zona Bar, by Three Bars (TB).

With such a distinguished broodmare band at his disposal, how could Jaguar have done anything but become a successful sire?

His first foal crop, a small one, hit the ground in 1957. From it came Jag, his first notable son. A bay stallion out of Leola, Jag won the 1959 Kansas Futurity and placed in the Pacific Coast Quarter Horse Racing Association Futurity. He achieved a speed index of 95 and $11,936 in earnings. Shown at halter, he earned 17 halter points and stood grand at the American Royal in Kansas City, at Sweetwater, Tex., and at Dewey, Oklahoma.

Jag qualified for his AQHA Championship in 1962 and was the first AAA AQHA Champion in the history of the association to have both a sire and dam who were AAA AQHA Champions as well.

Jaguar's 1958 foal crop was larger, and the number of champions to emerge from it went up proportionately.

Amber Jag, a brown stallion out of Amber's Star, achieved a speed index of 95 and earned 14 halter points. Cut Loose, a bay stallion out of Fanny's Finale; Lady Jag, a gray mare out of Whitcomb's Lady Hank; and Miss Hot Heels, a roan mare out of Hancock Mary, all earned AAA track ratings. Jagy Jr, a chestnut gelding out of Tippy Tuck, was an AQHA Champion.

Coy's Bonanza, a sorrel stallion out of Sparky JoAnn, and Jag's Jewel, a chestnut mare out of Mona Leta, were the stars of Jaguar's third foal crop.

Coy's Bonanza, bred by the highly respected Wyoming horseman Bill Coy, earned his racing Register of Merit in 1962, his Superior halter award in 1963, and his AQHA Championship in 1967. He was also the 1963 AQHA High-Point Halter Stallion. Under the ownership of Bill Moomey of Waukesha, Wis., Coy's Bonanza became one the premier sires of the breed.

Jag's Jewel, a home-bred Quincy Farms product, was both AAA and a multiple producer of the same.

With his AAA track rating, Jagalong, a 1960 bay stallion out of Black Fly, by King,

COURTESY THE QUARTER HORSE JOURNAL

Jag, a 1957 bay stallion by Jaguar and out of Leola by Leo, was the first AAA AQHA Champion with both a AAA AQHA Champion sire and dam.

COURTESY THE QUARTER HORSE JOURNAL

Jag's Jewel, a 1959 chestnut mare, was another classic example of the golden cross between Jaguar and Leo daughters. The streamlined mare, shown here as a 2-year-old at Quincy Farms, was out of Mona Leta. Jag's Jewel become a AAA runner and the dam of two AAA runners.

Here's Barjag, a 1961 bay stallion by Jaguar and out of Zona Bar, by Three Bars (TB). Shown here at Quincy Farms, the good-looking stallion was a AAA AQHA Champion with 21 halter points.

Jag On, a 1962 sorrel stallion by Jaguar and out of Star's Lass, by Star Lightning, was bred to be a show horse. He lived up to his heritage by becoming an AQHA Champion and a Superior halter horse.

Jaguar was a consistent sire of speed and good looks.

In addition to being AAA-rated on the tracks, Right Turn was also a top halter horse. The 1963 brown stallion, by Jaguar and out of Next Turn, by Bob Jr., is shown here after earning grand champion stallion honors at the 1966 National Western Stock Show in Denver. Pictured (from left) are Bud and Reba Warren, Ed Honnen, and Quincy Farms Manager Leonard Milligan.

Here's Jaguar Twister, a 1966 sorrel gelding by Jaguar and out of Jezebel Twist, by Hard Twist. A Superior hunter-under-saddle horse, Twister also earned 40 halter points.

PHOTO BY DAROL DICKINSON, COURTESY *THE QUARTER HORSE JOURNAL*

Mr Jaguar, a 1965 sorrel stallion by Jaguar and out of Zona Bar, was one of his sire's most popular get. He was an AQHA Champion, Superior halter horse, and the sire of great halter horses.

was the sole member of Jaguar's fourth foal crop to achieve any fame. But in 1961, four of Jaguar's get gained stardom.

Barjag, a bay stallion out of Zona Bar, was a AAA AQHA Champion. Three more earned AAA ratings: Imajag, a chestnut stallion out of Iamarose; Jag's Polleta, a chestnut mare out of Polleo; and Miss Jag, a chestnut mare out of Leo Liz.

Reaffirming that Jaguar was a consistent sire of speed and good looks, Jagit, a

1962 brown mare out of Etta Leo, raced her way to a AAA track rating, and Jag On, a 1962 chestnut stallion out of Star's Lass, was an AQHA Champion and a Superior halter horse.

Over the course of the next four years, it was more of the same.

Among the Jaguar get to achieve AAA race ratings were Pamie Jo Jag, a 1963 bay mare out of Pamie Jo; Quincy Miggi, a 1963 sorrel mare out of Leo Dale; and Right Turn, a 1963 sorrel stallion out of Next Turn.

Named as AQHA Champions were Custus Jaguar, a 1964 bay stallion out of Leo Dale; Jaguar's Misty, a 1964 bay mare out of Syralja; Fan Ran Jim, a 1965 sorrel gelding out of Bonnie Robb; and Mr Jaguar, a 1965 sorrel stallion out of Zona Bar.

Jaguar's Twister, a 1966 sorrel gelding out of Jezebel Twist, earned a Superior in hunter under saddle; and Sis Jaguar, a 1966 buckskin mare out of Abney's Ginger, earned a Superior in western pleasure.

A New Owner

In 1966 Jaguar changed hands for the third and final time. His new owner, Loraine Beresford, lived in New Vernon, N.J., and her Sheepfields Farm was already well known as the home of top race and show Quarter Horses. Jaguar wasted no time in adding his potent genes to the mix.

From his first East Coast foal crop in 1967, Jaguar Jr, Jag's Pride, and Isleaway Pride excelled.

Jaguar Jr, a bay stallion out of Spanish Tale, became an AQHA Champion. The well-known Spanish Tale, the first AAA AQHA Champion to be developed solely in the East, also produced Story Man, a AAA AQHA Champion who figured prominently in the Jaguar story at a later date.

Getting back to Jaguar and his initial East Coast foal crop, Jag's Pride, a brown stallion out of Warleta, earned a speed index of 91, and Isleaway Pride, a 1967 bay mare out of Bay Joan, earned a Superior halter award.

From that same 1967 foal crop came Jaguar's Go Go, a brown stallion out of I

Jaguar Jr, a 1967 bay AQHA Champion stallion out of Spanish Tale, was in Jaguar's first crop of New Jersey foals.

Wanta Go, who achieved a speed index of 100; and Palleo Jaguarett, a bay mare out of Sweet Palleo, who graded out at 95.

Two more AAA-rated runners emerged from the 1968 crop of hopefuls. Go Jaguar, a chestnut gelding out of I Wanta Go, had a speed index of 95, while Rainy Jag, a bay mare out of Rainack, achieved a rating of 97.

From Jaguar's 1969 foal crop, Hi Arrive, a brown gelding out of Hialeah Lady, had a speed index of 90 and won the 1971 Empire Futurity. Jaguar's Joetta, a gray mare out of Lady Pokey Joe, was an AQHA Champion.

The Jaguar stars of 1970 and 1971 were a pair of full sisters — to each other and to Coy's Bonanza, as well. Jaguars Fancy, a 1970 bay mare, earned Superiors in open and youth western pleasure. Jaguar's Bonanza, a 1971 bay mare, became an AQHA Champion and earned Superiors in halter and western pleasure.

For the first time in his 17-year siring career, Jaguar produced no AAA runner or AQHA Champion in his 1972 foal crop. His final noteworthy champion came the following year, from his final foal crop. That was Jaguar's Pip, a 1973 bay gelding out of Jubalynn, who earned 25 halter and 308 performance points, a Superior in western pleasure and four open and youth ROMs.

While owned by both Quincy Farms

PHOTO BY CONNIE, COURTESY *THE QUARTER HORSE JOURNAL*

Jaguars Fancy, a 1970 bay mare out of Sparky JoAnn, was an open and youth Superior western pleasure horse and a full sister to Coy's Bonanza.

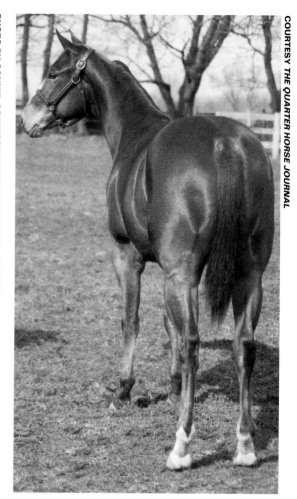

COURTESY *THE QUARTER HORSE JOURNAL*

Jaguar's Bonanza, shown here as a yearling, was a full sister to both Coy's Bonanza and Jaguars Fancy. Foaled in 1971, Jaguar's Bonanza earned an AQHA Championship and Superiors in halter and western pleasure.

and Sheepfields Farm, Jaguar was entered in a number of get-of-sire classes. In 1967 his get won that class at Pueblo, Colo., and in 1968 at Branchville and Frenchtown, New Jersey.

In 1974 Jaguar won six get-of-sire classes at Cape May, Frenchtown, Hopewell (twice), Millville, and Branchville, New Jersey. Those placings were enough to see him finish the year as the fourth high stallion on the AQHA's 1974 Leading Get-Of-Sire Class Winners list.

Jaguar passed away in 1972 at the age of 20.

Although he headed two of the best broodmare bands of his era — first at Quincy Farms and then at Sheepfields

Farm—Jaguar was never heavily bred. From 18 foal crops he sired only 184 foals.

Of these, an amazing 122, or 66 percent, were performers.

As race horses they earned 49 ROMs and $101,892. As open show horses they amassed 12 AQHA Championships, 11 Superiors in halter and performance, 23 ROMs, and 1,585 points. As youth and amateur show horses they added one performance Superior, seven ROMs, and 510.5 points.

The Next Generation

In keeping with their heritage, the next generation of Jaguars was outstanding as well. Jaguar's sons, particularly Coy's

Here is Jaguar's Pip, a 1973 bay gelding by Jaguar and out of Jubalynn, a full sister to Sparky JoAnn. Pip was a Superior western pleasure horse who earned 25 halter and 308 performance points in open and youth competition.

In keeping with their heritage, the next generation of Jaguars was outstanding as well.

Bonanza, Jag, Cut Loose, Jag On, Custus Jaguar, and Mr Jaguar, did their part in perpetuating the line.

Destiny Leo Jag, a 1962 bay stallion by Jaguar and out of Lady Sophia, was unshown due to a broken leg. Used exclusively as a sire, he contributed such get as AQHA Supreme Champion Destiny Jagetta to the family tree.

The Jaguar daughters proved just as good. As racing matrons, they produced 188 starters who amassed 117 ROMs and earned $761,105.

As show producers, they contributed 267 performers who earned 6 AQHA Championships, 19 Superiors in halter and per-formance, 43 ROMs, and 3,816.5 points in all divisions combined.

On the racing end, Jackie's Pride, a 1958 bay mare by Jaguar and out of Jackie Leo, stands out. She produced 14 performers, of whom 12 earned racing ROMs. Four had speed indexes of 100 or higher; two more were rated at 90 or higher; and four were Superior race horses.

Jagalena, a 1960 sorrel mare out of Frye's Breeze, was also a top speed producer. Bred to four stallions, she produced four offspring who achieved speed indexes of 90 or higher.

In addition, Lady Jag, the AAA-rated daughter of Jaguar and Whitcomb's Lady

Destiny Jagetta, a 1965 chestnut mare by Destiny Leo Jag and out of Herfano, by Victory Chief, was one of Jaguar's most-accomplished paternal grandget. An AQHA Supreme Champion and Superior halter horse, she is shown here winning the 2-year-old mare class at the 1967 Montana Winter Fair in Bozeman.

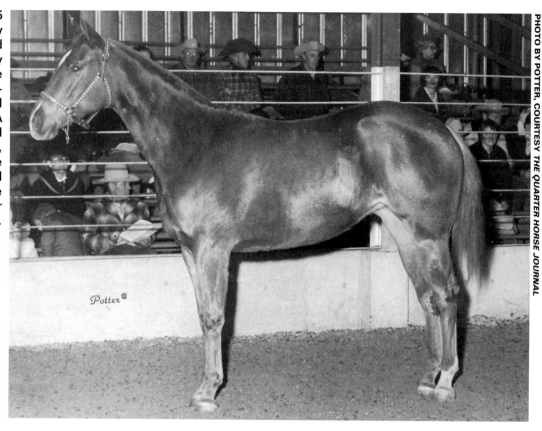

PHOTO BY POTTER, COURTESY THE QUARTER HORSE JOURNAL

Jaguar Rocket, a 1967 gray stallion by Rocket Bar (TB) and out of Lady Jag, was Jaguar's top money-earning maternal grandget. Winner of the Sunland Spring Futurity and Monita Stakes, Jaguar Rocket was a Superior race horse and earned $65,158 during his straightaway career.

Story Man was chosen by Mrs. Beresford as her junior sire, specifically to be bred to the Jaguar daughters.

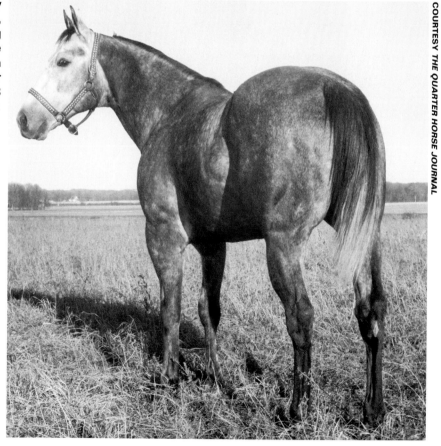

COURTESY THE QUARTER HORSE JOURNAL

PHOTO BY DAROL DICKINSON

Ed Honnen (left) with Jaguar and Leonard Milligan. Date and location are unknown.

Hank, produced four racing ROMs. Her 1967 foal, Jaguar Rocket, had a speed index of 100. With $65,158 in earnings, he was also Jaguar's top money-earning grandget.

Miss Leo Jaguar, a 1964 bay mare by Jaguar and out of Lady Sophia, produced six ROM runners, including two with speed indexes of 95 or higher, and two who were Superior race horses.

On the show front, Jaguar Speed Girl and Squaw Jag Bars were the top producers.

Jaguar Speed Girl, a 1970 brown mare out of Brown Lace, produced Itsa Long Story, a Superior western pleasure horse; Itsa Nother Story, an AQHA Champion and Superior western pleasure horse; and Hezacoy Story, an amateur and youth Superior western pleasure horse.

Squaw Jag Bars, a 1967 bay mare out of Tonabar, produced Mrs B's Story, an AQHA Champion and a Superior halter and western pleasure horse; and Mrs M Story, an open and youth Superior western pleasure horse.

All five of the above top-notch performers were sired by Story Man, who was AAA on the track and an AQHA Champion and Superior halter and western pleasure horse. The son of Go Man Go and Tattle Tale, Story Man was chosen by Mrs. Beresford as her junior sire, specifically to be bred to the Jaguar daughters.

Other top producers by Jaguar were Jaguar's Tale and Jill St John.

Jaguar's Tale, a 1968 brown mare out of Spanish Tale, produced Some Kinda Jaguar, a runner with a speed index of 93, and Tales Teddy Too, a Superior halter horse.

Jill St John, a 1959 brown mare out of Sally's Blue Bonnet, produced Jill's Lady Jane, an open and youth AQHA Champion and open Superior western riding horse; and Skipper Jill, a Superior halter horse.

First as an early day champion, then as a sire who headed two great breeding programs, and finally as a horse whose influence has carried down through the generations, Jaguar met every challenge head on and came away a winner.

He couldn't help but do so. On both sides of his pedigree, it was in his blood.

JACKIE BEE

By Frank Holmes

A well-balanced, athletic horse, he became an all-time leading sire.

"IF JACKIE BEE had been a man instead of a horse, he'd have been the kind of man you'd like to partner up with; the kind of man you'd be proud to call a friend."

High praise indeed, but it is exactly how Duane Walker of Canton, Kan., feels about the big gray stallion with whom he shared 23 years of his life.

When Walker introduced the Jackie Bee line of horses to the AQHA show world in the early 1970s, it was seen by much of the country as a completely new, male-based strain. Walker doesn't disagree with that assessment, but knows that there's a bit more to the story.

"Looking back," he says, "I guess I'd have to agree with those folks who thought Jackie Bee founded a new family of

A 1967 photo of Jackie Bee taken shortly after Duane Walker purchased him.

PHOTO COURTESY DUANE WALKER

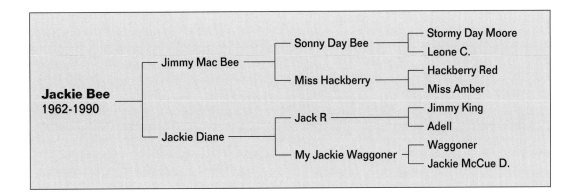

```
                                          ┌─ Stormy Day Moore
                          ┌─ Sonny Day Bee ─┤
         ┌─ Jimmy Mac Bee ─┤               └─ Leone C.
         │                 │               ┌─ Hackberry Red
         │                 └─ Miss Hackberry ┤
Jackie Bee ┤                                └─ Miss Amber
1962-1990  │                                ┌─ Jimmy King
         │                 ┌─ Jack R ──────┤
         └─ Jackie Diane ──┤               └─ Adell
                           │                     ┌─ Waggoner
                           └─ My Jackie Waggoner ┤
                                                 └─ Jackie McCue D.
```

Quarter Horses. They were unique in their *look* and consistent in their size, structure, muscling, and color. And they bred true to type.

"Where I'd tend to disagree is that I don't think Jackie did it all by himself. He had a little help along the way, both from the outstanding line of foundation Quarter Horses he came from, and the outstanding foundation Quarter Horse mares he was bred to. It was a combination of those factors that created the new line."

Sunflower Roots

When it comes to Kansas Quarter Horses and their breeding, Walker should know what he's talking about. A Sunflower State native, he was born and raised near the small town of Brookville.

After graduating from high school in 1953, Walker went to work for a local grain elevator. Shortly thereafter, he married his childhood sweetheart, Jo Hanssen, who hailed from nearby Lorraine. In 1958 he became the manager of a grain elevator in Canton and relocated there.

By the mid-1960s Walker was firmly settled into life as a grain elevator part-owner and manager, and head of a family that included four children: Tim, Kathy, Cindy, and Dennis.

It was at this point that he decided to seriously pursue what had always been one of his major interests—Quarter Horses.

"For as far back as I can remember," Walker says, "I've liked horses. Even when I was a kid, I always had horses around. By my late teens, I began to realize that there

Halter and Performance Record: None.

Progeny Record:

Foal Crops: 26	Superior Halter Awards: 12
Foals Registered: 1,009	Performance Point-Earners: 222
AQHA Champions: 7	Performance Points Earned: 3,966
Youth AQHA Champions: 9	Performance Registers of Merit: 91
World Champions: 3	Superior Performance Awards: 8
Halter Point-Earners: 168	Race Starters: 1
Halter Points Earned: 3,913.5	

were several Kansas Quarter Horse families that were head and shoulders about the rest.

"The Ready Money W. line was one of them. Ready Money was an Oklahoma Star-Bert-bred horse. He was owned by Hunter Wheat of Allen, Kan., and was a five-time state cutting champion.

"The Hackberry Red line was another good one. Hackberry was a double-bred King horse owned by Earl Hubbard of Maple Hill, Kansas.

"Then there were the Jimmy Mac Bee horses owned by Ronnie Crowther of Gypsum, Kansas. Jimmy was a Waggoner's Rainy Day-bred horse.

"Jimmy's dam, Miss Hackberry, was one of the early day greats. She was foaled in 1954 and won her class at the Kansas State Fair as a weanling and yearling. When she was 15, I showed her at the American Royal in Kansas City, and she won the broodmare class.

"These horses all possessed the top bloodlines of the day and were owned by horsemen I knew and admired. When I decided

This is Jimmy Mac Bee, Jackie Bee's sire. Bred and owned by Ronnie Crowther of Gypsum, Kan., the 1958 dun was sired by Sonny Day Bee and was out of Miss Hackberry, by Hackberry Red.

"She cost me $300, and I borrowed the money from his bank."

—*Duane Walker*

to get into the Quarter Horse business, it seemed only natural that I would draw from their blood."

A Matched Pair

Duane Walker did not kick off his breeding program with Jackie Bee, but with a pair of closely related mares.

"Frosty Money and Tee Jay Rusty were both daughters of Jimmy Mac Bee," he says, "and they were the first two good Quarter Horse mares I ever owned. Frosty was out of Red Dee Money, by My Red

Money, and I bought her from a local banker in 1964 when she was a yearling. She cost me $300, and I borrowed the money from his bank.

"Tim, my oldest boy, showed Frosty quite a bit, and she was the first AQHA high-point youth halter mare in the nation, an AQHA Champion and a Superior halter horse. Later, I sold her for $10,000, and she went on to produce The Continental and Robert Redford, both of whom were top show horses and sires.

"I bought Tee Jay Rusty, who was out of Kenny Linn, by Boys' Buck, a year or so

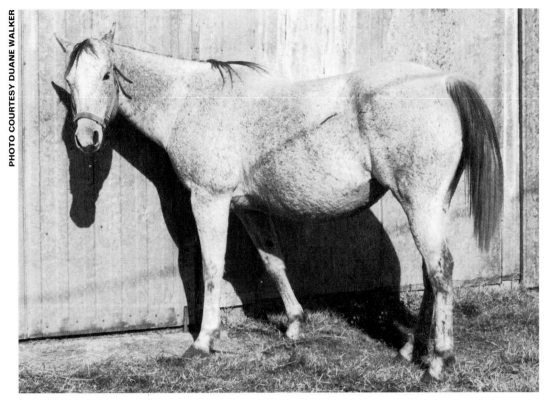

PHOTO COURTESY DUANE WALKER

Jackie Diane, a 1957 roan mare by Jack R. and out of My Jackie Waggoner, was the dam of Jackie Bee.

PHOTO BY GUY KASSAL, COURTESY DUANE WALKER

This photo of Jackie Bee was taken in 1980 when he was in his prime.

Prior to buying Jackie Bee, Walker showed Jackie's paternal half-sister Frosty Money to an AQHA Championship and a Superior in halter. Frosty Money went on to produce The Continental and Robert Redford, who both became top halter horses and sires.

Walker first laid eyes on the typey youngster when he was 1 day old.

later. Like Frosty, we showed Rusty to her Superior in halter, and then sold her too.

"We enjoyed so much success with Frosty," he continues, "that I bought her dam and her granddam, Irvin's Babe. By 1966, I had accumulated some additional mares, so I leased My Red Money to breed them to.

"My Red Money was a 1952 bay stallion by Ready Money W. His dam was Miss Amber, a Matador Ranch mare who, through her daughters Miss Hackberry, Roney's Babe, and Miss Showdown, figured prominently in my early breeding program.

"My Red Money was a good stallion and a fair sire, and I kept a couple of his daughters as broodmares. But I didn't buy him because, by that time, I had my eye on another horse I liked a little better."

Taking On a Partner

That horse was Jackie Bee, a 1962 gray stallion by Jimmie Mac Bee and out of Jackie Diane, by Jack R.

Although Walker first laid eyes on the typey youngster when he was 1 day old, Duane had to exercise a considerable amount of patience before being able to acquire him.

"Jackie Bee was bred by Glen Davis of Canton," Walker says. "Glen was a good friend of mine, and he kept his horses right on the edge of town. I happened to drop by his place on the day Jackie was born.

"I wanted that colt from the get-go, and it wasn't very long before I made Glen a firm offer to buy him. He turned it down, so the next year I made him another one.

"He turned that offer down, too, and this went on for several years. In the meantime, we were doing well with Jackie's half-sisters, and I even bred some mares to him when he got old enough.

"In January 1967 I was getting ready to attend the National Western Livestock Show in Denver. On the evening before I was to leave, I called Glen and told him I was headed west to buy a stud.

"I said when I got in the car the next morning my standing offer to buy Jackie was off. It was all a big bluff because I still wanted the horse. Later that evening, Glen called me back and told me Jackie was mine.

"It took me five years to get Jackie Bee, but that's how it came about."

By the time Jackie Bee and Duane Walker partnered up, the stallion was, for all practical purposes, past the age for a halter career. That didn't really bother Walker though. Jackie suited him to a "T", and he was convinced the big gray was just the horse to take his program to the next level.

"By the time I got Jackie," he says, "he had matured into quite an individual. He stood around 15.2 and weighed about 1,300 pounds. Structurally, he was very correct, with good bone and a good foot.

"He was a nice-headed horse, with a kind eye and little fox ears. He had a powerful front end and nice, high withers. His back was a little long, but that never bothered me because he had such a strong loin.

"If I had to fault Jackie, it would be that he didn't have as powerful a set of britches as I would have liked. But his foals did, so that kind of evened out.

"It was never our intent when we bought Jackie to try to turn him into a show horse," he continues. "But we did show him a couple of times in 1967, just to let folks know we had him. He never won any classes, but he always placed.

"One show that sticks out in my mind was at Rose Hill, Kansas. There were seven or eight horses in the aged stallion class that day. Jackie stood fourth or fifth, and the stud that placed right behind him was Tiny Watch, the 1965 and 1966 AQHA

PHOTO BY GUY KASSAL, COURTESY DUANE WALKER

Another 1980 photo of Jackie Bee that portrays him as the type of good-looking athlete Duane Walker has always tried to raise.

World Champion Quarter Running Stallion and a horse who went on to earn his AQHA Championship.

"Those two horses—Jackie Bee and Tiny Watch—didn't fit in with the rest of the studs in the class. But, as time would tell, they were the shape of things to come. And, although we never won any halter classes with Jackie, we did accomplish what we set

Tee J Black Jill was the first AQHA Champion sired by Jackie Bee. She was also a youth AQHA Champion and earned Superiors in halter and western pleasure. The Tee J (or Jay) prefix, by the way, comes from the first letters in the names of Walker's son, Tim, and wife Jo.

A New Look

Walker and Jackie Bee wasted little time in introducing their product to the Quarter Horse world. Predominately gray and black, the Jackie Bee offspring were also easily recognizable by the Tee J (or Jay) prefix that most had before their names and the fact that they consistently possessed more size than typical for the day and age.

"When I broke into the halter horse game in the mid-1960s and early 1970s," Walker points out, "I was surrounded by tough horses. They were from such families as Paul A., Bert, Wimpy II, King, Poco Bueno, Star Duster, and Pat Star Jr.

"And they were all basically the same type. They'd carry quite a bit of muscle distributed over a frame that stood anywhere from 14 to 15.1 hands. They were the old bulldog type.

"The top side of Jackie's pedigree was full of those same type of horses, but his bottom side was a little different. Jackie Diane, his dam, was by Jack R, who was from the My Texas Dandy line of running horses. Jackie Diane had a real breedy, Thoroughbred look to her, and I think she had a lot to do with the extra size Jackie sired."

Along with the running blood behind Jackie Bee's dam, Walker is again quick to credit Jackie Bee's broodmare band for much of the early success he enjoyed as a sire.

"People have always asked me what criteria I looked for in a broodmare," Walker says. "I told them I just demanded that two things be present. First, they had to be close by, and second, they had to be affordable.

"That might seem to be a trite kind of answer, but those two things really did have a lot to do with how I assembled my original band of mares.

"I did like certain foundation families, and I did like size and body volume," he continues, "so I tried to pick up mares who had those traits. But we weren't rich people. We were building our grain elevator business, raising a family, and starting a Quarter Horse breeding program. So we bought whatever mares we could afford. And they worked for us."

out to do. We wanted to get him out before the public. They liked him, they bred to him, and they bought his foals, and that enabled us to build up our breeding program and stay in the horse business."

PHOTO BY GEORGE AXT, COURTESY DUANE WALKER

George Axt
Calif. - Texas - Ohio - New York

FORT WORTH

This Jackie Bee son, Tee J Black Jack, earned 31 halter points. He's shown here with Jerry Wells after winning the 2-year-old stallion class at the 1970 Southwestern Livestock Exposition and Horse Show in Fort Worth.

PHOTO BY HAROLD CAMPTON, COURTESY DUANE WALKER

Harold Campton

Tee Jay Janie, shown here with Stretch Bradley, typified the Jackie Bee look of the 1970s. The 1971 gray mare was the 1977 AQHA High-Point Halter Horse.

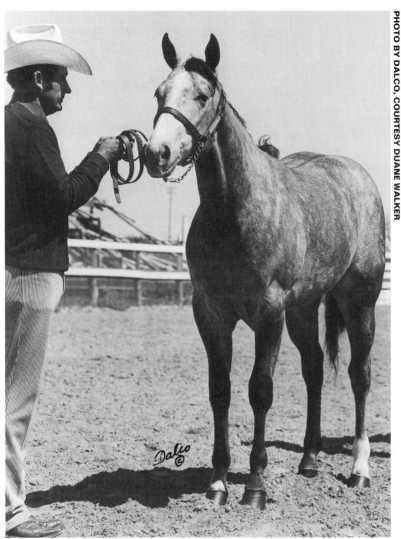

Jay Kay Billy Jack was the first horse sired by Jackie Bee to win a world championship. The earner of 184 youth and 331 open halter points, he was the 1975 Youth World Champion Aged Gelding.

Shades of Gray

The first Duane Walker-Jackie Bee foal crop out of his "cost-effective" broodmare band hit the ground in 1968. From it came the stallion's first two show ring stars: Tee J Black Jack, a black stallion out of Roney's Babe, and Tee J Black Jill, a black mare out of Wedel's Flit Leo.

Jack earned 31 halter points and became a successful sire. Jill was an open and youth AQHA Champion, and a Superior halter and western pleasure horse.

Over the course of the next decade—from the early 1970s to the early 1980s—the Jackie Bees became a fixture in the halter

ring. Four of the stallion's brightest stars during this era were Tee Jay Janie, Te Jay O'Hara Miss, Jay Kay Billy Jack, and Tee Jay Jackie Sue.

Janie, a 1971 gray mare out of Sally Ann Jane, was the 1977 AQHA High-Point Halter Horse, the 1974 Youth AQHA Reserve World Champion 3-Year-Old Mare, an AQHA Champion, and a Superior halter horse.

O'Hara Miss, a 1973 gray mare out of Irvin's Peppy, was the 1978 AQHA High-Point Halter Horse, the 1976 AQHA World Champion 3-Year-Old Mare, the 1978 AQHA Reserve World Champion Aged Mare, and a Superior halter horse.

Billy Jack, a 1971 gray gelding out of Miss Dorothy, was the 1975 AQHA High-Point Junior Halter Horse and Halter Gelding, the 1975 Youth AQHA World Champion Aged Gelding, and the 1976 Youth AQHA Reserve World Champion Aged Gelding. In addition, he was a youth AQHA Champion, an open and youth Superior halter horse, and a youth Superior showmanship horse.

Jackie Sue, a 1973 gray mare out of Tee Jay Sue Bar, was the 1975 Youth World Champion 2-Year-Old Mare, and a Superior halter horse.

Other Tee Jay stars of the 1970s included: Tee Jay Shasta, an AQHA Champion; Tee Jay Showman, a two-time youth AQHA Champion; Tee Jay Rob, a Superior halter and western pleasure horse; Tee Jay Poco Jack and Tee Jay Della, Superior halter horses; Two Way Split and Tee Jay Babe Sis, Superior western pleasure horses; and Tee Jay Judy, a Superior hunter under saddle horse.

Also featured during this period were the sons and daughters of what Walker came to view as one of his golden crosses—Jackie Bee on Badger Gal 50.

"Badger Gal was a Burnett Ranch mare," he explains. "She was a 1954 sorrel mare sired by Grey Badger II and out of Triangle Lady 50, by Red Buck.

"I never owned the mare. She belonged to Marshall Hoy of El Dorado, Kansas. Marshall was an old-time cowboy, and he had received the filly as a yearling from the rancher he worked for.

"Marshall kept Badger Gal for years.

PHOTO BY HAROLD CAMPTON, COURTESY DUANE WALKER

Tee Jay Della, who earned a Superior in halter, was another Jackie Bee star of the 1970s. Mary Anne Paris is at the halter.

He bred her off and on and then, when she was 15 or so, retired her. I had always liked the mare and asked Marshall if he'd consider selling her.

"He said he wouldn't because he'd gotten her as a gift, and it wouldn't be right to sell her. But he told me to just take her and raise a foal from her. I told him that didn't seem fair, but I would take her, raise a foal, and send her back to him in foal. We both figured that sounded okay, so we shook hands on it.

"I bred Badger Gal to Jackie for the first time when she was 17. She went on to have seven foals in a row by him — four fillies and three colts. They were some of the best horses I ever raised, and I kept most of them. The ones that were Marshall's, I either bought or sold them for him. It was a good deal for both of us."

Of the seven Jackie Bee-Badger Gal 50 foals, six were shown. Tee Jay Bee Bee, a 1971 sorrel mare, and Tee Jay Hancock, a 1974 gray gelding, were youth AQHA Champions and Superior halter horses. Tee Jay Badger Bee, a 1972 sorrel mare, was an AQHA Champion and a Superior halter horse.

Tee Jay Misty Dawn, Tee Jay Badger Mac, and Tee Jay Badger were all halter and performance point-earners. Tee Jay Badger also served as a Walker herd sire for more than a decade.

"We both figured that sounded okay, so we shook hands on it."

Te Jay O'Hara Miss, a 1973 gray mare by Jackie Bee and out of Irvin's Peppy, was the 1978 AQHA High-Point Halter Horse. The handler is George Freeman.

PHOTO BY HAROLD CAMPTON, COURTESY DUANE WALKER

One of the few palominos sired by Jackie Bee, Tee Jay Bee Money was the 1979 PHBA World Champion Aged Mare.

PHOTO BY CATHERINE VAN DER GOES, COURTESY DUANE WALKER

PHOTO BY JILL LANDERS, COURTESY DUANE WALKER

The cross of Jackie Bee and Badger Gal 50 produced a number of champions, including Tee Jay Bee Bee, a 1971 sorrel mare who earned 180 halter and 28 performance points, a youth AQHA Championship, and a Superior halter award. She's shown here with Scott Merritt, Gering, Nebraska.

PHOTO BY DAROL DICKINSON, COURTESY DUANE WALKER

Tee Jay Badger Bee, a 1972 sorrel mare shown here with Sunny Jim Orr, was an AQHA Champion and Superior halter horse. And she was a full sister to Tee Jay Bee Bee.

Throughout the 1970s, people bought the Jackie Bees primarily for their halter potential.

209

A willing friend of all, Jackie Bee was noted for his easy-going disposition and above-average intelligence. He's shown here with 2-year-old Trenton Prieb, the Walkers' grandson.

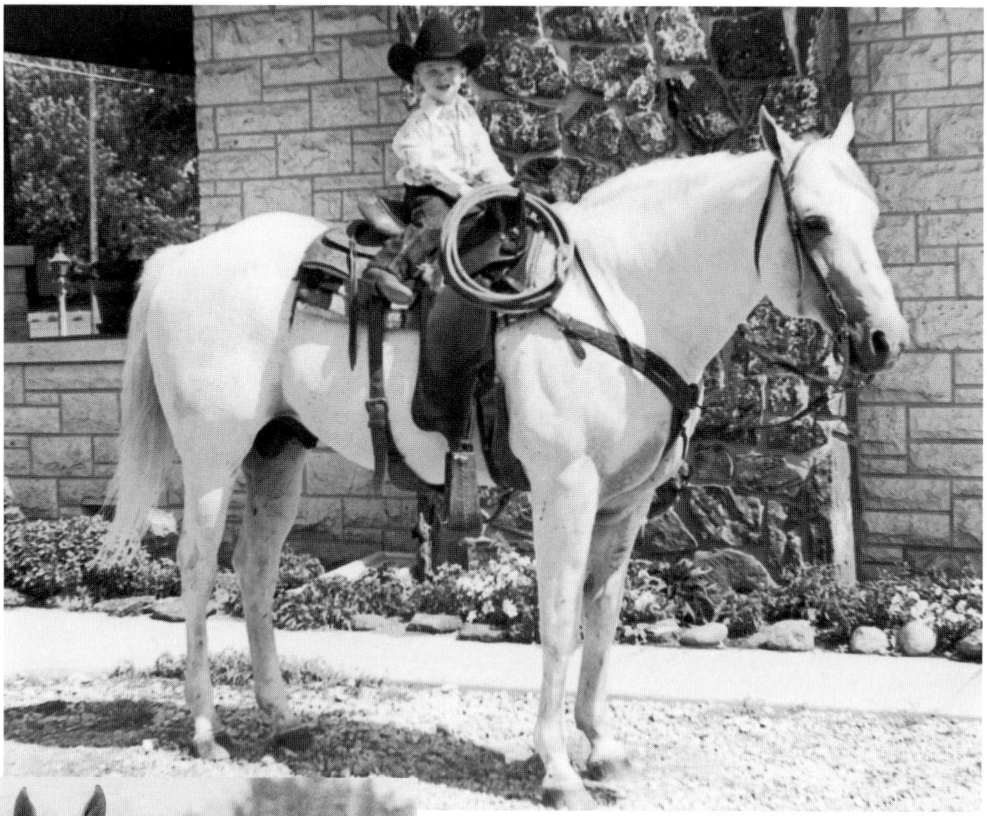

COURTESY DUANE WALKER

Tee Jay Bee Hancock was a tough gray gelding by Jackie Bee. He earned 78 halter points, 43 performance points, 29 youth halter points, and 9 amateur points. He's shown here with Sunny Jim Orr of Pueblo, Colorado.

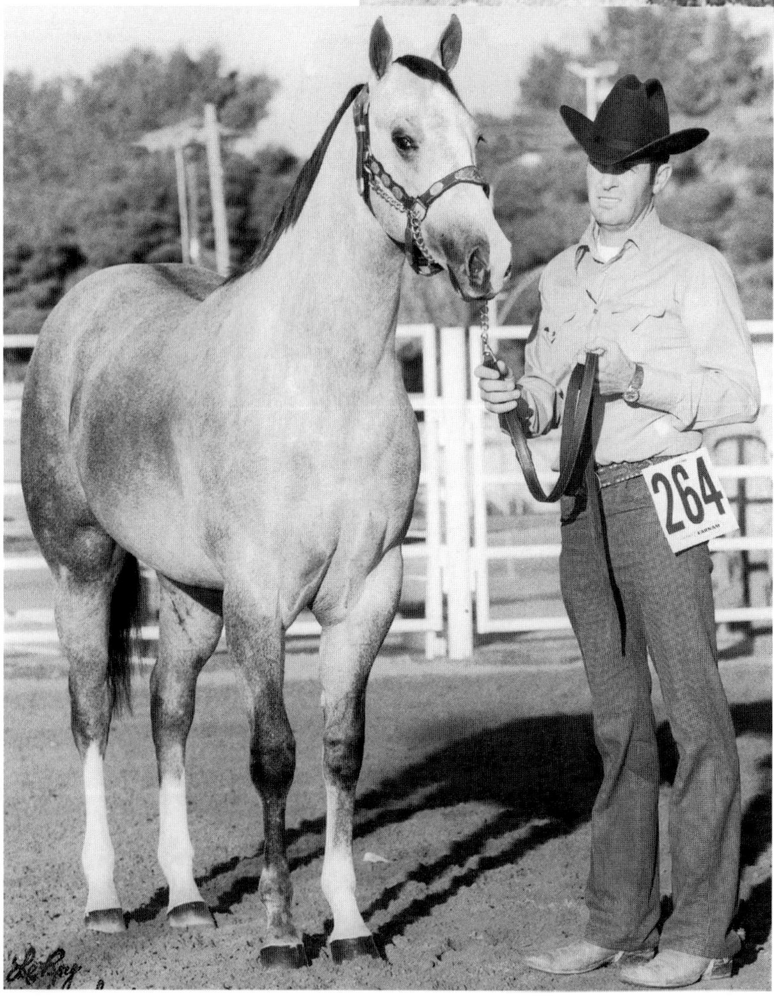

PHOTO BY LEROY WEATHERS, COURTESY DUANE WALKER

The "Look" Changes Again

With the arrival of the 1980s, the look of the halter horse changed once more. The specialized, ultrarefined Impressive horses displaced the bigger-boned, more functional Jackie Bees.

And yet the line remained popular. Whereas throughout the 1970s, people bought the Jackie Bees primarily for their halter potential, from the 1980s on they purchased them for their performance ability.

"For Jackie and me," Walker say, "that whole thing of winning in the halter ring was simply a matter of being in the right place at the right time.

"When we began concentrating on halter, it just so happened that the type that began winning was exactly the type Jackie was siring. It was a horse who was taller and breedier. You still needed a well-muscled horse, but the muscle had to be spread out over a taller frame.

"When the look changed again in the 1980s, we opted not to change with it. We

PHOTO COURTESY DUANE WALKER

Tee Jay Roman, a 1974 gray stallion, earned his AQHA Championship in 1980. Owned by Howard Dahlof of Walnut, Iowa, he went on to become a top sire in his own right.

felt we would have to give up too many traits we'd striven to breed into our horses for a decade and a half—traits like functional leg and hoof structure, disposition, athletic ability, and the willingness to use it.

"So from the early 1980s on, we put our emphasis more on performance and less on halter. It wasn't hard to do. When you get right down to it, the Jackie Bees were always bred to work."

In keeping with the program's realigned emphasis, the 1980s did not see a single Jackie Bee-sired Superior halter horse. What it did see was more and more performance stars.

Starting out the decade were horses like Tee J Ro Bee, the 1981 AQHA High-Point Junior Calf Roping Horse, 1981 AQHA High-Point Calf Roping Mare, and a Superior calf roping horse; Tee Jay Roman, an AQHA Champion; and Tee Jay Showman, an open and youth AQHA Champion.

Such horses as Lil Ms Jackie Bee, Beeville, and Tee J Robin Bee—all of whom earned their AQHA Championships—followed them. Tee Jay Jack Steel was also

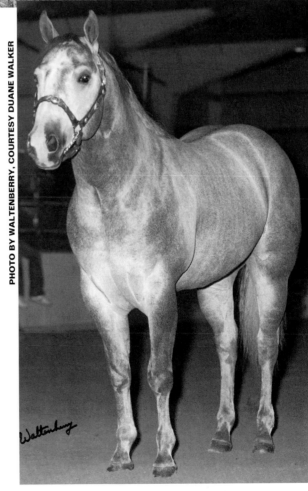

PHOTO BY WALTENBERRY, COURTESY DUANE WALKER

Tee J Jack Steel was one of Jackie Bee's most versatile get. The 1978 gray stallion was an AQHA Champion and earned 90 performance points in reining, working cow horse, western pleasure, calf roping, heading, and heeling.

211

PHOTO BY GUY KASSAL, COURTESY DUANE WALKER

Diamond Tender played a pivotal role in the Tee Jay Ranch breeding program, as he proved to be an outstanding sire when crossed on the Jackie Bee mares.

just as well-known as a sire of ranch and arena working stock.

Likewise, Tee Jay Black Jack, Tee Jay Super Jack, Tee Jay Badger Bee, Tee Jay Scamp, Bobcats Jay Bee, and Tee Jay Rob all enjoyed successful careers at stud.

By 1974, Walker had retained enough of Jackie's daughters that he needed a non-related junior sire. That year, he signed a five-year lease on Diamond Tender, a 1962 sorrel stallion by Diamond Signal and out of Brandetta. An AQHA Champion with points in halter, trail, and western pleasure, Tender proved to be an excellent cross on the Jackie Bee mares.

By the time the lease expired, Tender's owner had passed away. His widow then transferred ownership of the stallion permanently into Walker's name.

In 1984 Walker added another junior sire to his stallion battery. This was Gold Fingers, a 1972 gray stallion by Eddie Red Rose and out of Sadie Lace. Like Diamond Tender, Gold Fingers was an AQHA Champion. In addition, he was also the 1976 AQHA World Champion Junior Heeling Horse and the 1976 AQHA High-Point Steer Roping Stallion.

The Producers

Bred to Diamond Tender and Gold Fingers, plus a host of outside stallions, the Jackie Bee mares began proving their mettle as producers.

Tee Jay Janie, Tee Jay Babe Sis, Te Jay O'Hara Miss, Tee Jay Misty Dawn, and My Lady Diamond were the dams of AQHA world or reserve world champions, or AQHA high-point horses.

Tee J Frosty Money, Tee Jay Barlita, Jackie McEchols, Tee Jay Bar Maid, and My Lady Diamond were all AQHA Champion producers.

In addition, 13 Jackie Bee daughters produced 17 Superior halter horses, and 11 more produced the earners of 29 Superior performance awards.

By the late 1980s, on the basis of what his first and second generations of performers had accomplished, Jackie Bee

an AQHA Champion and one of Jackie's most versatile get, with points earned in halter, reining, calf roping, working cow horse, western pleasure, and heeling.

By this time the Jackie Bee sons were also doing their part to keep the family name near the forefront.

Tee Jay Roman, owned by Howard Dahlof of Walnut, Iowa, became widely respected as both a sire and maternal grandsire of world-caliber halter horses.

Tee Jay Three Bars, owned by Bill and Carole Smith of Thermopolis, Wyo., became

How D Mae Bee, a 1979 gray stallion by Tee Jay Super Jack, by Jackie Bee, was the 1983 AQHA World Champion Junior Reining Horse and the 1984 AQHA World Champion Senior Reining Horse. He was owned at that time by Tom McFadden, Hazard, Neb., and trained and shown by Doug Milholland.

Richard Bergquist, Marietta, Okla., bought the horse later and he's the rider shown here.

Bill and Carole Smith of Thermopolis, Wyo., have been long-time fans of the Jackie Bee line. At their 17th Annual WYO Quarter Horse Sale held in May 2000, Wyo Gray Bars Butch, a 1992 gray gelding by Tee Jay Three Bars and out of Gray Bee Jay, by Gold Fingers, sold for an eye-popping $81,000.

Gold Fingers was another stallion who crossed very successfully on the Jackie Bee mares. He was a 1972 gray stallion by Eddie Red Rose, by Eddie Cinco, and out of Sadie Lace, by Blue Gold.

My Lady Diamond, shown here with Billy Allen in the saddle, was another of the top-producing Jackie Bee daughters. Among her foals was Zan Parr Primrose, the 1990 AQHA Reserve All-Around High-Point Horse and the 1990 AQHA All-Around High-Point Junior Horse.

was listed on virtually every AQHA all-time leading sires and all-time leading maternal grandsires list.

"By this time," Walker says, "Jackie had truly become a member of our family. To give him just part of the credit due, I can honestly say that he helped pay for our ranch, build our home, and educate our kids. I've always said that the grain elevator business made our living, and Jackie Bee made our living better.

"And, he was such a nice horse to be around. If you wanted him to act like a breeding stallion, he would. If you wanted to ride him and have him act like a gelding, he'd do that too.

"Jackie liked people," he continues. "He'd come up to anyone, anywhere, to be petted and scratched. He didn't like to be treated rough, but then, there never was any reason to."

Indicative of the big gray stallion's tem-

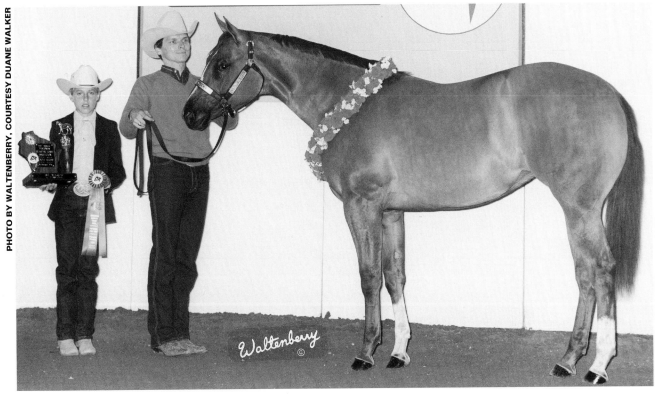

Lois Layne, a 1984 red dun mare by Sonny Supermann and out of Tee Jay Babe Sis, by Jackie Bee, was the 1985 AQHA Amateur World Champion Yearling Filly and the 1986 AQHA Amateur World Champion 2-Year-Old Mare. She was owned by Mary Ellsworth, Elkhorn, Wisconsin.

Here's Heavenly Ohara, a 1986 sorrel mare and maternal granddaughter of Jackie Bee. She was by Mr Conclusion and out of Te Jay O'Hara Miss. The earner of 277.5 halter points, Heavenly Ohara was the 1988 AQHA World Champion 2-Year-Old Mare, 1988 AQHA Youth World Champion 2-Year-Old Mare, 1989 AQHA World Champion 3-Year-Old Mare, and the 1991 AQHA High-Point Halter Mare.

Duane Walker and Jackie Bee spent more than two decades together and created an enduring family of horses who not only excelled in all phases of show competition, but also as working ranch, rodeo, and recreational trail horses.

"That would go on until they both got tired, and then you'd see that dog down in the shade between Jackie's legs, taking a nap."

perament was his long-time friendship with an Australian Shepherd dog named Smoke.

"It was in the mid-1970s," Walker remembers, "when Sandy Hollar, a South Texas cutting horse trainer, gave me Smoke as a gift.

"For most of Jackie's life, we kept him in a pen right to the south of the house. Every day, Smoke would run into that pen and growl and bark and snap at Jackie. Jackie would take after him like he was going to eat him alive, and run him out of the pen.

"That would go on until they both got tired, and then you'd see that dog down in the shade between Jackie's legs, taking a nap. Jackie would just stand there, like he was protecting him. They had quite a relationship."

By the fall of 1990, the Duane Walker-Jackie Bee tandem was ready to take life a little easier. They had slowed down to the point where a near-dispersal sale was in order, and it was scheduled for Nov. 3-4 at the ranch.

In the sale catalog, Walker announced that he would retain the then-28-year-old Jackie, three of his daughters, and one Gold

Fingers mare. He further commented that every year he wondered if Jackie would be around for the next one. Unfortunately for both Walker and the Quarter Horse world, the wondering soon came to an end.

"When Jackie was about 23," Walker says, "he lost the muscle tone in his esophagus. Sometimes when he was eating, he would choke. At first, we could always get him through it.

"We could no longer let him graze though, or bed him in straw. We ground all of his rations together, and then moistened them. Then he could swallow.

"Occasionally, though, he would still choke. We'd work him through it and relieve him. He wouldn't eat for two or three days after each episode, but finally he'd come around and get going, and he'd be all right for six months or so.

"By the time we were getting ready for our dispersal sale, we knew Jackie's breeding days were over. Other than that, he seemed to feel good. In fact, Jo and I were out with him on a Sunday, two weeks before the sale.

PHOTO COURTESY DUANE WALKER

Jackie Bee nuzzles Smoke, his long-time canine friend.

"He came out of the barn and showed off for us a little bit — he kind of tried to rear up and whirl around. It didn't work as well for him as it had when he was 4 or 5 years old, but he still felt good.

"On Tuesday, two days after that, he choked again. We got him through it, but he wouldn't eat or drink at all. On Thursday, I had the vet do something we had never done before. We gave Jackie IV fluids to get him going. We decided not to do that again.

"Orville Burtis, a past AQHA president from Manhattan, Kan., had died that week. On Saturday morning, Oct. 28, I left to attend his funeral. When I got home, Jackie had just died.

"I guess it was time.

"There's really no way," he continues, "that people could really understand how much of an effect on a person a horse like Jackie could have.

"I guess I was probably more emotionally attached to him than most people would have been. But how could I not be? He was such an important part of our family as far as our lifestyle went. We shared so

PHOTO COURTESY DUANE WALKER

After Jackie Bee's death at the age of 28, the Walkers buried him in front of the pen that had been his home for most of his life.

many experiences and met so many people together — some of whom went on to become lifelong friends.

"I knew it at the time, but I wasn't as aware of it as I am now. It's hard to describe a horse like Jackie, hard to put him into words. I guess the best I can do is just say he was a great partner, and one of my best friends."

217

17 CHICADO V

By Ty Wyant

She left her timeless mark on the Quarter Horse breed through her sons and daughters.

EVERY ONCE in a long while a horse comes along who just does everything asked of him, or her. Chicado V was such a horse. Foaled in 1950 on Frank Vessels' ranch in Los Alamitos, Calif., Chicado V excelled on the race track despite a fragile constitution and then left her timeless mark on the Quarter Horse breed through her sons and daughters.

A little brown mare, Chicado V was sired by Chicaro Bill (*Legends 1*) and was out of Do Good. Chicaro Bill is best remembered as a terrific sire of broodmares. Another of his daughters was Flicka, who produced several AAA runners.

Do Good, owned by the Vessels, also produced Senor Bill, a full brother to Chicado V, who was AAA on the track and who sired several ROM race and per-

Chicado V was not impressive-looking— at least not in this photo taken when she was a 3-year-old, but she had speed to burn and became a great producer.

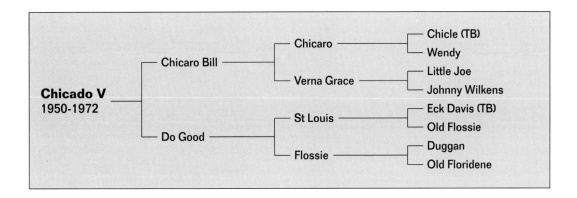

```
                                                    ┌── Chicle (TB)
                                    ┌── Chicaro ─────┤
                                    │                └── Wendy
                  ┌── Chicaro Bill ─┤
                  │                 │                ┌── Little Joe
                  │                 └── Verna Grace ─┤
Chicado V ────────┤                                  └── Johnny Wilkens
1950-1972         │
                  │                 ┌── St Louis ────┤── Eck Davis (TB)
                  │                 │                └── Old Flossie
                  └── Do Good ──────┤
                                    │                ┌── Duggan
                                    └── Flossie ─────┤
                                                     └── Old Floridene
```

formance offspring and one AQHA Champion, Senora Michele.

In addition to her racing and producing accomplishments, Chicado V was also a sweetheart. Standing just 15 hands, Chicado V probably had a heart as big as a washtub. She had to, in order to race with such blazing speed on legs that were less than ideal.

But let's back up a little bit.

Earl Holmes, a cantankerous man with a soft heart, lived a life that was connected, on and off, to the Vessels family for over four decades. He started as a groom cleaning stalls, and in 1952 he was given the responsibility of caring for Chicado V.

After working as a groom on many of Vessels' horses, Holmes became a public trainer and later saddled the 1972 World Champion Quarter Running Horse, Mr Jet Moore, and a laundry list of other major stakes winners. Holmes retired from the track in the early 1990s to manage the showplace Vessels Stallion Farm. He held that position until he died of heart disease in 1995.

"Chicado V was gentle, real gentle—in everything," Holmes said in a 1990 interview. "She was born broke, I tell you, and you wouldn't know she was in the barn. She was real kind."

Bay Meadows is a track south of San Francisco. Its saddling paddock is indoors, surrounded by noise and commotion. It was designed with gamblers in mind, not horses. Just about any 2-year-old, or older horse for that matter, comes unglued when he first sees this intimidating cavern in the grandstand.

Holmes remembered Chicado V's first appearance at Bay Meadows as a 2-year-old.

Race Record: Had six official starts on the track. Won three and placed second, and third once each. Earned $5,215, 18 points, and AAAT rating. Was 1952 Co-Racing World Champion 2-Year-Old Filly.

Produce of Dam Record:

Triple Chick	1955 stallion by Three Bars (TB)
War Chic	1956 stallion by War Bam (TB)
	1958 Racing World Champion 2-Year-Old Colt
	Racing Register of Merit
Table Tennis	1957 mare by Spotted Bull (TB)
	1960 Racing World Champion 3-Year-Old Filly
	Racing Register of Merit
Three Chicks	1959 brown stallion by Three Bars (TB)
	Open AQHA Champion
	Racing Register of Merit
Chicado Chick	1960 stallion by Three Bars (TB)
	Open AQHA Champion
	Racing and Performance Registers of Merit
Anchor Chic	1961 stallion by Anchor Watch (TB)
	Racing Register of Merit
The Ole Man	1963 stallion by Three Bars (TB)
	Racing Register of Merit
Successor	1953 stallion by Go Man Go
	Racing Register of Merit
Alisal	1968 mare by Double Bid

"She just walked in (the saddling paddock), looked around, and put her head underneath my arm, like a scared little rabbit. And she looked like a rabbit in the starting gate. When she was in the gate, it was like she was standing on her toes—she had big ears, and that's all you could see, she was so little."

Holmes' boss in the Vessels operation was trainer Farrell Jones, who didn't like

These photos were taken at Pomona, Calif., in October 1953 when Chicado V set a track and world record for 3-year-olds of 17.9 seconds for 350 yards.

CHICADO V. -AAA.
BY CHICARO BILL OUT OF DO GOOD by ST. LOUIS
OCT. 3, 1953   POMONA   350 YDS. - 17.9
NEW TRACK RECORD & NEW WORLDS RECORD FOR 3 YR.-OLDS

TRACK RECORDS
5201 POM 9/27/52
5263 BM 10/10/52
6539 POM 10/3/53

WORLD RECORDS
5201 POM 9/27/52
6539 POM 10/3/53

Jones quickly decided he wanted to train Chicado V and she rejoined his stable.

Chicado V when she was initially placed in training. Jones had good reason. Chicado V was calf-kneed, and she always lagged behind the other horses in training gallops. Those were hardly the characteristics of a future champion, and Jones knew it.

"But jockey Louie Juarez was working for Jones, and the first time he breezed her, he told me the filly could really run," Holmes recalled.

Nonetheless, Jones sent Chicado V home, and Frank Vessels Sr. then sent her to trainer Eddie Moreno. In her first start, with Moreno training her, Chicado V set a track record at Pomona and ran the

fastest 350 yards ever run by a 2-year-old (18.1 seconds).

After that remarkable racing debut, Jones quickly decided he wanted to train Chicado V and she rejoined his stable.

Chicado V was like a car with a huge engine and weak suspension. She was fast, incredibly fast, but her calf-kneed legs could not stand up to a constant racing schedule.

After her record-setting debut at Pomona, she only made one more start as a 2-year-old. That was her first trip to Bay Meadows. She beat the fleet mare Bardella by a length, and her 17.2-second time for the 330 yards equaled the track record.

As a broodmare, Chicado V became one of the premier producers in the Quarter Horse industry. The date and location of this picture are not known, but it obviously was snowing.

Farrell Jones, the legendary southern California horseman who trained Chicado V and many other greats.

Scoop Vessels (left), grandson of Frank Vessels Sr. and the current manager of Vessels Stallion Farm, with the late Earl Holmes, a longtime manager of the farm. Scoop's dad, Frank Vessels Jr., was the breeder of Chicado V.

Despite just making two starts as a 2-year-old, Chicado V's brilliance was easily recognized, and she was named co-champion 2-year-old filly with Bardella.

Those two starts took their toll on the fragile filly, and Chicado V was rested for 11 months before returning to racing as a 3-year-old. She made only four starts as a 3-year-old, winning once and placing second and third once each. In her only win she defeated the older stallion Robin Reed while lowering her Pomona 350-yard track record to 17.9 seconds.

Her fourth race that year, in December, marked the end of her racing career. "She was calf-kneed, and she was sore," Holmes recalled. "In those days, horsemen didn't know a helluva lot about what to do about that kind of thing. She never broke down; she just got real sore on those knees."

Chicado V achieved a speed rating of AAAT and earned $5,215 and 18 racing points.

Chicaro Bill, the sire of Chicado V, is featured in *Legends 1*. He was a wonderful broodmare sire.

Do Good, the dam of Chicado V and several other good horses, was foaled in 1938.

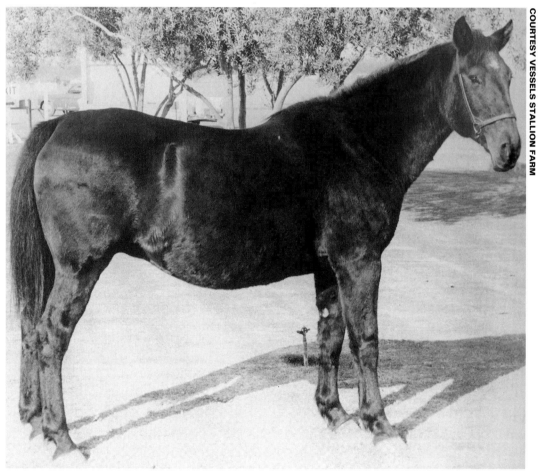

Foaled in 1955, Triple Chick, by Three Bars (TB), was Chicado V's first foal. Although unraced, he became an outstanding sire.

Broodmare Record

Chicado V was destined to be a broodmare. She was blessed with speed and had one of that era's best pedigrees. As already mentioned, she was by leading sire Chicaro Bill and out of the Vessels' great mare Do Good. This made Chicado V a full sister to the top sire Senor Bill, and a half-sister to track-record-holder Clabber II and the iron-legged gelding Do Win. The latter finished among the top three horses in 126 of 224 races over a 10-year span.

Chicado V produced nine foals from 1955 through 1968, and the majority of those foals are still leaving their genetic mark. Her offspring included:

- Leading sire Triple Chick, by Three Bars (TB).
- The 1958 champion 2-year-old colt War Chic, by War Bam (TB).
- The 1960 champion 3-year-old filly Table Tennis, by Spotted Bull (TB).
- Multiple-stakes winner and AQHA Champion Three Chicks, by Three Bars (TB).
- The AAA AQHA Champion Chicado Chick, by Three Bars (TB).
- Anchor Chic, by Anchor Watch (TB), racing ROM.
- The multiple stakes winner and great sire The Ole Man, by Three Bars (TB).
- Successor, by Go Man Go, racing ROM.
- Alisal, a bay mare by Double Bid.

Table Tennis, Chicado V's 1957 foal by Spotted Bull (TB), started a small dynasty of her own when she was retired from the track. She was the dam of the 1965 World Champion 2-Year-Old Filly Rapid Volley, by Three Bars (TB). Later, when Rapid Volley was bred to Go Man Go, she produced Really Rapid, who, in turn, produced leading sire By Yawl, by Dash For Cash.

When Rapid Volley was bred to Easy Jet, she produced Perks, a 1977 brown mare who earned a racing ROM. Perks, in turn, produced 15 foals, 12 of whom earned their racing ROM. Among them were:

- Lady Classic Cash, foaled in 1983 and sired by Dash For Cash, was a major stakes winner of $252,883 and earned a Superior title in racing.
- The barrel racing sire Dash For Perks

Table Tennis started a small dynasty of her own.

Table Tennis, foaled in 1957, was by Spotted Bull (TB) and out of Chicado V. The brown mare became the 1960 Quarter Racing World Champion 3-Year-Old Filly. She then became an excellent producer when retired to the broodmare band.

The Ole Man, out of Chicado V and by Three Bars (TB), became one of the breed's all-time great sires, and certainly one of its most prolific. He sired 1,876 foals from 28 crops, and his get included 15 stakes winners and 10 AQHA Champions. This photo appeared in a Roy Browning Ranches ad in *The Quarter Horse Journal*, December 1987.

Joseph P. Wilson
Purcell, OK

was foaled in 1987 and sired by Dash For Cash.

- Cash Perks, a 1984 brown mare by Dash For Cash, was the 1986 World Champion 2-Year-Old Filly.

Despite the success of her daughter Table Tennis, Chicado V is far and away best known through three of her sons sired by Three Bars (TB): Triple Chick, Three Chicks, and The Ole Man.

Scooper Chick was a AAA AQHA Champion grandson of Chicado V. He was by Triple Chick and out of Scoop Bam, by War Bam (TB).

Triple Chick

Foaled in 1955 and Chicado V's first foal, Triple Chick never made it to the track because he foundered as a yearling. However, his sensational pedigree and striking good looks earned him a future as a stallion.

Triple Chick's foals did well on the track and in the show ring. He sired 28 stakes winners and 8 AQHA Champions.

Triple Chick's sons included Scooper Chick, Boston Mac, and Triple's Image.

Scooper Chick was an AQHA Champion often described as one of the best-looking Quarter Horses in history. He won five stakes races and defeated the great world champion Jet Deck in Jet Deck's final race.

Boston Mac, a 1968 black stallion, qualified for the All American Futurity, earning his ROM in racing, and then became a top halter stallion with 90 halter points and a Superior title. He went on to become a leading sire of halter and performance horses.

Triple's Image was a Superior halter horse and AQHA Champion who became a top show horse sire.

Triple Chick's daughters included Chickamona and Cookie's Gay Way. Chickamona, out of the great mare Monita, was second in the All American Futurity and the Raton Futurity.

Cookie's Gay Way, who set a 400-yard track record at Sunland Park, became a Superior halter horse and an AQHA Champion.

Three Chicks

This 1959 brown stallion was Holmes' favorite offspring of Chicado V. "Three Chicks resembled his mother more than Triple Chick did, in height and build. He was a real kind horse to train too," Holmes said.

Triple Chick's sensational pedigree and striking good looks earned him a future as a stallion.

Frank Vessels Sr., an oilman in Long Beach, Calif., bought a ranch in nearby Los Alamitos and started hosting match races there in 1947. After California began pari-mutuel wagering on Quarter Horses in 1951, Vessels founded Los Alamitos Race Course, adjacent to the ranch. Meanwhile, Vessels had also begun his breeding operation, which became one of the nation's finest. In 1984, after the Los Alamitos track sold to Hollywood Park, the Vessels' stallion farm was moved to Bonsall in northern San Diego County.

Cash Perks, the 1986 Quarter Racing World Champion 2-Year-Old Filly, traces to Chicado V through her maternal great-granddam, Table Tennis. Cash Perks, a brown mare foaled in 1984, was sired by Dash For Cash.

Three Chicks won the now grade 1 Go Man Go Handicap and gained his AQHA Championship in the show ring. He went on to sire 39 stakes winners and 5 AQHA Champions.

Three Chicks' leading son was 1968 All American Futurity winner Three Oh's, who sired the earners of $4.8 million from just seven crops to race.

Another son, Chick's Deck, won the Kansas Futurity and was third in the Rainbow Futurity.

Three Chicks' daughters included Miss Three Wars, Le Etta Chicks, Triple Depth, and Chick Called Sue.

Miss Three Wars won the Rainbow Futurity over Easy Jet and was second to Easy Jet in the All American Futurity.

Le Etta Chicks won 11 stakes races and set 6 track records.

Triple Depth produced the 1979 champion aged stallion Azure Three.

Chick Called Sue, the 1975 champion 2-year-old filly, won the Rainbow Futurity and was second in the All American Futurity.

The Ole Man

A 1963 sorrel stallion, The Ole Man won only two minor stakes races and had career earnings of $20,657. But then he became one of the most prolific sires of race and show horses in AQHA history. His numbers are incredible. Standing much of his career at the Roy Browning Ranches in Ada, Okla., The Ole Man sired 1,876 foals from 28 crops. His final crop hit the ground in 1995 when he was 32 years old.

The Ole Man sired 15 stakes winners and 10 AQHA Champions. His offspring earned

War Chic, by War Bam (TB) and out of Chicado V, was foaled in 1956 and was the 1958 Quarter Racing World Champion 2-Year-Old Colt. The jockey here is L.G. Littell, and the trainer was C,M. Kiser. This photo was taken after War Chic won the Signal Hill Lions Club Purse at Los Alamitos, December 1960.

$1,077,061 on the track; 232 earned their racing ROMs; 78 earned 1,335.5 halter points; and 104 earned 1,430 performance points.

On the track, his top earner was Ole Sport, with winnings of $103,696. Other good racing offspring included My Old Gal Nancy, Cee Lady Bar, three-time stakes winner Be Sure Ole Lady, and the two-time stakes winner Cee Bar Girl.

In the show ring, several of The Ole Man's offspring included:
- Tee Jay Ole Jackie, a youth world champion aged gelding.
- Anna Three, a youth world show aged mare finalist and an AQHA Champion.
- Ole Sugar Ma'm, a junior hunter under saddle world show finalist and AQHA Champion.
- Ole Sompin Special, an open and youth AQHA Champion.

Wrapup

One year when Chicado V was at Sid Vail's ranch in Arizona to be bred to Three Bars (TB), she got loose in the middle of the night. The commotion woke Vail up. He looked outside and saw a horse standing there. Vail figured the horse was from a neighbor's ranch, and he was too sleepy to catch it. So he threw some rocks to scare the horse into returning home

The horse just stood there ... and then Vail realized it was Chicado V. She knew where she was supposed to be and was just hanging around.

Chicado V, a champion on the track and in the broodmare band, is still hanging around in the pedigrees of many good horses.

She died in February 1972 while in foal to Alamitos Bar.

18

MR BAR NONE

By Alan Gold

He was a great race horse and went on to become a great sire of speed horses.

FOR A "short horse," Mr Bar None covered an awful lot of miles. At ages 2 and 3, he cut a path across the Southwest like a sorrel tornado, blowing away the fastest horses of the day at tracks in five states.

Mr Bar None's story bridges the eras — not just from match racing on abandoned roads to the pari-mutuel future, but also the transition of the horse from an animal of utility to one of recreation.

Even after he retired from the track, Mr Bar None kept on the move. He was a pioneer breeding-farm commuter, going up the road a piece each day to meet his mares.

All that mileage was fitting for a horse bred, raised, and cherished by a Ford dealer. In fact, it was a burned-out headlight on a Model T that started the chain

The well-made Mr Bar None burned up the tracks in 1957 and '58.

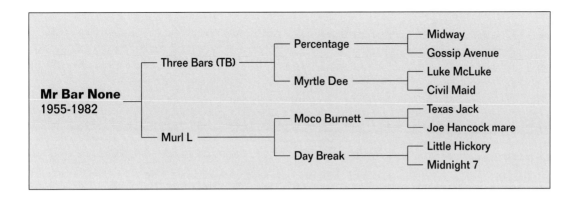

```
                                      ┌─ Midway
                         ┌─ Percentage ─┤
                         │              └─ Gossip Avenue
          ┌─ Three Bars (TB) ─┤
          │              │              ┌─ Luke McLuke
          │              └─ Myrtle Dee ─┤
Mr Bar None ─┤                          └─ Civil Maid
1955-1982    │                          ┌─ Texas Jack
          │              ┌─ Moco Burnett ─┤
          │              │              └─ Joe Hancock mare
          └─ Murl L ─────┤
                         │              ┌─ Little Hickory
                         └─ Day Break ──┤
                                        └─ Midnight 7
```

of events that led to a horse who rewrote the record books.

Oscar "June" Jeffers Jr. met his future wife, Zelma, when she came into his garage to get her headlight fixed. He did the work, but because of a glitch in the Model T's electrical system, she was back the next day with the same problem. However, the electricity between the two of them worked just fine. They got married and later moved to Wagoner, Okla., where Jeffers ran a Ford dealership selling cars, trucks, and farm equipment.

From top steer roper Barton Carter, June bought Zelma a spotted horse called Tony, who showed some speed.

As horses faded from the farming scene, Jeffers took plenty of them in on trades for new tractors and pickups. "Every time I got a new horse," Jeffers once said, "I'd take him behind the garage and test him out to see if he was fast enough to outrun Zelma and Tony. I finally outran her on a horse called Brown Jug."

Brown Jug also outran the local competition, so Jeffers hauled him down to Eagle Pass, Tex., where he met Curly Tyndall, who wanted to set up a match race. Tyndall showed him a few stout-looking horses, but Jeffers backed off. Finally Tyndall pointed to a slight-built filly.

"She didn't look like she had been weaned very long," Jeffers once recalled. "I said, 'Now I can outrun one like that.' And he said, 'Aw, now, Mr. Jeffers, you wouldn't want to do that to me, would you?'"

They settled on a $500 match and Jeffers never had a chance with Brown Jug.

"She just went by my horse like he was

Race Record: 36 starts, 22 wins, 10 seconds, 1 third; 46 racing points; $72,126.
1958 Racing World Champion
1958 Racing World Champion 3-Year-Old Stallion
1958 Racing World Champion Stallion
1958 Racing High-Money Earning Horse
1957 Racing World Champion 2-Year-Old Colt

Progeny Record:

Foal Crops: 23	Performance Point-Earners: 17
Foals Registered: 367	Performance Points Earned: 181
AQHA Champions: 4	Performance Registers of Merit: 5
World Champions: 3	Race Starters: 290
World Championships: 4	Race Money Earned: $1,156,677
Halter Point-Earners: 20	Race Registers of Merit: 183
Halter Points Earned: 190	Superior Race Awards: 7
Leading Race Money-Earner: Bar None Doll ($166,843)	

standing still," Jeffers admitted. "That lil' ol' thing outran us so bad it wasn't funny. I learned a little lesson from that race."

Jeffers also met Byrne James of Raymondville, Tex., who owned the filly, as a result of the race. James was showing Jeffers around his place when a mare named Murl L caught his eye. The Oklahoman's offer was rebuffed, but several months later James changed his mind about selling Murl L.

"I beat it down there and bought her," Jeffers said. The price was $2,500.

Murl L was by Moco Burnett and out of Day Break, by Little Hickory. She had earned a reputation as a top match-race mare in south Texas and Oklahoma, running under the name of Adelita. She achieved a AA rating at Enid, Okla., the highest rating given at the time.

Mr Bar None burning a hole in the wind with an exercise rider in the irons.

Jeffers bred her to Leo in 1951, and in August of that year, she won a 220-yard match race in Enid in :12.7. The next day, she was shown at halter and won the reserve championship. The foal she was carrying was Miss Adelita, a AAA winner of six races, including the Oklahoma Futurity. Miss Adelita went on to produce six winners of her own.

Murl L's second foal was Hy Adelita, a 1953 Hysition (TB) mare who won three races and ran second in the Oklahoma Futurity.

In 1955 Murl L produced Mr Bar None by Three Bars (TB). He was foaled on a cold February night in the paddock behind the Jeffers' home in Wagoner. The Jeffers had high hopes for the grandly named colt. June once told a *Daily Racing Form* reporter, "The first time I saw Mr Bar None right after he was born, he lifted up his head and

nickered like a big horse. Yes sir, he looked like a champion to me when he was just a few minutes old."

But after Jeffers broke Mr Bar None to saddle, the hopes began to dwindle when it looked like the colt was going to be a lazy son of a gun. The late Richard Jeffers admitted that his parents had even put a price on Mr Bar None at that point. But June lined up Tecumseh Stark, who had ridden the Jeffers' record-breaking mare NR Negraletta, to test the youngster. Stark worked the baby against NR Negraletta herself. The result restored the Jeffers' faith in Mr Bar None.

Jeffers went to a bush track at Porter, Okla., and matched Mr Bar None against a mare named Queenwood, and then against a top race horse named Vinegar Bend, winning both races.

COURTESY RICHELLE JEFFERS

A picture of Mr Bar None as a 4-month-old with his dam, Murl L.

COURTESY RICHELLE JEFFERS

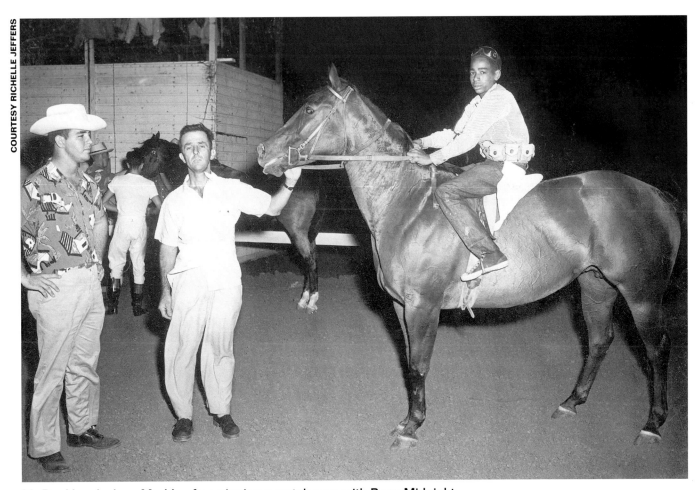

Mr Bar None's dam, Murl L, after winning a match race with Roan Midnight.

Describing this photo, Richelle Jeffers (the Jeffers' granddaughter) says: "Here's the truck and van Grandpa hauled Mr Bar None in. Eventually the van rotted and is gone, but we still use the truck to haul hay. Pictured with Grandpa is the world champion heavyweight wrestler Dick Hutton (left)."

On the Road

June Jeffers handed the keys to his Ford dealership over to his sons and loaded Mr Bar None into a 1957 model truck that had a van on the back emblazoned with "Oscar Jeffers Quarter Running Horses" and "Mr Bar None Ranch." It would be the home for the horseman and his one-horse stable for the next seven months.

"When Granddad hauled Bar None to the race tracks, he would back this van up to the stall door and let Bar None out into the stall," said granddaughter Richelle Jeffers. "He would keep the van there and he used to joke that you couldn't poke a straw between the back of the van and that stall opening. He would even sleep in the van."

Richelle isn't sure just why June kept the van smack dab against the stall door, but suspects it was possibly to keep Mr Bar None safe from any unscrupulous characters hanging around the tracks.

Mr Bar None made his official debut on March 9, 1957, at Rillito Park in Tucson. He became the first 2-year-old to earn a racing Register of Merit that year.

Three weeks later, he ran second in the Southwestern Futurity at Rillito, and then went on to Los Alamitos in southern California, where he was second in the Juvenile Championship. From there, he won

Zelma and June Jeffers with Mr Bar None, circa 1959.

Mr Bar None handily won the Autumn Championship in December 1958 at Los Alamitos, which was his last race.

233

MAID OF COTTON
ALLOWANCE •
1958

RUIDOSO DOWNS

HORSE *Mr Bar None*

OWNER *Oscar Jeffers, Jr.* DISTANCE *350 yards*

TRAINER *Owner* TIME: *17.6 N.T.R.* DATE *6-29-58*
Trans-Photo Lab

JOCKEY *Kenneth Chapman* RUIDOSO DOWNS, RUIDOSO, N. M.
"World Record"

At Ruidoso Downs in June 1958, Mr Bar None set a world record for 350 yards (17.6 seconds) in the Maid of Cotton Allowance. Among those in the winner's circle are movie and TV star Dale Robertson (right) and Richard, Zelma, and June Jeffers on the left, closest to the horse.

the Kansas Futurity and Rocky Mountain Futurity at Centennial Race Track outside Denver, the Oklahoma Futurity at Enid, the Pacific Coast QHRA Futurity back in California, and the Winner-Take-All in Albuquerque. At one point in his campaign, he won four races in a fifteen-day span, by an average margin of a length and a half.

Mr Bar None's 2-year-old campaign added up to 10 wins and 8 seconds from 18 starts for earnings of $24,008, the second-highest earnings of any horse running that year, and the highest ever for a freshman. He was named 1957 Racing Champion 2-Year-Old Stallion. He tied the AQHA 2-year-old records of 16.0 for 300 yards in the Oklahoma Futurity and of 17.1 for 330 yards in the Kansas Futurity.

He also tied the track record at Pomona

despite an unorthodox treatment for a cold. Some years ago Richard Jeffers told writer Lyn Jank, "They draped blankets over his head to form a tent over a tub of real hot water laced with lots of Vicks (VapoRub). That did the trick. He was bright eyed and breathing easy by the time he went into the post parade the next day."

Kenneth Chapman, the leading jockey of 1957, called him the best Quarter Horse he'd ever ridden. "He runs straight, hard, and true," Chapman said, "and is a very good gate horse. He has the very best disposition I have ever seen in a horse, and his intelligence is equal to any horse I have ever known."

After wintering back home, Jeffers set out on another cross-country campaign in 1958 with Mr Bar None. This time he took along Murl L for a return engagement

COURTESY RICHELLE JEFFERS

Zelma and June at home in Wagoner with Mr Bar None and some of his racing trophies.

with Three Bars (TB) in California. But he lost the mare when she colicked on the road in New Mexico.

In his seasonal debut as a 3-year-old, Mr Bar None won a warm-up by daylight at Rillito Park, but followed that with seconds in Rillito's Quarter Horse Convention Stakes and the Los Alamitos Inaugural, and a third in the Los Alamitos Derby trials. He bounced back to collect his biggest check to date, $10,500, in the Pacific Coast QHRA Derby.

From May to September, he was undefeated in a nine-race streak that included six stakes: the Bay Meadows Handicap, the California Horse Racing Association Handicap, the Ruidoso Derby, Centennial's Wonderland Stakes and Rocky Mountain Derby, and Albuquerque's Shue Fly Stakes.

After a couple months off, Mr Bar None ran dismally when he returned to Los Alamitos, finishing off the board in the Clabbertown G and the Hard Twist. Jeffers was about ready to take his star home for good when a top leg man diagnosed the problem as sore feet, caused by a sloppy farrier.

Jeffers made it known that he would give the champ one more race before retirement. The poor showings in the previous two starts lengthened his odds in the Los Alamitos Autumn Championship, despite

PHOTO COURTESY THE QUARTER RACING JOURNAL

Bayou Bar, a 1962 son of Mr Bar None, set four track records and was the 1965 Racing World Champion 3-Year-Old Colt and a Superior race horse. He also had a career in the show ring with trainer Harold "Huddy" Hudspeth, Bixby, Okla., shown here. Hudspeth described the sorrel stallion as having "unbelievable athletic ability." Bayou Bar earned five halter points and three in barrel racing.

235

330 YARDS   THE OKLAHOMA FUTURITY   MAY 26, 1962
      1st: MR JUNIPER BAR OSCAR JEFFERS, JR, own & tr   KENNETH CHAPMAN, up
    3   2nd: KAMALETA   O. M. WOODSON, owner & trainer   CHARLES WATTERSON, up
        3rd: MONTECARLO BAR OSCAR JEFFERS, JR, owner & trainer   TON HIX, up

In the 1962 Oklahoma Futurity, Mr Bar None offspring finished an unprecedented first (Mr Juniper Bar), second (Kimaleta), and third (Montecarlo Bar), something that rarely happens in racing. June Jeffers owned the first and third horses, and O.M. Woodson owned the second-place horse. (*Note*: The correct spelling of the second-place horse is Kimaleta, not Kamaleta.)

Mr Bar None in the winner's circle after winning his 1958 RMQHA Derby Trial at Centennial. That's June at the head and Kenneth Chapman in the irons.

the fact that he'd beaten chief rivals such as Go Man Go earlier in the season.

June Jeffers was an astute horseman, always looking for a new and better way to get something done. Richelle Jeffers related how he was a self-taught lay veterinarian who set up his own lab with a microscope, centrifuge, and the works. Once he took a mare to a vet to have the follicle checked. A little later, the vet spotted a trailer at the side of the road and a man with his arm up the mare's rear end.

"He stopped and saw it was Grandpa," Richelle said. "Grandpa was wanting to learn what the follicle that the vet had tested felt like, so he could build his own vet work."

June and Zelma's son Robert apparently inherited his dad's fascination with gadgets. He rigged a tape recorder and sound system to capture June's phone call after the Autumn Championship on December 13, 1958.

"I don't feel too good," June said.

"What?" Richard Jeffers asked.

"I don't feel too good . . . (long pause) . . . we won! He liked to tear those gates up when he left there."

"What did he close?" Richard asked.

"He closed 9-2."

"Did you bet my money?"

"No, I didn't bet a nickel. I wanted to save your money. He walked around there like an old horse with lice falling off him. Hell, I didn't think we'd win it. I got up this morning, I tried to get him to trot, he wouldn't trot. He wouldn't gallop. But he came out of there (the starting gate) just like a cannon! Twenty yards out, Chap hit him once and he just took off."

In the Autumn Championship, he beat three-time world champion Go Man Go, world-champion-to-be Vandy's Flash, three-time world champion mare Vanetta Dee, and 1959 World Champion Racing Stallion Double Bid.

"I'd be lying if I'd said I wasn't nervous,"

"He walked around there like an old horse with lice falling off him."

Kimaleta, a 1960 sorrel mare by Mr Bar None and out of Bonna Lita, by Leo, set four track records in her career and won three stakes.

"That was the sweetest race, in my mind, that he ever ran."

Jeffers told a reporter. "This was definitely going to be Mr Bar None's last race, and I sure wanted him to win it.

"That was the sweetest race, in my mind, that he ever ran. He outran seven of the top horses of that time, won the biggest purse in his career ($11,000), and he retired a big winner. It sure made a nice trip coming home."

With a record of 12 wins, 2 seconds, and 1 third from 18 starts and earnings of $48,116, Mr Bar None was named 1958 World Champion Racing Stallion. He had earned more money than any other Quarter Horse that year. And in a single year, he had made more than the career earnings of all but three Quarter Horses.

Mr Bar None's lifetime record stood at 22 wins, including 13 stakes, from 36 starts, for earnings of $72,126.

In the Breeding Shed

While he was on the road with his one-horse stable, Jeffers had also been building up his broodmare band. "I didn't have hardly any mares to breed to him," he once said. "While I was running him around the country in '57 and '58, I would hear about good mares. I bought them one or two at a time and sent them back home. By the time we were finished running, I had about 15 good mares to breed to him."

There were plenty of others in line too. In his first crop (1960), Mr Bar None sired:

- Mr Juniper Bar, out of Red Juniper, by Red Man, the 1962 Racing World Champion Gelding.
- Kimaleta, out of Bonna Lita, by Leo, a multiple stakes-winner who set a world record for 330 yards.
- Montecarlo Bar, out of NR Negraletta, by Johnny Fleet, a six-time stakes winner who set several track records and earned a Superior in racing.
- Buck's Bar None, Gates Bar, Mr Minnie Bars, My Bar None, and Nelly Bars, all stakes winners.

Several more of Mr Bar None's most outstanding get from subsequent foal crops included:

- Bayou Bar, a 1962 stallion out of Bayou Bar, by Bob Jr., the 1965 Racing Cham-

Bar None Doll was Mr Bar None's biggest winner. The 1963 sorrel mare earned $166,843 and was the 1966 Racing World Champion 3-Year-Old Filly, the 1967 Racing World Champion Aged Mare, and a Superior race horse.

Mr Juniper Bar, a 1960 gelding by Mr Bar None, was the 1962 Racing World Champion 2-Year-Old Gelding, earned his racing ROM, and set a track record at Enid, Okla., for 350 yards.

pion 3-Year-old Colt and a Superior race horse with earnings of $27,433.

- Bar None Doll, a 1963 mare out of Negra Creek, by Afton Creek (TB), the 1967 Racing World Champion Aged Mare and a Superior race horse with winnings of $166,843.
- Mister Te Jay, a 1978 stallion out of Miss Top Rocket, by El Charro Rocket, a Superior race horse with earnings of $90,246.

Like his racetrack career, Mr Bar None's breeding life was marked by travel. June and Zelma kept him in the paddock behind their house in town, and hopped him in the trailer each day for his rendezvous with the broodmares at the ranch. The unorthodox routine didn't seem to hurt his performance: His progeny include 30 stakes winners from 290 starters foaled from 1960 to 1982.

Although Mr Bar None covered a lot of miles during his lifetime, he died on a cold, rainy day in 1982, just a few feet from the place where he was foaled, behind the Jeffers' house in Wagoner, Oklahoma.

AUTHOR PROFILES

Frank Holmes

DAROL DICKINSON

FRANK HOLMES has been penning horse-related feature articles and historical books for more than 35 years.

He sold his first feature article involving Quarter Horses to *Hoof and Horns* magazine in 1965. Frank is also considered one of the foremost historians of the Appaloosa and Paints breeds as well as Quarter Horses, and his many features on the founding sires and dams of all three breeds stand as benchmark contributions to the collective lore of the western horse.

After 18 years of working for the federal government, Frank began pursuing a full-time career as a free-lance writer in 1991. Then, between 1994 and 1996, he was a staff writer for *Western Horseman*. During that time, he contributed to the *Legends* series and authored *The Hank Wiescamp Story*.

In 1996 Frank became the features editor of the *Paint Horse Journal* in Fort Worth. There, through his articles and photographs, he combined his love for history, horses, and the horsemen and horsewomen behind them.

Frank left Fort Worth and returned to Colorado in 2000, to rededicate himself to his first love — researching and writing horse history.

Alan Gold

ALAN GOLD got his introduction to the horse world when he took a job with the *Australian Stock Horse Magazine* in the mid-1970s. He also got hooked on horse racing while living in Australia. "People pull over to the side of the road to listen to the Melbourne Cup on their car radios," he says. "I learned a lot about enthusiasm for horses while I was in Australia. I even met people who could repeat the call of a race the way a student might recite Shakespeare."

When he returned to the States in 1982, Alan took a job with *The Quarter Racing Record* and eventually became that magazine's editor. His stories have appeared in dozens of magazines on three continents.

Alan founded Fifth Leg Publishing, which offers a selection of quality books for horse lovers at **www.fifthleg.com**. "An Aussie race caller inspired the name," he explains. "When the favorite made up a hopeless deficit in the homestretch, the announcer shouted, 'He grew a fifth leg!' Sometimes, that's all it takes."

Alan lives in Arlington, Texas.

Ty Wyant

TY WYANT has been involved with equine journalism for 25 years since graduating from Colorado State University with a journalism degree.

Currently, Ty is the managing editor of three publications, *RIDE with Bob Avila*, *Spin To Win*, and *The Trail Less Traveled*. He is the national Quarter Horse columnist and writes a weekly column for *Daily Racing Form*. He is a member of the American Quarter Horse Association's racing committee.

Ty was the editor of *QuarterWeek* magazine, a magazine devoted to Quarter Horse racing, and worked in the public relations and marketing department at Los Alamitos Race Course. He has written Quarter Horse pedigree and breeding columns for two publications.

"I started showing horses in youth programs and then migrated to racing after college graduation," Ty said. "I've been blessed with the opportunity to write about horses and horsemen. I relish the writing process and dealing with horsemen."

But Ty has more pride in his two sons, Jeff and Ben, than in his writing accomplishments. Jeff is a high school honor student and Ben is a midshipman at the United States Naval Academy.

Ty lives in Louisville, Colorado.

Sally Harrison

SALLY HARRISON, a former English teacher and Arabian horse owner, has been writing about and photographing horses since 1981. Her articles and photographs have appeared in numerous publications and she has written three books: *Cutting: A Guide for the Non-Pro Competitor*; *Matlock Rose, The Horseman*; and *The Cowboy Life of James L. Kenney*. She also co-authored *Pride in the Dust*.

A nationally recognized equine photographer, Sally has turned her lens on countless great Quarter Horses and Thoroughbreds over the past 20 years. Says cutting legend Buster Welch, "Sally is the only person I know who can head a cow and take a picture at the same time."

Sally, who also owns an equine advertising and marketing business, lives in Arlington, Tex., with her husband, writer Alan Gold.

PHOTO INDEX

NOTES

The *Western Horseman*, established in 1936, is the world's leading horse publication.
For subscription information: 800-877-5278. To order other *Western Horseman* books: 800-874-6774.
Western Horseman, Box 7980, Colorado Springs, CO 80933-7980. Web-site: **www.westernhorseman.com**.

Books Published by Western Horseman Inc.

ARABIAN LEGENDS by Marian K. Carpenter
280 pages and 319 photographs. Abu Farwa, *Aladdinn, *Ansata Ibn Halima, *Bask, Bay-Abi, Bay El Bey, Bint Sahara, Fadjur, Ferzon, Indraff, Khemosabi, *Morafic, *Muscat, *Naborr, *Padron, *Raffles, *Raseyn, *Sakr, Samtyr, *Sanacht, *Serafix, Skorage, *Witez II, Xenophonn.

BACON & BEANS by Stella Hughes
144 pages and 200-plus recipes for delicious western chow.

BARREL RACING, Completely Revised by Sharon Camarillo
128 pages, 158 photographs, and 17 illustrations. Teaches foundation horsemanship and barrel racing skills for horse and rider, with additional tips on feeding, hauling, and winning.

CALF ROPING by Roy Cooper
144 pages and 280 photographs covering roping and tying.

CUTTING by Leon Harrel
144 pages and 200 photographs. Complete guide on this popular sport.

FIRST HORSE by Fran Devereux Smith
176 pages, 160 black-and-white photos, about 40 illustrations. Step-by-step information for the first-time horse owner and/or novice rider.

HORSEMAN'S SCRAPBOOK by Randy Steffen
144 pages and 250 illustrations. A collection of handy hints.

IMPRINT TRAINING by Robert M. Miller, D.V.M.
144 pages and 250 photographs. Learn to "program" newborn foals.

LEGENDS by Diane C. Simmons
168 pages and 214 photographs. Barbra B, Bert, Chicaro Bill, Cowboy P-12, Depth Charge (TB), Doc Bar, Go Man Go, Hard Twist, Hollywood Gold, Joe Hancock, Joe Reed P-3, Joe Reed II, King P-234, King Fritz, Leo, Peppy, Plaudit, Poco Bueno, Poco Tivio, Queenie, Quick M Silver, Shue Fly, Star Duster, Three Bars (TB), Top Deck (TB), and Wimpy P-1.

LEGENDS 2 by Jim Goodhue, Frank Holmes, Phil Livingston, Diane C. Simmons
192 pages and 224 photographs. Clabber, Driftwood, Easy Jet, Grey Badger II, Jessie James, Jet Deck, Joe Bailey P-4 (Gonzales), Joe Bailey (Weatherford), King's Pistol, Lena's Bar, Lightning Bar, Lucky Blanton, Midnight, Midnight Jr, Moon Deck, My Texas Dandy, Oklahoma Star, Oklahoma Star Jr., Peter McCue, Rocket Bar (TB), Skipper W, Sugar Bars, and Traveler.

LEGENDS 3 by Jim Goodhue, Frank Holmes, Diane Ciarloni, Kim Guenther, Larry Thornton, Betsy Lynch
208 pages and 196 photographs. Flying Bob, Hollywood Jac 86, Jackstraw (TB), Maddon's Bright Eyes, Mr Gun Smoke, Old Sorrel, Piggin String (TB), Poco Lena, Poco Pine, Poco Dell, Question Mark, Quo Vadis, Royal King, Showdown, Steel Dust, and Two Eyed Jack.

LEGENDS 4
Several authors chronicle the great Quarter Horses Zantanon, Ed Echols, Zan Parr Bar, Blondy's Dude, Diamonds Sparkle, Woven Web/Miss Princess, Miss Bank, Rebel Cause, Tonto Bars Hank, Harlan, Lady Bug's Moon, Dash For Cash, Vandy, Impressive, Fillinic, Zippo Pine Bar, and Doc O' Lena.

LEGENDS 5 by Frank Holmes, Ty Wyant, Alan Gold, and Sally Harrison
The stories of Little Joe, Joe Moore, Monita, Bill Cody, Joe Cody, Topsail Cody, Pretty Buck, Pat Star Jr., Skipa Star, Hank H, Chubby, Bartender, Leo San, Custus Rastus (TB), Jaguar, Jackie Bee, Chicado V, and Mr Bar None fill 248 pages, including about 300 photographs.

PROBLEM-SOLVING by Marty Marten
248 pages and over 250 photos and illustrations. How to develop a willing partnership between horse and human to handle trailer-loading, hard-to-catch, barn-sour, spooking, water-crossing, herd-bound, and pull-back problems.

NATURAL HORSE-MAN-SHIP by Pat Parelli
224 pages and 275 photographs. Parelli's six keys to a natural horse-human relationship.

REINING, Completely Revised by Al Dunning
216 pages and over 300 photographs showing how to train horses for this exciting event.

ROOFS AND RAILS by Gavin Ehringer
144 pages, 128 black-and-white photographs plus drawings, charts, and floor plans. How to plan and build your ideal horse facility.

STARTING COLTS by Mike Kevil
168 pages and 400 photographs. Step-by-step process in starting colts.

THE HANK WIESCAMP STORY by Frank Holmes
208 pages and over 260 photographs. The biography of the legendary breeder of Quarter Horses, Appaloosas, and Paints.

TEAM PENNING by Phil Livingston
144 pages and 200 photographs. How to compete in this popular family sport.

TEAM ROPING WITH JAKE AND CLAY by Fran Devereux Smith
224 pages and over 200 photographs and illustrations. Learn about fast times from champions Jake Barnes and Clay O'Brien Cooper. Solid information about handling a rope, roping dummies, and heading and heeling for practice and in competition. Also sound advice about rope horses, roping steers, gear, and horsemanship.

WELL-SHOD by Don Baskins
160 pages, 300 black-and-white photos and illustrations. A horse-shoeing guide for owners and farriers. The easy-to-read text, illustrations, and photos show step-by-step how to trim and shoe a horse for a variety of uses. Special attention is paid to corrective shoeing techniques for horses with various foot and leg problems.

WESTERN HORSEMANSHIP by Richard Shrake
144 pages and 150 photographs. Complete guide to riding western horses.

WESTERN TRAINING by Jack Brainard
With Peter Phinny. 136 pages. Stresses the foundation for western training.

WIN WITH BOB AVILA by Juli S. Thorson
This 128-page, hardbound, full-color book discusses traits that separate horse-world achievers from also-rans. World champion horseman Bob Avila shares his philosophies on succeeding as a competitor, breeder, and trainer.